# Sport Facility Operations Management

*Eric C. Schwarz, Stacey A. Hall
and Simon Shibli*

**ELSEVIER**

AMSTERDAM • BOSTON • HEIDELBERG • LONDON • NEW YORK
OXFORD • PARIS • SAN DIEGO • SAN FRANCISCO
SINGAPORE • SYDNEY • TOKYO
Butterworth-Heinemann is an imprint of Elsevier

Butterworth-Heinemann is an Imprint of Elsevier
The Boulevard, Langford Lane, Kidlington, Oxford OX5 1GB, UK
30 Corporate Drive, Suite 400, Burlington, MA 01803, USA

First edition 2010

Notice
No responsibility is assumed by the publisher for any injury and/or damage to persons or
property as a matter of products liability, negligence or otherwise, or from any use or
operation of any methods, products, instructions or ideas contained in the material
herein. Because of rapid advances in the medical sciences, in particular, independent
verification of diagnoses and drug dosages should be made

**British Library Cataloguing in Publication Data**
A catalogue record for this book is available from the British Library

**Library of Congress Cataloging-in-Publication Data**
A catalog record for this book is available from the Library of Congress

ISBN: 978-1-85617-836-5

For information on all Butterworth-Heinemann
publications visit our web site at elsevierdirect.com

Printed and bound in Great Britain
10 11 12 10 9 8 7 6 5 4 3 2 1

Working together to grow
libraries in developing countries

www.elsevier.com | www.bookaid.org | www.sabre.org

ELSEVIER    BOOK AID International    Sabre Foundation

Loughborough
COLLEGE est 1909

# Sport Facility Operations Management

# Contents

# Preface

Sport facilities of all shapes and sizes are an ingrained part of global sport management culture. As such, it is inevitable that students who enter into the field of sport management will interact with the management and operations of a sport facility at some point during their career. This book is being published with the sport management educator and student in mind, specifically aimed at those sport management programs that require a facility management unit as a part of their curriculum.

Most sport facility management books currently on the market go into the basic theoretical framework of sport facility management, but fail to relate many of the concepts to the traditional operations management units taught in business management. In addition, there is limited relevant practical professional experience infused through the books. Finally, there is a lack of identification, interpretation, and recognition of the individual differences in managing and operating facilities across the globe. **Sport Facility Operations Management: A Global Perspective** strives to address these limitations by bringing the most comprehensive and significant sport facility management textbook to market that addressed this important area of sport management from a global perspective. This is crucial in textbooks within this field of study, as the sport industry is truly global, and education must reflect this.

This book brings together three authors with significant experience in teaching sport management in the United States, Europe, and Australia; conducting research related to sport facility management and operations around the globe, and having practical experience in sport facility operations management. With this background, the purpose of the textbook is to provide the theoretical foundation for sport facility operations management, and would be supplemented both in the text and in the appendices with practical applications via case study scenarios and functional documentation that can be utilized by the sport facility manager. In addition, each author would infuse research and experiences from sport facilities around the world (North America, Europe, Middle East/ Asia, Australia, and New Zealand) to ensure that a global perspective for the textbook is achieved.

The initial chapter of the book serves to provide an overview of sport facility operations management, including a basic review of those topics commonly covered in an introductory sport facility operations management course. The remainder of this text will provide the reader a framework understanding of sport facility operations management from a global perspective by: (1) connecting the behind-the-scene concepts that must be understood before even entering into management and operations of sport facilities, (2) implementing management and operations in sport facilities and the ancillary and support issues inherent to sport facility operations management, and (3) providing methods for measuring and evaluating the performance of operations and management for sport facilities that aid in the successful implementation of activities that meet the needs, wants, and desires of users.

# Section I – Pre-management and pre-operational issues

## Ownership structures

The reader will be presented with the various business, ownership, and governance structures for sport facilities across the globe. Sport facility owners must first understand the legal authority under which the sport facility can operate as a business, including as a sole proprietorship, a partnership, or under a number of forms of corporations. At the same time, the sport facility owners must determine how they want to structure their sport business – either as a public entity, a non-profit business, or a commercial enterprise; and also whether the governance structure will be as a public entity, a private entity, a public–private partnerships, or under a voluntary structure. In addition to these structures, the reader will be presented with models of organizational effectiveness that can assist in efficiently managing the ownership structure.

## Financing

The reader will gain an appreciation of the intricacies of financing sport facilities as related to various business issues, the costs of ownership, life-cycle costing, cost-effectiveness/efficiency, and the principles of economic impact analysis. The understanding of these issues will then allow the reader to recognize and understand the different sources of financing to be used for sport facilities, including public sector funding, private sources of revenue, public–private partnerships, and the influence of the voluntary sector.

## Planning, design, and construction processes

The reader will learn about the various stages of the planning, design, and construction processes, including preliminary planning; the development of design; actual construction; and preparation for training and management of facilities. By understanding these issues in advance, the reader will have a stronger conceptual underpinning of the management framework applied to sport facilities, and be able to more clearly connect that knowledge with the implementation processes inherent to management and operations of sport facilities.

# Section II – Implementation of management and operational structures

## Organizational management

The reader will learn how to distinguish, identify, and classify the important concepts of organization management as related to individual and group behavior in sport facilities. These will include the principles of motivation, stress management and well being, leadership, use of power and authority, politics, conflict management, decision making, and problem solving. The reader will then be able to connect these concepts with various leadership and organizational management concepts that affect international and global sport facility operations, including determinants of organizational culture and change, and the effects of cultural diversity and global organization behavior.

## Human resource management

The reader will be presented with an overview of the increased growth, interest, and complexity of human resource management in sport facilities, with significant emphasis on managerial competencies, the strategic importance of human resource management, and the implications of legislative, governance and ethical issues in terms of employees, volunteers, and customers of sport facilities. This will be accomplished by providing the reader with foundational concepts regarding the individual differences in people and their interactions in groups, which in turn will lead to an explanation of how to effectively manage those groups strategically through the integration of strategic human resource management and performance management processes.

## Financial management

The reader will be presented with numerous financial functions that a sport facility manager must understand. This includes an overview of why financial skills are an integral part of the sport facility manager's overall portfolio of management of skills, how finance is the 'language' of business, the importance of being fluent in financial language both in terms of understanding it and being able to communicate in it, and the need for sport facility managers to continuously develop and enhance their financial skills.

## Operations management

The reader will gain an understanding of the various maintenance, control, and organizational activities that are required to produce products and services for consumers of the sport facility. This will include an explanation of how the operational structure integrates with the operation of the sport facility, the need for a comprehensive, structured approach that seeks to improve the quality of facility services, and the general sport facility operating procedures that need to be managed within governmental guidelines and budget parameters.

### Legal concerns for owners and managers

The reader will be provided with an overview of the relationship between legal issues and sport facility operations. With it being impossible to make the reader a legal expert, and impractical to cover all the specific laws worldwide that affect sport facility operations management, the authors strive to articulate the effects of the legal environment on sport facilities by dispelling the myth that law and risk management in sport facilities are one in the same. Therefore, the reader will be provided with an overview of the major legal principles and standards related to the management and operations of sport facilities, and recommendations regarding the level of legal expertise a sport facility manager should have – including when they should defer to individuals with a higher level of proficiency in the law.

## Section III – Ancillary issues in management and operations

### Sponsorship

The reader will gain an appreciation of the significant role sport marketing and communications play in sport facility operations management. The goal is for the reader to develop knowledge and skill in the marketing process as it relates to understanding the sport consumer, logistics, promotions, and public relations activities in sport facilities that focus on studying and understanding the consumer in terms of marketing a sport facility, developing marketing strategies for the sport facility, clarifying the needs and goals for a sport facility, and implementing sport marketing plans to support the management and operations of a sport facility.

### Event planning in facility management

The reader will gain an understanding about the relationship between facility operations and management and event planning. The concepts in this chapter will specifically focus on the role facility management plays in supporting event management through the sport facility event planning process; the role of the sport facility management and personnel before, during, and after an event; and the evaluation processes integral for staging future events.

### Risk assessment in facility management

The reader will recognize that sport facility managers must plan for all types of emergencies that may disrupt normal operations. In order to manage and mitigate potential incidents, facility managers need to possess a sound knowledge of risk management practices. Therefore, the reader will gain knowledge about risk management concepts including risk assessment, risk control strategies, and risk planning options.

### Security planning for facility management

The reader will gain an appreciation of the ever-growing global security issues involved in protecting sports facilities from threats and risks. Security best practices, systems, and planning options are provided to equip the twenty-first century sport manager with an all-hazard's approach to facility security planning.

## Section IV – Effectiveness of management and operations

### Benchmarking and performance management

This final chapter will bring together the various strands of performance management referred to throughout the book, providing the reader with an understanding that anything a facility manager does gets measured. Therefore, facility managers need to be clear about what their priorities are and what measures they need to monitor in order to demonstrate personal, team, facility, and corporate effectiveness. The chapter will specifically discuss the concept of benchmarking, and how measuring performance helps sport facility managers achieve better results by enabling them to understand the drivers of performance and how to influence them. The chapter also provides techniques that a sport facility manager can utilize to integrate benchmarking and performance management within the organizational culture, how it provides the basis for a clear focus on business essentials, and offers courses of action for continuous improvement of the sport facility.

## Pedagogical features

Sport Facility Operations Management: A Global Perspective enhances learning with the following pedagogical devices:

- Each chapter opens with a chapter outline and a list of chapter objectives.
- Key terms are highlighted and defined in the text when it first appears. They are also defined alphabetically at the end of the book in the glossary.
- Each chapter has real-world scenarios or a case study embedded within the text to enhance critical thinking related to real-world concepts associated with the chapter material. Questions associated with each case study allow the learner to apply theoretical knowledge to the scenarios.
- A comprehensive chapter review at the end of each chapter that reviews the chapter objectives and pertinent information from the chapter.

## Critical thinking

One of the most important skills for students to develop through their college and university years is critical thinking. This mental process of analyzing and evaluating information is used across all disciplines, and serves as a process for reflecting on the information provided, examining facts to understand reasoning, and forming conclusions and plans for action.

The authors of this book have provided a series of opportunities for students to enhance their critical thinking skills while also verifying their understanding of the materials presented in this text. A test bank has been provided for each chapter with 10 multiple-choice questions that provide students the opportunity to verify their comprehension of the chapter's main concepts. To supplement that verification, there are also four discussion questions. These questions, which can be used as essay topics or in-class discussion issues by instructors, are based on the information provided in the chapter, the research available in the specific aspect of sport facility operations management, and the education and experiences of the authors.

In addition, embedded within each chapter are either real-world scenarios or a case study to enhance critical thinking as related to real world concepts associated with the text material. These scenarios are a collection of 'real-world' situations to provide the reader with the maximum opportunity to analyze, evaluate, and ponder possible solutions to the specific situation. Questions associated with each case study will help the student focus their efforts on key theoretical aspects from the chapter, and apply that knowledge to deal with the specific scenario.

This text provides a unique opportunity for critical thinking and application in association with sport facility operations management. An online appendix has been provided with diagrams, schematics, manuals, and forms that will provide additional information for the reader about the role and responsibilities of sport facility managers and owners, as well as provide the reader with actual documentation they can modify for use when they enter the profession of sport facility operations management.

## Supplements

Sport Facility Operations Management – A Global Perspective provides the instructor with the following teaching aids:

- PowerPoint presentations for each chapter.
- An electronic test bank.
- Case studies and scenarios within each chapter with suggested discussion topics.
- Appendices with diagrams, schematics, manuals and forms.

# Acknowledgements, dedications, epigraphs

## Dr. Eric C. Schwarz

I would like to dedicate this book to my wife Loan. Your unconditional love in life, and your continued support for my work and my writing is the foundation for all of my success. Your calming influence and belief in my abilities give me the strength to be the best person and professional that I can be. I love you more than anything in this world, and thank you for making me a better person every day!!!

In addition, I would like to show my appreciation to my co-editor and co-author on this book, Stacey Hall. Your assistance as a second set of eyes for all parts of this project, and the quality of your input and suggestions significantly enhanced the quality and strength of this text. In addition, your expertise in risk assessment and security planning has provided current and cutting edge information that will provide the readers with information most other books have yet to address. Thank you for your professionalism and involvement in this project.

I would also like to recognize the efforts of my other co-author, Simon Shibli. Although you came to this project after it had been accepted, your influence, professionalism, and expertise in financial management and benchmarking/performance management, as well as input on a number of different topics, has added significant depth and quality to this book. Thank you for all of your efforts.

Finally, I would like to acknowledge the Chair of the Department of Sport Business and International Tourism at Saint Leo University, Phil Hatlem. This project was contracted and completed during my first year of employment at Saint Leo, and without your support and input, this project could not have been completed. Thank you.

## Dr. Stacey A. Hall

I would like to thank my family in Northern Ireland for their unconditional love and support in both my professional and personal endeavors. I would also like to thank my friends and colleagues at Southern Miss for their support and guidance. Lastly, I thank Dr. Eric C. Schwarz for the opportunity to contribute to this book. Eric's leadership skills and professionalism made this project an enjoyable experience.

## Prof. Simon Shibli

My contribution to this book is dedicated to my wife Tracey, and our three children Alice, James, and Mary.

# About the authors

## Dr. Eric C. Schwarz

Dr. Schwarz completed his first year as an Associate Professor of Sport Business within the School of Business at Saint Leo University in Florida in 2008–2009. Before coming to Saint Leo, he was at Daniel Webster College in New Hampshire for 9 years, serving as Assistant, then Associate Professor and Program Coordinator of Sport Management within the School of Business, Management, and Professional Studies. During the 2006–2007 academic year, he took a sabbatical leave to serve as Visiting Senior Lecturer and Researcher at the University of Ballarat in Australia.

Dr. Schwarz received a B.S. degree in Physical Education from Plymouth State University in 1991; an M.Ed. in Administration and Supervision from Salisbury University in 1992; and an Ed.D in Sport Management from the United States Sports Academy in 1998.

Dr. Schwarz has presented on various topics in sport marketing, sport facility management, and experiential learning at conferences in the United States, Canada, Europe, and Australia, and has been published in leading business and sport management journals including the *International Journal of Entrepreneurship and Small Business* and the *International Journal of Sport Management and Marketing*.

Dr. Schwarz is the lead author of *Advanced Theory and Practice in Sport Marketing*. Published by Butterworth-Heinemann/Elsevier in 2008, this university-level textbook filled a much needed niche in sport management curriculum support by breaking new ground in pedagogy by providing both in-depth theoretical discussions and practical applications in sport marketing. In addition, he has contributed to two books: *The Sports Event Playbook*: *Managing and Marketing Winning Sports Events*; and *The Encyclopedia of Sports Management and Marketing*.

Dr. Schwarz has been involved with numerous consulting projects, including facility management and marketing for sport facilities in New Hampshire, development of a retail management plan for a minor league baseball team in New Hampshire, and an economic impact analysis for a Senior PGA Tour event in Massachusetts. Dr. Schwarz also served as an expert witness in Physical Education and Sport Management for an attorney in New Hampshire; has worked with a variety of sport-related organizations in high school athletics, college athletics, and campus recreation programming; and previously owned his own summer camp, clinic, and coaching training business.

Dr. Schwarz lives in Zephyrhills, Florida with his wife Loan.

## Dr. Stacey A. Hall

Dr. Stacey Hall is the Associate Director of the National Center for Spectator Sports Safety and Security (NCS[4]) and an Assistant Professor of Sport Management at The University of Southern Mississippi. She has earned a Bachelor's degree in

Management, a Master's in Business Administration, and a Ph.D. in Human Performance (Teaching & Administration) with an emphasis in Sport Management.

Dr. Hall's expertise is in the area of sport security management. She has been published in leading sport management, homeland security, and emergency management journals, and is lead author on a sport event security textbook to be published in 2011. Dr. Hall has presented at international and national conferences, and conducted invited presentations for United States federal and state agencies, college athletic conferences, and professional sport leagues, including Major League Soccer (MLS).

Dr. Hall has been the Principal/Co-Principal Investigator on external grant awards in excess of $4 M. Funded projects included awards from the United States Department of Homeland Security to: develop risk management curriculum for sport security personnel at National Collegiate Athletic Association (NCAA) institutions; conduct risk assessments at college sport stadiums; and develop training programs for sport venue staff.

Dr. Hall has been involved in several service projects, including development of a risk assessment tool for United States sport stadiums in conjunction with the Department of Homeland Security and International Association of Assembly Managers; and development of a disaster mitigation plan post-Katrina for the Mississippi Regional Housing Authority.

Dr. Hall teaches undergraduate and graduate sport management courses in economics, law, finance, and security. She developed a graduate level emphasis area in sport security management for the Master's program at Southern Miss. Dr. Hall also developed a professional certificate program in sport security and currently serves as program director.

A native of Northern Ireland, Dr. Hall has resided in the United States since 1997, currently living in Hattiesburg, Mississippi. She is a former collegiate soccer athlete at Southern Miss, and a former player and captain of the Northern Ireland Women's International Soccer team.

## Prof. Simon Shibli

Simon Shibli is Professor of Sport Management at Sheffield Hallam University in the United Kingdom, and is a Co-Director of the Sport Industry Research Centre. He is a qualified accountant with the Chartered Institute of Management Accountants (CIMA). Simon graduated from Loughborough University in 1985 after studying Physical Education, Sport Science and Recreation Management. After leaving university, Simon worked for 7 years as a facility manager in the arts and entertainments industry. In 1992 Simon returned to academic life as a lecturer specializing in finance, and he wrote his first book *Leisure Manager's Guide to Budgeting and Budgetary Control* in 1994. He has subsequently developed a research career and has peer-reviewed publications in numerous peer-reviewed journals notably *Managing Leisure: An International Journal*. Simon lives in Sheffield, England with his wife Tracey, and three children Alice, James, and Mary.

# Prologue

# 1 Introduction to sport facility operations management

## Chapter outline

## Chapter objectives

The purpose of this prologue is to provide the reader with some initial background on the concept of sport facility operations management. First will be an explanation of the concepts of facility management and operations management in general terms followed by how these concepts interact with each other in terms of sport facilities. This will be followed by a presentation of global scenarios where poor management and/or operations of a sport facility led to significant problems. This prologue will conclude with an explanation of how this book will help the reader learn to deal with the scenarios presented, and much more. This will be accomplished through a description of the discipline of sport facility operations management in terms of the various concepts that will be covered in this textbook.

## What is sport facility operations management?

In order to effectively understand sport facility operations management, it is important to understand the two root concepts – facility management and operations management. Facility management is an all-encompassing term referring to the maintenance and care of commercial and non-profit buildings, including but not limited to sport facilities, including heating, ventilation, and air conditioning (HVAC); electrical; plumbing; sound and lighting systems; cleaning, groundskeeping, and housekeeping; security; and general operations. The goal of facility management is to organize and supervise the safe and secure maintenance and operation of the facility in a financially and environmentally sound manner.

There are numerous associations that oversee the profession of facility management worldwide. These associations have further clarified the definition of facility management and also provide guidance and education for those who are employed in the field. The world's largest and most widely recognized international association for professional facility managers is the International Facility Management Association (IFMA). According to their website (www. ifma.org), they support more than 19,500 members in 60 countries through 125 chapters and 15 councils. They define facility management as 'a profession that encompasses multiple disciplines to ensure functionality of the built environment by integrating people, place, process and technology' and further clarify this definition as 'the practice or coordinating the physical workplace with the people and work of the organization; integrates the principles of business administration, architecture, and the behavioral and engineering sciences.' Other organizations include the British Institute of Facilities Management (BIFM – www.bifm.org.uk), the Facility Management Association of Australia (FMA Australia – www.fma.com.au), and the International Association of Assembly Managers (IAAM – www.iaam.org).

While facility management focuses on the overall maintenance and care of a building, operations management focuses on administrating the processes to produce and distribute the products and services offered through a facility. This would include the processes of production (tangible and intangible), inventory control, supply chain management, purchasing, logistics, scheduling, staffing, and general services – with the goal of maintaining, controlling, and improving organizational activities. The operations management field also has numerous associations that support the profession. The largest is the Association for Operations Management (APICS – www.apics.org), whose mission is to build knowledge and skills in operations management professionals to enhance and validate abilities and accelerate careers. Other organizations that support the profession of operations management globally include the European Operations Management Association (EurOMA – www.euroma-online.org), the Production and Operations Management Society (POMS – www.poms.org), and the Institute of Operations Management (www.iomnet.org.uk).

## Why sport facility operations management is important?

Every day, thousands of facilities around the globe host sport, recreation, and leisure activities with minimal or no problems. But when a problem occurs, or there is a lack of planning ahead for activities, the results can be harmful and damaging. This can range from damage to the facility or equipment to injuries to personnel, participants, and visitors – with the injuries ranging in severity from minor (cuts, bruises, sprains) to major (broken bones, torn ligaments, back and eye injuries) to catastrophic (loss of limb, paralysis, death). Sport facility operations management seeks to maintain and care for public, private, and non-profit facilities used for sport, recreation, and leisure to ensure safe and secure production and distribution of products and services to users.

The discipline of sport facilities operations management has many different components that need to be understood. However before an explanation of these various sub-disciplines is provided, let us take a look at a number of real scenarios where poor facility operations and management have led to significant problems...

- In 1972, 11 Israeli athletes (along with one German police officer and five terrorists) were killed by the Palestinian terrorist group Black September due to inadequate security at the Munich Olympic Games. Eight Palestinians, with bags of weapons, were able to scale the fence that surrounded the Olympic village, and then they proceeded to enter the Israeli accommodation and take the athletes hostage.
- In 1985 at Valley Parade football stadium, the home of Bradford City, a flash fire broke out during a match with Lincoln City. The fire consumed one side of the stadium, killing 56 people and injuring over 250. The fire was believed to have been caused by either a match or cigarette that fell through a hole in the stands and into rubbish below. Even though the fire brigade was called, there was no way to keep the fire at bay as fire extinguishers were removed from passageway's to prevent vandalism.
- Also in 1985, Liverpool and Juventus were facing each other in the European Cup final at Heysel Stadium in Belgium. Before the match started, Liverpool supporters reacted to taunts from the Italian fans by charging through the lines of Belgian police. The Juventus fans could do nothing, but retreat as far as a wall, which collapsed under the pressure and onto their own fans below. In the ensuing panic 39 supporters died and over 600 were injured. Another contributor to the problems based on the inquiries and also concerned voiced before the event – 58,000 people coming to watch the game at a stadium that only holds only 50,000 and was crumbling from disrepair (including people being able to kick out parts of walls from the outside to gain admittance without a ticket) made it a potential death trap.
- In 1988 in Katmandu, Nepal, 80 soccer fans seeking cover during a violent hail storm at the national stadium were trampled to death in a stampede. The reason – the stadium doors were locked.
- In 1989 at Hillsborough Stadium (the home of the Sheffield Wednesday Football Club), there was a human crush that occurred during an FA semifinal match with Liverpool that resulted in the deaths of 96 people. This deadliest stadium-related disaster in British history (and one of the worst in international football history) could have been prevented, as the inquiry into the disaster (the Taylor Report) named the cause as failure of police and security control.
- In 1993, during a quarterfinal tennis match in Hamburg, Germany, a fan ran from the middle of the crowd to the edge of the court between games and stabbed Monica Seles between the shoulder blades. The individual (who was deemed to be 'psychologically abnormal' by the courts) was a fan of Seles' rival, Steffi Graf (whom was not Seles' opponent in this match). While her injuries were not life-threatening, she did not return to professional tennis for over 2 years.
- In 1996 at the Mateo Flores National Stadium in Guatemala City (seating capacity 45,800), Costa Rica and Guatemala were playing a World Cup qualifier. According to FIFA, the world soccer association, forgers apparently had sold fake tickets to the match, bringing far more people to the stadium than could fit (estimated at over 60,000). This, combined with gate-crashers (people without tickets), pushed into the bleachers through a concrete causeway, overwhelmed other fans below, and caused

a mass of people to tumble down on top of one another. Ticket takers were seen to also continue admitting fans even after bleachers were clearly filled to capacity.

- In 2007 at the Australian Open tennis tournament a brawl between Serbian and Croat spectators erupted outside a merchandise tent when the two groups began trading insults. Punches, bottles, and beer cups were thrown as about 150 members of the two rival groups clashed. No injuries were reported, but 150 people were ejected from the event, and Tennis Australia announced the need to revise plans for handling these types of situations in the future.
- Multiple reports published between 2006 and 2009 have examined significant risks to players and spectators due to air poisoning from exhaust systems from zambonis because of lack of ventilation in ice arenas. Medical studies have shown that the results can cause a significant increase in asthma and chronic coughs in hockey players who play in poorly ventilated arenas due to carbon monoxide and nitrogen dioxide poisoning.
    - Ventilation problems have also been related to 'sick pool syndrome' in aquatic centers/natatoriums due to the high humidity and the contaminants caused by chemicals and biologics.
- In 2009 at the Dallas Cowboys practice facility, a thunderstorm ripped the roof off the inflatable bubble and collapsed the infrastructure, injuring 12 people including the paralysis of one coach. The question of negligence on behalf of the Cowboys has arisen due to a number of factors, including (1) was this an adequate and safe facility to be holding practice during the tornadic weather conditions, (2) was there substandard maintenance on the facility to withstand the winds from the storm, and (3) show the Cowboys have used Summit Structures LLC to build the facility when they had prior knowledge that similar type of facility built for the Philadelphia Regional Port Authority collapsed under similar weather conditions (which are more regular in Texas).
- Also in 2009, Stan Kroenke and Kroenke Sport Enterprises, owners of the Pepsi Center in Denver, signed a contract with World Wrestling Entertainment (WWE) to hold their Monday Night Raw wrestling show that is televised worldwide on Memorial Day. A the same time, the Denver Nuggets of the NBA (also owner by Kroenke) made it to semifinals of the NBA playoffs, which resulted in Game 4 of the playoffs being scheduled the same day at the WWE event. The WWE, who had a legal and binding contract, were bumped from the facility for the Denver Nuggets – less than 1 week before the event.

So, how would you deal with each of these scenarios? Could they have been prevented? What would you have done differently? You probably cannot answer those questions right now, but the goal of this book is to provide you with a body of knowledge in sport facility operations management that can be transferred to any type of facility around the globe. As with any textbook, the theoretical foundations presented offer the reader the opportunity to conceptualize the practices within a subject, then take that knowledge and apply it in practical settings. While this book will not and cannot cover every individual unique aspect of sport facility operations management from the viewpoint of every type of facility – this would be impossible – it does provide a framework that will allow an individual to enter a sport facility operations management situation, have a base understanding of what is happening, and conceptually understand how to start the process of managing the situation.

# The discipline of sport facility operations management

The first section of the book seeks to provide the reader with an understanding of behind-the-scene concepts that must be understood before even entering into management and operations of sport facilities. First is an explanation of the various business, ownership, and governance structures for sport facilities across the globe. It is equally important to understand the legal authority under which the sport facility can operate as a business, as well as the business, governance, and organizational effectiveness structures. Second is an analysis of the intricacies of financing sport facilities, including the costs of conducting business, life-cycle costing, cost-effectiveness/efficiency, and the importance of economic impact analyses. By understanding these financing concepts, sport facility operations managers can connect the financing options to the ownership and governance structures, and understand how the facility came into being. Furthermore, this information serves as a foundation for looking at the current and future trends that will affect the management and operation of sport facilities. The third and last concept for this section is the planning, design, and construction processes for sport facilities. While not all individuals will be involved in these processes from the initial concept of a facility, it is inevitable that facility management professional will be involved with modification, refurbishment, and/or expansion of a facility sometime in their career. The goal is to provide background about preliminary planning, developing designs, construction processes, and preparation planning for training and management of the facility.

The second section of the book will focus on the implementation of management and operations in sport facilities, including organizational management, human resource management, financial management, operations management, and legal responsibilities. Organizational management involves the planning, organizing, leading and coordinating functions within a business to create an environment that supports continuous improvement of personnel, the organization, and the customers. Human resource management is the logical and strategic supervision and managing of the most important asset within an organization – the employees. Without a quality group of individuals working for the facility, goals and objectives could not be met, tasks would not be completed, and customers would not be served. Understanding the various types of human resources and the generally accepted practices of human resource management is crucial to the success of sport facility operations management. Equally important is financial management, as concepts such as financial reporting, budgeting, and break-even analysis are vital to the fiscal health of the sport facility, and hence the ability to continue business operations. All of these concepts above lead into actual operations management, which is the maintenance, control, and improvement of organizational activities that are required to produce products and services for consumers of the sport facility. In order to effectively manage operations, a sport facility manager must understand how the operational structure integrates with the operation of the sport facility in terms of total quality management and generating operating procedures to be utilized in various facility operations and services. In addition, general legal concerns for sport facility owners and managers will be covered, including the effects of the legal environment on sport facilities, general legal principles and standards inherent to sport facility operations management, and an explanation of the level of legal expertise an owner or manager needs.

The third section of the book will focus on ancillary issues in sport facility operations management, including marketing, event planning, risk planning, and security planning. In the marketing chapter, basic theories and principles of global sport marketing and communications will be covered to provide the reader with broad knowledge and skill in marketing process related to understanding the sport consumer, logistics, promotions, and public relations activities. As far as event planning, while without events a facility would have no purpose, it is important to understand that the goals and operational procedures of facilities are often not the same as that of an event manager. Hence the intent is to articulate the role facility management plays in supporting event management through the sport facility event planning process; the sport facility's role in pre-event, during event, and post-event operations, including the activation of a facility event marketing plan, actual event implementation, the level of involvement in managing events, preparing for unexpected circumstances, and evaluation events after they have taken place. As with almost any activity related to sport, recreation, or leisure, there is some element of risk. The next chapter will articulate the need to plan for all types of emergencies that may disrupt normal operations through knowledge about risk management practices and being able to identify potential facility threats, vulnerabilities, and security countermeasures. Security will be expanded upon in the final part of this section by introducing security best practices, systems, and planning options to equip the twenty-first century sport manager with an all-hazard's approach to facility security planning through the development of plans, policies, and protective measures.

The final section of the book focuses on benchmarking and performance management. Benchmarking is the process of measurement based on a specific set of standards of comparison. Performance management is a visionary process of setting goals and evaluating progress toward accomplishing those goals. Both are equally important concepts for facility managers so they can understand the drivers of performance and how to influence them; provide a detailed process for reporting and evaluating performance; and by integrating these processes as part of organizational culture, they provide the basis for a clear focus on the business essentials and a direction for continuous improvement in connection with all the concepts covered within this book.

## Chapter review

Facility management is an all-encompassing term referring to the maintenance and care of commercial and non-profit buildings, with the goal of organizing and supervising the safe and secure maintenance and operation of a facility in a financially and environmentally sound manner. Operations management focuses on administrating the processes to produce and distribute the products and services offered through a facility, with the goal of maintaining, controlling, and improving organizational activities. Therefore, sport facility operations management seeks to maintain and care for public, private, and non-profit facilities used for sport, recreation, and leisure to ensure safe and secure production and distribution of products and services to users. In order to be a successful sport facility owner or manager, they must understand the various components of sport facility operations management, including (1) pre-management and pre-operations issues (ownership structures, financing, and planning/design/construction), (2) the implementation of management and operations (organizational management, human resource management, financial management, operations management, and legal concerns), (3) ancillary issues in management and operations (marketing, event planning, risk assessment, and security planning), and (4) measuring effectiveness of management and operations (benchmarking and performance management).

# Section One

## Pre-Management and Pre-Operational Issues

# 2 Ownership structures

## Chapter outline

## Chapter objectives

This chapter will cover the various business, ownership, and governance structures for sport facilities across the globe. Sport facility owners must first understand the legal authority under which the sport facility can operate as a business, including as a sole proprietorship, a partnership, or under a number of forms of corporations. At the same time, the sport facility owners must determine how they want to structure their sport business. Sport business organizations are generally structured in three ways: public, non-profit, or commercial. While these categories are general and independent in definition, many sport business organizations can operate under multiple structures. As a result, the ownership must also make choices regarding the governance of the structure, which may be as a public entity, a private entity, a public–private partnerships, or under a voluntary structure. Each of these structures will be examined to provide the reader with a holistic understanding of the various configurations of sport facility ownership. In addition, models of organizational effectiveness will be presented to assist the sport facility manager to efficiently manage the ownership structure. Models to be covered will include the goals model, the system resource model, the process model, and the multiple constituency model. The chapter will conclude with an explanation that ownership and sport facilities managers, in order to be most effective and efficient, must use a contingency approach in all they do, because there is no other best model – which is only an optimum solution for a specific set of circumstances.

## General business structures for sport facilities

As with any type of business, a sport facility must operate under a specific legal business structure to be a viable business. Understanding these various business structures and the operational framework each is crucial to the operations and management of a sport facility from a legal and functional standpoint. The three main categories of business structures are sole proprietorships, partnerships, and corporations. While these main structures are generic in nature, partnerships and corporations have numerous sub-structures that need to be considered for the maximum effectiveness and efficiency in managing the sport facility business.

## Sole proprietorships

The most basic form of business ownership is a sole proprietorship. A sport facility under this form of ownership has only one individual who owns the facility, and hence that individual is responsible for the overall administration of the sport facility. In addition, the sole proprietor is accountable for all business operations, including the management of all assets, and having personal responsibility for all debt and liabilities incurred by the sport facility. This includes the tax liability, which is incurred by the owner as part of their personal income tax. Sole proprietors will often pass their business down to their heirs, as in the case of most family-owned sport facilities.

In addition to having complete control over the decision-making and management processes of the sport facility, there are a number of additional advantages of a sole proprietorship. There are relatively minimal legal costs and few formal business requirements to create a sole proprietorship, and if the owner choose to sell the facility, they can do so without consultation from others. Sole proprietorship businesses can usually open their doors fairly easily; however it is important to recognize the unique licensing, legal, and zoning regulations that are present in different jurisdictions. A further advantage of sole proprietorships, and arguably a disadvantage for other ownership types, is the degree of scrutiny that outside bodies can have on the financial performance of a sole proprietor. In practice the financial affairs of a sole proprietor are confidential between him or her and the tax authorities. As you will discover later in this chapter, one of the prices to be paid for the more complex types of business entity is the requirement for a higher level of scrutiny over an entity's financial affairs.

There are some disadvantages to sole proprietorship for sport facilities over and above the personal liability of the sport facility from business operations. First, the owners are personally liable for the actions of their employees – hence any act of negligence or other illegal conduct related to the sport facility will become the legal responsibility of the sole proprietors. Second, since investors and venture capitalists usually will not invest in sole proprietorships it is difficult for businesses of this type to raise additional funding (or capital) for expansion and development. Most sole proprietors rely on profits, bank loans and personal assets to finance their sport facility initially, which has the effect of limiting the funding that can be sourced to support a business. In the future, if and when the business grows, the sole proprietor may choose to take on partners or incorporate to secure additional funding, but obviously that would change the entire structure of the business.

## Partnerships

A partnership is an ownership structure where more than one individual share the overall administration and business operations of the sport facility. There are a number of partnership structures utilized for sport facilities including general partnerships and limited partnerships.

### General partnerships

The most basic form of partnership is a general partnership, where two or more partners are responsible for all business operations and management responsibilities of a sport facility. The structure is similar to that of a sole proprietorship in that there is personal responsibility for all debt and liabilities incurred by the sport facility including tax liability, but where it differs is that the liabilities are shared by the partners based on the percent of ownership each partner has in the sport facility. In addition to the shared financial commitment and the relative ease of creation, a partnership allows for a stronger top management structure, as multiple owners bring multiple strengths to the business, and often one partner's strength is another partner's weakness. This allows for more effective and efficient management of the sport facility, a stronger business plan, and the potential for acquiring additional resources and investors.

However, if the partners have different personalities, especially as it comes to how each view the management and administration of the sport facility, problems can occur. This is especially true if the goals and vision of the partners differ, and consensus cannot be reached. This can become even more contentious if there is a majority partner who tries to drive the business because of his/her majority ownership in the sport facility. Another disadvantage of a partnership, which is the same as a sole proprietorship, is that the partners are personally liable for the negligence or illegal conduct of their employees when acting as an agent of the sport facility. This disadvantage is elaborated in a partnership because each partner is liable for all decisions made and actions taken by the other partner(s), including any debts they incur in the name of the partnership. As a result of these disadvantages, general partnerships should have agreements that are drawn up by lawyers, mutually agreed upon and signed, and include provisions for the dissolution of the partnership. Reason for dissolution may include death or disability of one or more of the partners, if a partner wishes to sell his/her share of the sport facility, or choose to cease involvement in the business.

### Limited partnerships

Limited partnerships are different from general partnerships specifically in the way the roles and responsibilities that are undertaken by the partners. Also known as a limited liability partnership (LLP), the limited partner provides financial backing, but does not take an active role in the day-to-day operation and management of the sport facility (this responsibility reverts solely to the general partner(s) in the limited partnership). This is an attractive financial investment for an individual who does not have the expertise or time to run the sport facility. The limited partner(s) still have a say in major decisions that affect the sport facility and take on the financial risk of the sport facility, however they do not take on the liability risk because they are not involved with the management or day-to-day operations. However, this does not include protection from personal negligence related to a limited partner's actions in the sport facility, or that of an employee acting under the direct supervision of a limited partner.

## Corporations

A corporation is a business structure created under the laws and regulations of governmental authority made up of a group of individuals who obtain a charter authorizing them as a legal body where the powers, rights, authority, and liabilities of the entity are distinct from the individuals making up the group. The individuals in charge of the corporation are normally referred to as shareholders, and the corporation acts as a legally recognized entity in its own right – eligible to enter into contracts, obtain assets, be responsible for liabilities, and conduct the day-to-day management and business operations.

The process of incorporation or company formation is a very complex process that may vary from jurisdiction to jurisdiction, and based on the type of corporation chosen for the business – such as a C-Corporation, a close corporation, an S-corporation, a limited liability corporation, a publicly traded corporation, or a non-profit corporation. Generally, there is a three-step process to incorporate. First is to determine a name for the corporation and verify with the appropriate jurisdiction that the company name is available for incorporation. The name must be unique and cannot create deception in its similarity to another incorporate business. The second step is to file all the necessary documentation as required by the specific incorporation. This documentation is usually referred to as the Articles of Incorporation, but can also be called a Certificate of Incorporation, a Corporate Charter, or Articles of Association. These articles of incorporation include the name of the corporation, names and contact information of the directors of the corporation, information about membership (if applicable), where the registered office and/or principal location are, the purpose of the corporation, the limitations of the corporation, the activities of the corporation, and how the corporation would be dissolved. The final step is to pay any fees charged by your jurisdiction. This may include governmental fees, franchise taxes, and business initiation fees. In addition, if you have any legal representation assisting in the incorporation of the business, fees incurred would also need to be paid.

There are numerous advantages to setting up a sport facility as a corporation. The major reason is because of the limited liability that is provided to owners, the personal assets of owners is not at risk for the debts or liabilities of the corporation. This is extended to tax liabilities since the corporation is a separate legal entity – the corporation pays the taxes, not the owners. Corporations are also generally considered to be attractive investments; therefore it is often easier to attract investors to improve the corporation. From an employee standpoint, there are a few interesting advantages. For general employees, there are opportunities for profit sharing and stock ownership – a benefit that often attracts higher-quality employees. For owner-employees, many of the general expenses incurred by the individual, including insurance, are often able to be reimbursed through the corporation, or used as a tax deduction at the end of the year. From a structural standpoint, the management structure is usually very clear and ordered, and the organization will have perpetual existence until all of the shareholders either dissolve the corporation or merge with another.

There are also disadvantages to incorporating a sport facility, not the least of which is the cost to file the articles of incorporation, pre-pay taxes, file governmental documentation, and pay for legal fees. Paperwork is very extensive, including corporate reports, tax filings, banking and accounting records, minutes of corporate actions and shareholder meetings, and documents related to any licenses and certifications. In addition, the formalities required to run a corporation are significant, hence why many meetings use Robert's Rules of Order or the Democratic Rules of Order; and why there is a need for such a strict organizational structure. In addition, the dissolution of a corporation is very time consuming and complex, as a result of the processes related to liquidating assets, organizing payments to creditors, and distributing remaining cash value to shareholders.

## Types of corporations

There are a variety of legal structures a corporation can take for sport facilities, including C-Corporations, close corporations, S-corporations, limited liability corporations, publicly traded corporations, or non-profit corporations. The general structure discussed in the previous section on corporations is indicative of the most common structure – a C-Corporation. A C-Corporation is for profit-driven, incorporated sport facilities and provides a structure that allows an unlimited number of owners, shareholders, and shares of stock. Another type of corporation – a close corporation – is similar in structure to a C-Corporation, however it is designed for sport facilities that have a corporate structure with as few one owner (a sole proprietor who chooses to use a corporation structure) to a maximum of usually no more than 50 owners/shareholders.

The other types of corporations have some unique characteristics that may be beneficial to various sport facility owners. For example, while the S-Corporation is formed in a similar manner to C-Corporations and close corporations, its tax structure is very different because taxes are paid similarly to a sole proprietor-ship or partnership – where the income from the S-Corporation is passed on to the shareholders, and they pay the taxes on the profit (or take the deduction in case of a loss) rather than the corporation. The advantage of this type of corporation for the owners of the sport facility is that they can act as a sole proprietor of partnership with all the tax and liability benefits of a corporation, and also allows the owners to seek investors as a corporate structure – which is often more attractive. On the negative side, there are significant regulations on S-Corporations, including limits on the number of shareholders, and close scrutiny by governmental agencies regarding compensation of shareholders who are also employees of the sport facility. S-Corporations are relatively expensive to set up in comparison to sole proprietorships and partnerships, and have unique governmental regulations that vary from jurisdiction to jurisdiction. In addition, to avoid any legal problems, the owners need to be diligent to keep personal financial records and corporate financial record separate.

Similar to a limited liability partnership (LLP), a limited liability corporation (LLC) has the characteristics of both a partnership and a corporation. Over the past decade, this has become the single most popular form of ownership for sport-related business entities not only because of its hybrid structure, but also as a result of the status of the individuals who act as the owners. An LLC is formed by members of the organization, not shareholders. In the case of a sport facility, they create an operating agreement to run the facility without the strict guidelines and organizational structures of a corporation. This includes not having to write annual reports, run structured meetings, and deal with shareholder issues. By not having to operate under these strict formalities, the ownership can focus on the operation of the facility, have more flexibility in the management of the facility (including developing and implementing contracts, assigning human and physical resources, and allocating income), and meeting the needs of their clients. In addition, the LLC provides the same personal liability protection as any other corporation

Publicly traded (or publicly owned) corporations have a number of meanings based on the part of the world. In general the concept of a public corporation refers to a business entity that has registered securities such as stocks and/or bonds that can be sold to the general population through stock offerings. Public corporations have also be referred to as government-owned corporations because of the public ownership of the assets and because the benefits provided by the business entity are for the interest of the public. This latter reference is most commonly used globally in terms of sport facilities. The benefits of being a public-owned/government-owned corporation center are the ability to have better access to capital through the sales of stocks and/or bonds, and a higher level of support as a result of governmental backing. However, this type of corporation requires total public disclosure of all financial and operational actions.

A final corporation that is prevalent in sport business, but not as widely seen in the ownership structure of sport facilities (however it is prevalent in many of the events and companies that use sport facilities) is the non-profit corporation. A non-profit corporation is a business whose purpose is not to make a profit, but rather to offer services that are beneficial to the general public. Most non-profit corporations are tax exempt because of their nature as a public benefit business. Examples of sport facilities that may be categorized under non-profit status include those related to religious, charitable, and educational purposes. Many facilities that have the purpose of fostering international sports events are often categorized as non-profit, such as those hosting the Olympics. In addition, facilities that are owned and operated by civic leagues and recreational clubs are often classified under non-profit corporation status. These types of corporations are kept under close scrutiny by the government as a result of the benefits they receive.

## Sport facility ownership and governance structures

In looking at the general business structures for sport facilities as discussed previously, we can categorize the types of sport business facility ownership into three basic categories. Public sport facilities are usually operated under governmental or quasi-governmental ownership either through federal, regional, or local jurisdictions. Non-profit sport facilities are those managed by volunteer executives and hire paid staff to carry out day-to-day operations, with the ultimate goal not based on profit but on public benefit. The main goal of commercial sport facilities is to make a profit.

While the three sport facility ownerships structures are generic in nature, the methods employed to govern these structures can vary. For sport facilities, there are four main governance structures that are prevalent globally – public governance, private governance, non-profit/voluntary governance, and governance via trusts. It is important to remember that these governance structures can be applied individually, or can also be applied in combination with each other, such as public–private governance.

### Public

Public governance of sport facilities is usually conducted as a responsibility of an elected public body for a governmental jurisdiction, and usually assigned as the main responsibility of a specific appointed governmental official. The main reason for a public-owned facility is often related to the importance of offering high-quality facilities for the use of the population based on their needs. When it comes to larger facilities for the purpose of holding large events and/or having a professional team, municipalities believe that these sport facilities are important engines of economic development – especially in urban areas. These officials believe that the sport facilities contribute new spending and jobs in the municipality, hence providing justification for public subsidies for the construction and maintenance of these sports facilities.

In this type of governance, the facility manager usually reports directly to these government officials, and must work within the operational efficiency constraints, regulations and procedures evident in bureaucratic management. This often has a direct effect on many of the operational functions of a sport facility manager, including purchasing processes (which often must go through either a tedious bidding or approval process), contract approvals (which must go through the various levels of legislative bureaucracy), and human resource management (hiring, promoting, and firing – which all must go through governmental approval and clearance procedures). There are also challenges when the governmental officials/bodies who are overseeing the public facilities are politicians who truly do not understand the managerial processes of a sport facility. As a result of this, many public-governed sport facilities have commissioned independent boards to oversee the facilities – made up of individuals who understand facility management, but still report back to the government agencies. Another viable option is noted below

## Private management of public facilities

In many cases, public bodies have chosen to outsource the management of municipal sport stadiums, arena, and recreational facilities by hiring private management groups to manage the day-to-day operations of the sport facility, and provide reports back to the governmental agency. Two of the major companies in the world who offer this type of service to sport facilities are SMG and Global Spectrum.

SMG (www.smgworld.com) is one of the largest companies in the world focused on venue management, marketing and development. They manage convention centers, exhibition halls and trade centers, arenas, stadiums, performing arts centers, theaters, and specialized-use venues, and have partnerships and relationships with both municipal and private clients. SMG has global reach in sport arena and stadium management – just a few examples of prominent sport facilities include the United States (Reliant Stadium, Arena, and Astrodome in Houston; and the Superdome in New Orleans); and Europe (König Pilsener Arena in Oberhausen, Germany; Manchester Evening News Arena in England; and Odyssey Arena in Belfast, Northern Ireland). SMG is also in the process of expanding their operations into Latin America and Asia.

Global Spectrum (www.global-spectrum.com) provides management, marketing, operations and event booking services for public assembly facilities, including arenas, civic and convention centers, stadiums, ice facilities, equestrian centers and theaters. In addition to providing full scope-of-services for existing facilities that decide to privatize, Global Spectrum also provides pre-opening design and constructing consulting services for the development phase of facilities under construction. The global reach of this company is growing – some examples of current facilities around the world managed by Global Spectrum include the United States (Wachovia Sports Complex and Citizens Bank Field in Philadelphia, and the University of Phoenix Stadium in Arizona); Canada (John LabattCentre in London, Ontario; and Abbotsford Sports and Entertainment Centre in British Columbia); and are expanding into Europe (Spaladium in Split, Croatia) and Asia (Singapore Sports Hub – Arena, National Stadium, and Indoor Stadium).

*Continued*

## Private management of public facilities—cont'd

*Sources*:

1. **Global Spectrum**. (2009). *Company Background*. Retrieved April 3, 2009 from http://www.global-spectrum.com/
2. **SMG**. (2009). *About SMG*. Retrieved April 3, 2009 from http://www. smgworld.com/ company_history.aspx

### Suggested discussion topics

1. What are the advantages and disadvantages to outsourcing the management of public sport facilities?
2. Other than SMG and Global Spectrum, identify three other private management companies for sport facilities. Compare and contrast the mission and main service offerings – how each of those companies are similar to and different from SMG and Global Spectrum?
   a. Since SMG and Global Spectrum seem to be focused on the Northern Hemisphere, can you identify any facility management companies in the Southern Hemisphere in countries such as Australia, Brazil, and South Africa?

### *Private*

The fastest growing structure for governing sport facilities of all types is private governance. As public funding dries up because of changes in the economy the determination that other municipal projects are more needed, and the lack of human resources to appropriately manage and oversee sport facilities, private enterprises have evolved to meet the needs of communities. These private-managed sport facilities run as an independent business under any number of ownerships structures including sole proprietorships, partnerships, or corporations – and can be either commercial or non-profit. The owners have the ability to exercise their own power and authority over the entire governance structure of the sport facility, including the development of the mission and vision, determining who the users of the facility are, and the regulatory power for anything that happens within the sport facility.

### *Non-profit/voluntary governance*

Non-profit and voluntary governance organizations are an integral part of the sport business landscape, especially related to sport facilities that are part of educational, charitable, and religious sport entities. Involvement of individuals in the day-to-day operation of these sport facilities is usually voluntary in nature, although there may be some compensated employees within the organization.

However, the governance of the sport facility is usually voluntary. The main responsibilities as related to voluntary governance involves the ability to work within the external environments to secure resources from market operations, governmental subsidies, or from reciprocity (volunteering, donations) while pursuing the goals and objectives set forth for the sport facility. Organizations under a voluntary governance structure usually work under a constitution and a set of bylaws. The constitution is a document that outlines the purpose, structure, and limits of an organization. The bylaws are the rules adopted to define and direct the internal structure, policies, and procedures of the sport facility.

### Trusts

The importance of managers being aware of the jurisdiction in which they are working is well illustrated by the case of the United Kingdom where the use of sport and leisure 'trusts' is an increasingly common trend. The term 'trust' does not really have a legal definition and tends to be used as a catch all description for organizations that are specifically set up to run local authority leisure services independently, and for public good rather than individual gain. The essence of what a trust is can be appreciated from the three stage diagram presented below.

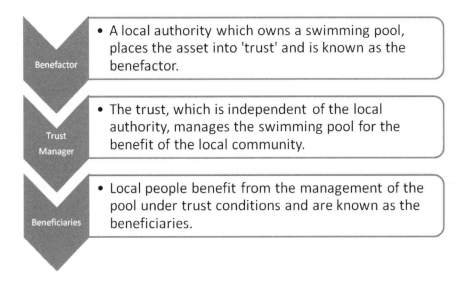

There are three types of trust that local authorities can consider using...

### A company limited by guarantee with or without charitable status

A company limited by guarantee is a legally recognized business entity in its own right – the same as any other limited company. However, unlike conventional limited companies where the owners' liability is limited to the extent of their investment in the business, in a company limited by guarantee there is no individual investment and the liability of the owners is limited to a guarantee of a fixed amount in the event of the company failing. In practice the amount that directors of companies limited by guarantee are asked to contribute in the event of failure is a nominal amount of around £1–£5 should it be called for. In order to achieve limited by guarantee status a company needs to have objectives that are for the public good, such as the provision of recreational or cultural opportunities for the community. A further distinguishing feature of a company limited by guarantee is that surpluses or profits are not allowed to be distributed to the directors or trustees. This does not mean that it is not permitted for companies of this type to make profits; rather those who control the company are not permitted to benefit financially from its trading performance. Indeed it may be essential for companies limited by guarantee to make profits in order to maintain their facilities and to reinvest in the business. For many facility providers in the UK achieving the status of company limited by guarantee is but a stepping stone to achieve charitable status. Charitable status provides desirable tax advantages for organizations whose objectives include: the relief of poverty, the advancement of education, the advancement of religion, or other purposes deemed beneficial to the community. The provision of sports facilities and sporting opportunities falls into the 'other purposes' category and there are plenty of precedents whereby charitable status has been awarded to sports organizations. The major financial benefits of charitable status are exemption from corporation tax on the profits plus mandatory relief of 80% of local authority business rates (a form of local taxation) with the potential to increase this to 100% at the discretion of the local authority. Thus simply from rate relief alone, registered charities have a significant financial competitive advantage over suppliers that are not registered charities. Some companies that are limited by guarantee do not pursue charitable status and are content with the protection that their status provides the directors of the company, that is, a nominal limit on their liability in the event of failure. Regardless of charitable status, one of the key benefits of being a company limited by guarantee is the ability to attract competent directors from the community who are happy to offer their expertise for free safe in the knowledge that their liability for debts is limited by the value of their (usually nominal) guarantee.

### An industrial and provident society with or without charitable status

Industrial and Provident Societies (IPS) are recognized as being legal entities in their own right and have broadly the same benefits as companies limited by guarantee. To achieve IPS status in the context of sport, applicants are required to demonstrate that they are providing benefits for the community and not just the membership. The key features of an Industrial and Provident Society are that it will have:

- a written set of rules which govern its activities;
- a recognized separate legal identity;

- the right to own property;
- the right to enter into contracts;
- additional legal requirements made of it such as company law;
- limited liability (i.e. the liability of the management committee is usually limited to a nominal amount); and
- a profit making ability, which is put back into the organization.

Greenwich Leisure Limited (GLL) is an innovative example of a staff led 'Leisure Trust', which uses the Industrial and Provident Society format. GLL manages more than 65 public leisure centers in Greater London. Not only is the legal format of the business an ideal way to run the trust, but also benefits from economies of scale in terms of procurement whereby it can negotiate bulk discounts on energy costs and other supplies. Like companies limited by guarantee it is also possible for Industrial and Provident Societies to qualify for charitable status and hence benefit from mandatory rate relief.

## Public interest companies (PICS)

Public Interest Companies are a relatively new legal format for delivering public services. A Public Interest Company (PIC) exists to deliver a specific public benefit such as providing equitable sporting opportunities for the community. This benefit cannot be changed without direct agreement from the appropriate publicly accountable body, protecting the public's interest in the services provided, and distinguishing PICs from commercial companies and the not for profit sector. PICs are independent bodies. The government cannot manage them directly nor interfere with management processes and day-to-day decisions. PICs can only be held accountable for their results and standards of delivery by government. This makes PICs different from public sector organizations and allows them to be entrepreneurial and responsive to the needs of users.

The intricacies of what type of business format to adopt is best left to those with up to date legal skills and experience to advise managers expertly. However, as a manager you should have a working knowledge of the available options and should be conversant with the advice that lawyers give you. It is therefore worthwhile knowing the strengths and weaknesses of various formats so that decisions are made using the best available information.

The strengths of 'trust' status are:

- Trusts operate as "social enterprises" which provides them with the ability to run as a business, whilst working towards the community's needs and a local authority's strategic direction.
- There is a proven record of trusts improving the performance of their partners through the achievement of social targets and the setting of clear strategic goals.
- Evidence gathered over a long period suggests that trusts reduce the cost of a service to the local authority which in turn reduces an authority's financial risk. Trusts do not pay tax on profits, they qualify for rate relief and tend to find it easier to fund raise for both revenue and capital projects than local authorities.
- Local authorities retain some control over trusts by agreeing shared targets to ensure that sport facilities are managed to optimize the achievement of an authority's

objectives. In practice, this is achieved through partnership working and service level agreements.

- Local authorities can retain influence on the board of a trust via the nomination of trustees who will protect the authority's interests.
- Sports facilities can be operated with greater financial and management autonomy, enabling them to respond to market changes dynamically and hence remain competitive.
- Trustees have the ability to develop business and financial plans over sustainable periods of time, creating the ability to plan for the future.
- Previous evidence suggests the trusts improve the opportunity for community involvement in service delivery.
- Trusts have the ability to deliver a wide spectrum of varying leisure facilities, as long as the activities can be considered to be 'charitable activity'. Examples include running sport facilities ('other purposes beneficial to the community') and arts facilities ('advancing education').
- The Trust option creates a perceived "middle ground" towards outsourcing public services and does not necessarily involve such a fundamental shift in political ideology as contracting facilities and services out to the private sector.
- The board of trustees, if appointed successfully, should add expert financial, business and marketing experience with no additional cost to the service as these are voluntary posts.

The weaknesses of 'trust' status are:

- There is a widely held view that establishing a trust is resource intensive both in terms of financial outlay and the time required to see the process through from inception to completion.
- By placing a facility or service into trust there is an inevitable loss of integration with other local authority services. For example, in case of an emergency the authority would not be able to convert a trust-managed sports hall into a temporary shelter for homeless people as easily as it could if the facility was managed in-house.
- The success or failure of a trust hinges crucially on the ability to recruit a suitable board of trustees, with the requisite skills, experience and knowledge to provide strategic direction and leadership. There is the danger that in deprived areas particularly, appropriate community leadership will not emerge and under these conditions trust status can be more of a hindrance than a help.
- In the early stages of running a trust it may be difficult to attract financing owing to the company's unproven trading record. As discussed in Chapter 8 (Finance) potential trading partners like to vet the accounts of companies they do business with. If a trust does not have a financial track record, and is unable to provide copies of its last three years worth of audited accounts, some firms may be reluctant to trade or will set punitive trading conditions such as payment in advance.
- Facilities often receive hidden subsidies from local authorities such as help with central administration and maintenance costs. These should be planned for so that there is no duplication of effort or that in reality the trust is more expensive to run than under the in-house model.
- If a trust fails financially there is potentially a large financial risk that may need to be borne by the Authority. This type of situation can be seen as local authorities

bearing much of the risk but not benefiting from the rewards. However, evidence to date indicates that in the last 20 years there have been very few trusts that have failed.

The essential points emerging from the information presented on the types of ownership structure presented in this chapter are twofold. First, there are numerous types of legal format available to the sports facility manager. The reality is that in the early part of your career this type of activity will have been taken care of and you will work in a predetermined ownership structure over which you have no strategic control. As your career develops and you take on a more strategic role, which could involve deciding the ownership model and legal identity of a facility, you will be required to explore and advise on various options accordingly. Second, issues around ownership structures and legal identity are complex. Whilst you should be conversant with the issues, it is also important to realize the limitations of your knowledge. Somethings are best left to specialists and a good manager is one who knows when to ask for help.

## Models of organizational effectiveness

To be able to appropriately govern a sport facility, a manager must have a clear understanding of the concept of organizational effectiveness. Organizational effectiveness is the concept of how efficient a business is in achieving the outcomes set forth in the planning processes. Measuring organizational effectiveness is central to the evaluation of what a sport facility delivers from programmatic, operational, and managerial perspectives. It is an integral process to prove the investors and donors that the money being provided is being used to accomplish the goals of the organization, to evaluate the communication processes and ethical actions of the business, and to serve as a foundational process for determining strategic growth.

For a sport facility to be effective and achieve its goals and objectives, the ownership and the governance structures must be able to successfully respond to changes in its environment. Changes in the environment may be internal to the sport facility organization/management/operation, or external (examples include customer's needs, the economy, politics, legal issues, and the media). At the same time, there is a need for an organization to understand the attributes of flexibility in correlation to control. Flexibility allows faster change, whereas control allows a firmer grasp on current operations. How these two concerns work in congruency in both the internal and external environments is a significant measure of organizational effectiveness.

Numerous models have been developed to help sport facilities measure organization effectiveness based on the varying levels of environmental and organizational attributes. The following chart articulates the major models of organizational effectiveness that are utilized in sport facilities globally.

| Model | Description |
|---|---|
| Goal (or rational goal) | • Where the achievement of specific organizational goals determine effectiveness.<br>  • Establish the general goal.<br>  • Discover objectives for accomplishment.<br>  • Define activities for each objectives.<br>  • Measure level of success.<br>  • Designed to enhance strategic planning by linking program goals and resource allocation levels.<br>  • Is output based and in measureable terms – not always good because all effectiveness is not output based. |
| Process (or internal process) | • Focuses on the effectiveness of the internal transformation process.<br>• Emphasis on control and the internal focus, and stresses the role of information management, communication, stability, and control. |
| Systems resources | • Where effectiveness is determined in terms of the ability to attract and secure valuable resources, such as operating capital, physical resources, and quality human resources |
| Multiple constituency | • Where effectiveness is not internally judged, but is based on the judgment of its constituents.<br>  • In the case of a sport facility, it may include spectators, promoters, resident teams, and vendors.<br>• Often used as a viable alternative to the goal and systems approaches. |
| Strategic constituencies | • Effectiveness is determined by the extent to which the organization satisfies all of its strategic constituencies.<br>• For a sport facility, it would include spectators, vendors, home teams, the media, sponsors, etc.) |
| Open system | • Effectiveness is measured as a result of the degree that an organization acquires inputs from its environment and has outputs accepted by its environment. |

*Continued*

| Model | Description |
|-------|-------------|
| Competing values | • Effectiveness that is measured based on the interaction between four sets of competing values:<br>  • Internal Focus and Integration;<br>  • External Focus and Differentiation;<br>  • Flexibility and Discretion;<br>  • Control and Stability. |
| High-performing system | • Effectiveness as a measurement that compare itself to other similar organizations. |
| Human relations | • Effectiveness measured based on the development of the organization's personnel.<br>• Places emphasis on flexibility and internal focus.<br>• Stresses cohesion, morale, and human resources as a development criteria for effectiveness. |
| Legitimacy | • Effectiveness measured by acting lawfully and ethically in the eyes of the internal and external environment. |
| Fault-driven | • Effectiveness seeks to eliminate traces of ineffectiveness in its internal functioning through the design of backup plans to be reliable even if some components fail. |

On a final note, sport facility managers and owners need to acknowledge a contingency approach to organizational effectiveness, as there is no best model. There are numerous variables that influence organizational effectiveness, including changes in the organizational structure, the implementation of new technologies, opportunities and threats in the environment that affect the sport facility, and the people using the sport facility (both customers and human resources) – to name a few. As a result, sport facilities owners and managers must take a situational approach to organizational effectiveness to attain an optimum solution for a specific set of circumstances that arise.

## Chapter review

A sport facility must operate under a specific legal business structure to be a viable business. Understanding these various business structures and the operational framework each allows is crucial to the operations and management of a sport facility from a legal and functional standpoint. The three main categories of business structures are sole proprietorships, partnerships, and corporations. The most basic form of business ownership is a sole proprietorship, where only one individual owns the facility and is responsible for the overall administration and liabilities of the sport facility. A partnership is where more than one individual who shares the overall administration and business operations of the sport facility. There are a number of partnership structures utilized for sport facilities including general partnerships and limited partnerships. General partners are directly involved with the day-to-day operations of the facility and have full liability, whereas limited partners have financial liability but not operational liability or responsibility. Corporations are business structure created under the laws and regulations of governmental authority made up of a group of individuals who obtain a charter authorizing them as a legal body where the powers, rights, authority, and liabilities of the entity are distinct from the individuals making up the group. There are various corporate structures for sport facilities including C-Corporation, a close corporation, an S-corporation, a limited liability corporation, a publicly traded corporation, or a non-profit corporation.

Sport facility ownership usually fall under one of three governance structures. Public sport facilities are usually operated under governmental or quasi-governmental ownership either through federal, regional, or local jurisdictions. Non-profit sport facilities are those managed by volunteer executives and hire paid staff to carry out day-to-day operations, with the ultimate goal not based on profit but on public benefit. The main goal of commercial sport facilities is to make a profit. A unique governance structure is governance by trust, where a benefactor places an asset (such as a sport facility) into a trust, that is managers by an assigned party (trust manager) to ensure the customers (beneficiaries) benefit from the services of the sport facility. These trusts can be either as a charitable organization, a non-profit without charity status, or a public interest company.

To appropriately govern a sport facility, a manager must have a clear understanding of the concept of organizational effectiveness, which is the concept of how efficient a business is in achieving the outcomes set forth in the planning processes. While there are multiple models of organizational effectiveness, it is important to recognize and acknowledge the need for a contingency approach to govern a sport facility, as there is no other best model – which is only an optimum solution for a specific set of circumstances.

# 3 Financing sport facilities

## Chapter outline

## Chapter objectives

This chapter will delve into the intricacies of financing sport facilities. Recurring themes in financing will be discussed, including business issues, the costs of ownership, life-cycle costing, cost-effectiveness/efficiency, and the principles of economic impact analysis. Their recurring issues have a direct effect on the source of financing to be used for sport facilities, such as public sector funding, private sources of revenue, public–private partnerships, and the influence of the voluntary sector. As significant economic change has taken place early in the twenty-first century, the effects on sport facility investment are significant, hence the chapter will conclude with a look at the current and future trends that will affect the management and operation of sport facilities.

## Financing concepts

Financing is defined as the act of obtaining or providing money or capital for the purchase of a business enterprise. For a sport facility, many of these financing issues are related to the types of financing available and the significant changes that have occurred in sport facility investment in the twenty-first century. However, prior to delving into those topics, it is important to understand recurring themes that are central to the understanding of basis financing themes. In addition to basic business issues related to financing sport facilities, other concepts to be understood include the costs of ownership/life-cycle costing; and the principles of economic impact analysis.

### Business issues

Developing new sports facilities is a risky process that invariably requires complex financial arrangements. These two points are interrelated. First, it is unlikely that any organization from any sector will have the spare cash available to develop and build a sport facility from the outset of a project. It is therefore current practice that the financing of sports facilities tends to be made with financial contributions from a variety of sources. For example, the new national football stadium in England (Wembley) cost an estimated £757M ($1.157 billion US) and was funded by the Football Association, distributions from the National Lottery, the London Development Agency and a series of commercial banks. As you will discover in Chapter 7 when we look at finance more closely, it is essential for businesses to make a profit and to be able to service their debts. In 2007, Wembley National Stadium Ltd had long term debts of £635M ($971M US) and paid £47m ($72M US) in interest to service those debts. Second, because of the risks involved and the scale of developing sports facilities, developers seek to share the risk involved in a project with partners. These are drawn from those who wish to risk their money on taking a stake in a business by buying the right to share in future profits (equity financing); and those who are prepared to loan money for the development in return for a fixed rate of interest and the knowledge that in the event of business failure they will get their money back (debt financing). The bigger the project, the more complex the web of relationships underpinning it is. When public sector money is involved there is also the scope for controversy as perhaps best demonstrated by adverse publicity surrounding the $450M US public sector subsidies provided by the New York authorities for the Yankee Stadium and the £120M ($183.5M US) provided by the National Lottery for Wembley Stadium.

When borrowed money (or debt) is used to finance a development the stance of those borrowing the money is the belief that they can make sufficient profit to be able to service interest costs and still make a profit. For the providers of loans, the stance taken is that the interest being paid on the loans justifies the risk of lending to the developer. In practice the two parties' fates are inextricably linked – for everyone to get a fair return on their investment the development has to succeed.

The complex nature of sport facility development helps to provide further insight into the role and responsibilities of the sports facility manager. At the most basic level it is important that day to day operations are profitable and sustainable. There is little point in using public subsidies and other people's money to develop a facility for sport only for further money to be required to underwrite operating losses. One of the first rules of business is that you need to make a profit is your business is to have a long term future. In the case of public sector facilities, for which there may be legitimate grounds to subsidize operating costs, managers must operate within the subsidy levels that have been allocated to them. The importance of appropriate financial performance can also be appreciated by looking at the bigger picture. If as a manager you do not deliver, then you place at risk the livelihoods of your staff, your suppliers and other stakeholders. Equally, by performing well you pave the conditions for growth, re-investment, higher salaries, more staff, and so on. Whilst this is a weighty responsibility in its own right, things do not stop at sound financial performance. Sports facilities are investments which have the potential to grow in value. Most properties tend to increase in value over time and sports facilities are no different. One method by which investors can profit from their initial investment in a sports facility is by selling it for a higher price than the facility cost to develop in the first place. Some of the key factors that determine how much a business is worth are:

- how well the business is performing financially;
- the condition of the land, buildings, fixtures, and local infrastructure; and
- the opportunity for future development in the locality.

Thus a further set of responsibilities for the sports facility manager is the importance of ensuring that the asset is well maintained and kept in a suitable condition such that it is attractive to potential purchasers or indeed new investors. Finally, the managers of sports facilities should be aware of the wider context in which they operate. When a facility is built, it supports jobs in the construction industry, and when the facility is operational numerous other people may be directly or indirectly dependent on the facility for some or all of their income. With this responsibility comes the importance of being a good corporate citizen, not only looking after your own interests but also those of the wider community. A good facility manager will operate at all three levels and look after the interests of the business, the facility and the wider community. You should now realize that effective sports facility management is much more than taking care of day to day operations.

## The costs of ownership/life-cycle costing

Considerations around financing sports facilities are not confined to how much a building costs to construct in the first instance. In our own lives we know that buying a car is simply the start of an expensive relationship with an asset which will require further expense in terms of tax, insurance, fuel servicing, parking and valeting. A second hand luxury car might cost the same as a new small car but we all know that the costs of owning the former will be much greater than the latter. The same type of commonsense thinking is applicable to sports facilities. For both buildings and equipment due consideration must be given to what are known as 'life cycle costs', which are defined by the Chartered Institute of Management Accountants as 'the maintenance of physical asset cost records over the entire asset lives, so that decisions concerning the acquisition, use, or disposal of the assets can be made in a way that achieves the optimum asset usage at the lowest cost to the entity.'

The importance of being aware of life cycle costing can be appreciated by the finding that as much as 90% of the lifetime costs attributable to an asset are determined by decisions made in the early part of the asset's life. For example, in the case of a swimming pool the purchase costs of an ozone treatment plant for water cleansing compared with a chlorine based plant might make the ozone option seem prohibitive on price. However, when the full lifetime costs of each option are evaluated to account for costs such as energy usage, chemical costs and plant maintenance, it may well be the case that the more expensive option to buy actually works out to less expensive to own and operate in the longer term than the cheaper option. It is important to avoid 'buy now pay later' situations as cheaper items may have higher running costs and a lower disposal value. Managers of sports facilities are routinely required to make long term judgments about the optimal solution for a given set of circumstances. For example, it is more cost effective to purchase gym equipment outright and to take responsibility for maintaining and replacing it, or is a better option to lease the equipment whereby maintenance is part of the service level agreement? By using the principles of lifetime costing, these decisions can be made on the evidence of the best information available and in the best interests of the business.

The evidence that lifecycle costing for an asset can be complicated is indicated in the range of considerations listed below:

- Purchase costs (how much does an asset cost to purchase?).
- Running costs (what are the operational costs of using an asset, such as the hourly costs of running air conditioning in a sports stadium?).
- Maintenance costs (how much does it cost to retain an asset in a fit for purpose condition?).
- Training costs (how much will it cost to train staff in the use of a new box office system?).
- Decommissioning and disposal costs (how much will it cost to wind down an asset and to dispose of it bearing in mind operational and environmental issues?).

In reality it is difficult to forecast what might happen in the future and lifecycle costing decisions are based on people's attitude towards risk and financial issues such as how quickly they want their money back. Nonetheless, the importance of making good decisions can be appreciated by examining the case of health and fitness clubs that are part of a chain. If proper lifecycle costing is carried out to inform an organization's business model, then when the model is rolled out to multiple sites the benefits will be reaped at every site. Conversely, if you get it wrong at one site and roll out a flawed business model, then the error will be compounded in every site affected. An alternative way of looking at lifecycle costing is to call it 'cost effectiveness' which is defined as an assessment, before a decision, of the available options, which are assumed to deliver the same outcomes, in terms of their relative costs.

Thus whether we are talking about the construction materials for a sports hall, the type of plant to use to clean the water in a swimming pool, or the purchase or leasing of fitness equipment; we should always be mindful of the importance of cost effectiveness and the impact our present decisions will have on costs in the future.

### The principles of economic impact analysis

The justification for financing many sport facilities is often based on arguments made about the economic benefits that the development will have on the local community. Indeed it is precisely this argument that developers present to public bodies in order to lever funding or other financially advantageous concessions for proposed projects. At the time of writing there is no higher profile example of economic impact arguments being used to justify investment in sports facilities than the London 2012 Olympic and Paralympic Games. During a time of global recession when there is a proven logic for governments to spend their way out of financial trouble, the expenditure of around £9.2 billion on sports facilities and supporting infrastructure can be considered to be a financial lifeline contributing to bring the economy out of recession rather than an expensive luxury.

Given the claimed benefits of investing in sports facilities, what is meant by economic impact and what are the benefits it brings? A simple definition of economic impact is 'the net economic change in a host community that is directly attributable to a facility or an event'. There are two points to note arising from this definition. First, the word 'net' means that it is important to take into account both positive and negative aspects of economic impact. Thus the opening of a new health club might not only create 30 new jobs, but it also might lead to the closure of a rival facility with the loss of say 20 existing jobs. The 'net' economic impact in this case would be 10 new jobs. Second, the words 'directly attributable' mean that the facility or event must cause the economic impact to occur. If people attending a conference in a city decide to attend a game of baseball as part of their visit, the economic impact is actually attributable to the conference and not to the game of baseball. That is to say, the visitors were in the area for a primary reason (the conference) and the baseball just happened to be on at the same time and was secondary to the main purpose of the visit. There is something of a culture in the sport industry for people to exaggerate the economic impact of facilities and events in order to make them look more attractive for public funding.

For sports facilities there are five key areas in which positive economic benefits can be delivered as discussed below.

- *Construction*: during the construction phase of a facility jobs will be supported or created in the building industry. In the UK, it is widely accepted by economists that every £100,000 ($153M US) of construction costs will support or create one job in the industry. It is therefore no surprise that in 2009 some 4500 construction workers are employed on the Olympic Park site in London. There can also be positive economic benefits in the construction supply change with increased demand for building materials and the fixtures and fittings needed to equip a new building.
- *Employment*: when a facility opens it will need staff to operate it and this leads to increased employment opportunities for the local community. Working in sport facility is a customer focused occupation and people can acquire useful customer care and operations management experience that is transferable to many other occupations.
- *Supply chain*: sports facilities need supplies such as food and drink to be sold to customers as well as services such as utilities. Those businesses which service new sports facilities will see an increase in the demand for their products as the ripples of economic impact spread wider.

- *Local income*: the presence of more money in the local community from the spending of employees, the increased demand in the supply chain and increased tax revenues means that the community as a whole will enjoy increased prosperity that can be linked to the opening of a new sports facility.
- *Events*: some new sports facilities change the local infrastructure and enable activities that were previously not possible to occur. For example, if a new stadium is built to host an NFL franchise there will be a guaranteed eight regular season home matches per year. The stadium will therefore have to be put to other uses such as staging concerts, conferences and exhibitions. Without the stadium these would not have been possible and the spending from out of town visitors at these events can provide a welcome additional revenue stream to the local community.

The manner in which potential economic impacts are quantified is by the use of specially commissioned 'economic impact studies'. These studies attempt to model the future economic impacts of a sports facility or to measure the actual economic impact of a facility or an event. They are as much art as science and radically different figures can be derived for the same development by consultants depending on who they are working for and the assumptions they use to drive their models. It is therefore important that economic impact studies are carried out independently and make full use of all of the data available. Furthermore, there should be a transparent audit trail of how the economic impact has been derived and what the key drivers of it are. As a manager you should have an awareness of the economic impact of your facility on the local community. Where appropriate you should also develop the skills necessary to exploit this knowledge for the benefit of your organization.

## Sources of financing for sport facilities

Financing of sport facilities come in three basic forms – public financing, private funding, and public–private partnerships. All three have had a significant effect on financing sport facilities throughout modern history. Public financing involves the collection of taxes from those who receive benefits from the provision of public goods by the government, and then uses those tax revenues to produce and distribute the public goods to the beneficiaries. Private financing is providing funding for capital investments by non-governmental individuals and/or businesses to provide products and services to the public under the management and operation of the private entity, and the public usually has to pay a fee to utilize the products and services. Public–private partnerships are agreements between government and the private sector regarding the provision of public services or infrastructure – the public municipality transfers the burden of capital expenditures and risks of cost overruns to the private entity, but maintains a partnership in the offering of products and services to the public.

## Public sector funding

As with any type of governmental funding, the appropriations have to come from some type of taxation. Public funding of sport facilities comes from both hard taxes and soft taxes. Hard taxes are assessments that are applied to the entire population, where soft taxes are assessments applied to specific product users, or to non-residents of a municipality.

Examples of hard taxes include the following:

- Real Estate Tax;
- Property Tax;
- Income Tax;
- General Sales Tax;
- Road Tax; and
- Utility Tax.

Soft taxes include the following examples:

- Tourist Development Tax;
- Lodging or Hotel/Motel Tax;
- Restaurant or Food Service Tax;
- Automobile Rental and Taxi/Limousine/Livery Service Tax;
- Sin Tax (Liquor, Tobacco);
- Players Tax;
- Team Tax;
- Business License/Permit Tax; and
- Lottery and Gaming Tax.

Bonds are interest-bearing certificates that are issued by either a jurisdiction or a business that is a binding promise to repay the initial investment of money (called the principal) and an agreed upon level of interest at a specified date in the future. Quality bonds are usually issued by businesses and/or jurisdictions with a good repayment history, and are bought by investors seeking the most favorable interest rates or tax benefits. Bonds have similar characteristics of long-term loans, as they are effectively contracts where a borrower makes payments on certain dates over a defined period of time in exchange from receiving repayment of the principal with interest at a date in the future. The advantages of investing in bonds include that they are relatively inexpensive – especially for those organizations that have a long history and a good credit rating, the bond market is fairly strong and established, and interest on bonds is tax deductable. Disadvantages of bonds are many which include the fixed interest that must always be paid – regardless of earning revenue/making a profit, and the principal that was borrowed must be paid on the maturity date – again regardless of earning revenue/making a profit. In addition, if a bond is secured with collateral, a jurisdiction or company cannot sell the collateral asset without bondholders' approval, and bondholders have the upper hand in collecting their principal and interest if a jurisdiction or corporation goes into bankruptcy.

There are various types of bonds, but most fall under two categories – taxable bonds and municipal bonds. Taxable bonds are usually issued by corporations, and do not offer the same tax exempt benefits of a municipal bond. These types of bonds are rarely used in the financing of sport facilities. The two types of taxable bonds most often used to finance sport facilities are private placement bonds and asset-backed securitizations. Private-placement bonds are long-term, fixed-interest certificates issued by a non-municipal organization developing a sport facility to venture capitalists and other private lenders of funds. These bonds are secured by the total revenues generated by the sport facility. Asset-backed securitizations are similar to private-placement bonds, however only the most financially viable revenue streams are bundled into the bond offering (example – naming right sponsorships, luxury suite, and PSL's be a part of the asset-backed security, concessions and parking revenues still to the facility).

On the other hand, municipal bonds are widely used to finance sport facilities. Municipal bonds are issued by a governmental agency, and the interest is tax exempt. There are a variety of bond options available under this category, either guaranteed or non-guaranteed. The most often used guaranteed bonds (also known as full-faith or credit obligations) utilized in financing sport facilities are general obligation bonds and certificate of obligation. General obligation bonds are bonds that are repaid with a portion of the general property tax – also known as an ad valorem tax, and is backed by the full faith and credit of the issuing body (in most cases the jurisdiction). Certificates of obligation are bonds that are secured by unlimited claims on tax revenues. These types of bonds usually have a low interest rate, and are easily obtained through governmental sources because the issuance does not require approval by vote of the population.

A variety of non-guaranteed bonds are utilized for the financing of sport facilities including revenue bonds, certificates of participation, tax increment financing, special authority bonds, straight governmental appropriations, and public grants. Revenue bonds are backed exclusively from the revenue that accrues from the sport facility or associated revenue sources. Certificates of participation (COP) involves a jurisdiction purchasing the sport facility and leasing parts of the facility back to the general public or associated agencies. The revenues from those lease payments are then utilized to pay off the capital expenses for the sport facility. Tax-increment financing (TIF) is utilized when there is an area identified as needing some type of renewal or redevelopment. The jurisdiction freezes the tax base in that area until the development or renewal takes place, and then taxes are raised to pay off the TIF. Special authority bonds finance through public organizations that have jurisdictional power outside the normal constraints of the government. This is most often used when there are public challenges to finance sport facilities, but the jurisdiction want the sport facility. So the jurisdiction uses these agencies, including power authorities, turnpike/roadway authorities, water works authorities, and other public works departments, to fund sport facilities through raised fees. Straight governmental appropriations is setting aside public funding from a municipality's budget for a specific purpose – such as financing a sport facility. Public grants to finance sport facilities are awards of financial assistance from a municipality to carry out a project of support or stimulation for the good of the public. This financing does not have to be repaid since it is technically not categorized as governmental assistance or individual loans.

In addition to these public finding options, there are other types of public sector contributions including the purchase of donated land; the funding of site improvements, parking garages, or surrounding infrastructure; direct equity investments; and the construction of related facilities. Regardless of the source of funding, there are always questions as to whether pubic financing is appropriate for the use of sport facilities. These questions center on uncertainty by the public about whether available alternative sources of private financing should supersede the use of public financing, and the contention that the economic returns accruing from public investments do not necessarily equate to the initial investment in the sport facility. However, there are alternate sources of spillover benefits that justify these public subsidies as documented in the chart below:

| | |
|---|---|
| Increased community visibility | A professional sport facility often results in a significant increase in the amount of media coverage for the municipality in which it is located. It also keeps the community's name in front of regional, national, and sometimes even international/global audiences. |
| Enhanced community image | Many municipalities engage in place marketing, which strives to sell the image of a place so as to make it more attractive to businesses, tourists, and inhabitants. The omnipresent popularity of sport in the media has persuaded many municipalities to realize that sport facilities may be useful vehicles to enhance their image. |
| Making a 'major league city' | There is a lot of public interest in the belief that a municipality cannot be considered a 'major league city' or 'first-tier city' without a 'major league' sports team. As such, it is near impossible to have a 'major league' sports team without a quality sport facility. In many municipalities, the facility is seen as being indicative of their character and as defining the external perceptions of the city. |
| Loss of a major sports team | If a municipality loses a sports franchise, it may create the impression that local businesses and governmental officials are not supportive of the community, that the community is declining, and that its residents lack civic pride. Hence, if a municipality does not provide quality sport facilities, they may create a worse image for themselves than if they never had the teams or facilities at all. |

*Continued*

| Stimulation of other developments | Municipalities believe that the investment in sport facilities will stimulate additional development and hence contribute to expansion of a city's tax base. There are three types of development to be addressed when financing a sport facility: |
|---|---|
| | • Proximate development is utilized to stimulate economic development as part of an integrated redevelopment plan around the sport facility. |
| | • Complimentary development comes from the need to support the proximate development around the sport facility, either as a result of the municipality's desire to host a hallmark or mega event, or to upgrade the level of service near the sport facility (restaurants, bars, retail stores, etc.). |
| | • General development goes beyond proximate and complimentary development into the increased availability of public services including roadways and public transportation. |
| Psychic income | Psychic income is the emotional and psychological benefit residents of a municipality perceive they receive, even though they do not physically attend events at the facility, and are not involved in organizing them. Sport facilities are a medium through which cities and their residents express their personality, enhance their status, and promote their quality of life to a regional, national, and even international/global audience. This is often measured using the contingent valuation method (CVM), which places currency values on goods/services not exchanged in the marketplace. |

## Private sources of revenue

A sport facility cannot be financed solely from public sources. Sport businesses need to create sources of revenue to enhance the financing efforts for a sport facility. When we look at the traditional forms of obtaining revenue in business, we typically look at donations of cash, gifts, in-kind contributions, bequests, endowments, trusts, and revenues from fundraising efforts. In sport facilities, there are numerous additional sources of revenue that play a crucial role as economic generators for a sport facility. The chart below depicts these various revenue sources:

| | |
|---|---|
| Naming rights and sponsorships | The entitlement to name a sport facility (or a part thereof) in exchange for financial considerations. |
| Lease agreements/building rentals | The amount of money earned by the facility for its use by tenants (usually sport teams but may include outside vendors who can fill spaces not used by the sport facility for sports), outside travelling events (examples include concerts, WWE, and monster truck shows), and local events (municipal gatherings, graduations, corporate gathering etc.). |
| Advertising rights | The percentage of revenue earned by the facility for signage and other advertisements within the sport facility. |
| Luxury suites and corporate/private boxes | Yearly leases of specialized seating typically located near the middle section of the sport facility that allows the best view of events. Usually has glass paneling that can open to the playing area; included amenities such as a bar, TV's, internet, private seats, and a bathroom; catered food service; and private parking and entrances to the facility. |
| Preferred/premium/club seating | A level below luxury boxes, but offers special amenities above and beyond general admission seating, including private restaurants, lounge areas, and merchandise stands. The main difference is that the seating is not enclosed as with the luxury box – it is open-air similar to general admissions – hence this specialty seating provides the elements of both. |
| Permanent/personal seat licenses (PSLs) | PSLs (known as debentures in Europe) is a fee paid to buy tickets for a specific seat within a specific sport facility. PSLs are usually limited to those buying season tickets. |
| Ticket sales | The percentage a sport facility gets back for every ticket sold for events within the facility. A higher percentage comes back for tickets sold through the box office. |

*Continued*

| Concessionaire exclusivity/restaurant rights | Organizations purchase the sole rights for all concessions within a sport facility. |
| --- | --- |
| Concessions revenue | The percentage of revenue that comes back to the sport facility for all food service and merchandising sold within the facility. |
| Parking fees | The amount a sport facility makes for allowing parking at the facility, whether it is the full parking price minus expenses when management is kept in-house, or the percentage of the fee when parking management is outsourced. |
| Ancillary entertainment revenue | Revenue earned from extras within the stadium such as amusement parks, halls of fame, museums, and facility tours. |

## Public–private partnerships

Many times, to effectively finance sport facilities, there is a need for a better relationship between municipalities and private entrepreneurs. The public sector has the authority to implement project funding through the governing process, while the private sector has the ability to contribute financing and management expertise in the area of sport facilities. While there are advantages in combining the funding and revenue resources as discussed in the previous two sections, there are two major challenges to facilitating a successful public–private partnership.

The first challenge is for public and private entities to understand, respect, and acknowledge the differences between each other, especially as related to value systems and customer expectations. Public sector organizations exist to meet the need and wants of their target population as related to social benefits and outcomes. Private business look to maximize financial return and/or return on investments (i.e. be able to pay off their investors), and hence target their efforts to those who can provide the greatest opportunity to earn revenue and make a profit. There is a need within these types of partnerships to ensure that social and financial considerations are included in the decision making process related to financing for a sport facility.

The second challenge is the concern that each elements only looks out for themselves – hence unfairly competing against each other through the partnership. It is usually the public agency that must address this issue, as many private entities serve to help the public sector satisfy the needs of their constituents in areas they cannot provide service for.

There are numerous models that have been created to articulate the various public–private partnerships evident in sport facility financing. The most often utilized modelsare documented below:

| | |
|---|---|
| Public sector leasing | This is the most common form of public–private sport facility partnership, where private entities pay a lease fee in order to use the public-funded and managed sport facility. |
| Leaseback agreements (private sector leasing) | Where a municipal agency uses a sport facility it has leased from a private owner. |
| Public sector takeovers | The seizing of a struggling or failing private sports facility should in the effort to keep an existing sport asset within the municipality because without it the sport/entertainment opportunity would cease to exist in the area. |
| Private sector takeovers | Where a private organization takes over responsibility for operation of a sport facility owned by the public sector because the municipality either does not have the expertise or finance to appropriately manage/operate the facility. |
| Private pump-priming | Where a private entity uses its assets to force a public entity to invest in a sport facility project. |
| Multiparty arrangements | Where multiple financial partners initiate complex agreement to finance the sport facility. These are usually seen in large-scale public–private sport partnerships, and are most often organized by independent quasi-governmental bodies that facilitate collaborative exchange between the various public and private entities involved with the project. |

# History of sport facility financing

Prior to understanding the specific sources of financing, it is important to understand the history of financing for sport facilities. Generally, the period before 1960 can be referred to as the Period of Antiquity for sport facilities. During this period, the government was the primary source of funding for sport facilities – although there were still privately financed stadiums and arenas (but very few). Most of these sport facilities were funded through the government through general obligation bonds, where the repayment of the bonds came from the general property tax.

During the 1960s (1960–1969), there was the start of a transformation as to how sport facilities were funded. This Period of Growth was where municipalities started building sport facilities that focused on multipurpose use and unique architectural designs – some of which became 'cookie-cutter' in nature; similar designs were repeated in numerous cities. From a financing standpoint, the money was still flowing from public sector funding through the government, however with the increase in need for funding the government started offering bonds secured through a multitude of hard (on the entire population) and soft (on targeted parts of the population) taxes.

The 1970s through 1983 saw significant public subsidy offer to sport facilities. This Period of Revitalization in sport facilities focused on building sport facilities in conjunction with improving the infrastructure of cities. As a result of the multipurpose function of financing, municipalities extended their public subsidies through more revenue bonds borne from taxes, continued the issuance of general obligation bonds from the general property tax, and enhanced both with annual appropriations from the government.

The Period of Discontinuance hit between 1984 and 1986. This was a significant time of change in the way in which sport facilities of the future would be financed. They were significant questions regarding the logic of dumping significant amounts of money into sport facilities when there were bigger economic and financial issues that needed to be addressed with governmental appropriations. In the United States, two laws were passed that had a direct effect of sport facility financing. The Deficit Reduction Act of 1984 mandated that because of the need to lower the national deficit, public funding of projects such as sport facilities was to be given a lower priority. This was followed up two years later by the Tax Reform Act of 1986, which significantly reduced the availability of tax exempt bonds for building sport facilities. Many other countries around the world followed this lead, exacting similar laws and regulations reducing the amount of public subsidy available for sport facility financing.

As a result, there was a need for change, and hence the period from 1986 to around 1995 is referred to as a Period of Change in sport facility financing. During this time, there was a transition from fully public financing to public–private partnerships, and there was some growth taking place in privatized facilities. The public–private partnerships that were indicative of this period involved public entities providing land, investment capital through debt or equity financing, some operating knowledge, and the ability to take of some of the risks associated with sport facilities. In turn, private entities paid taxes that resulted from facility operations and corporate guarantees; and also ushering in the introduction of alternative sources of revenue through luxury suites, premium seating, personal seat licenses, concessionaire rights, and naming rights.

Since 1995, sport facility financing has taken another shift into the Period of Partnerships, where the shift has gone to funding being provided by both private and public entities, and has extended into the running of sport facility operations. Since this era requires private owners to cover a percentage of the bill before governmental agencies will chip in, private entities are building new 'fully-loaded' stadiums and arenas with amenities including restaurants, fan experiences, and technology; and infrastructural designs such as retractable roofs and retractable field. The price tag for these new facilities are increasing exponentially, with new facilities opening in New York and Dallas in 2009 exceeding US $1 billion, and naming rights deal to help pay the private entities part of the bill around US $20 million per year over average terms of 20–30 years.

## Future trends in sport facility financing

So where does sport facility financing go from 2010 and into the future? Will there be a return to multipurpose facilities that can be justified by public subsidy? Perhaps total privatization of stadiums and arena, with municipalities showing their support as corporate sponsors? How about corporate ownership of facilities – taking it out of the hands of municipalities and team owners? Could changes in technology change how we watch the sport experience in the stadium/arena, and how spectators are viewed in the stadium by participants? What about a reduction in need of specialized seating, concessions, amenities, etc. (except for those deemed necessary for the participants to play), as a result of breakthroughs in technology such as through virtual fans who dial in from home and virtually sit in the stadium?

---

## Sport facility financing investment – 2010 and beyond

As the economy and public outcry create a reduction in public subsidy, there are concerns of where facility financing will come from. From a professional sport facility standpoint, if a municipality balked at providing funding for a new facility, the professional team would threaten to move and the municipality would eventually come up with the money (recent example would be the NHL's Pittsburgh Penguins getting a new facility agreement only hours before they were set to leave for Kansas City). However, there is a shift in this trend in recent times. In the NBA, the Seattle Supersonics and the City of Seattle could not come up with a viable solution to replace the aging Key Arena, so the team picked up and moved to Oklahoma City.

---

*Continued*

# Sport facility financing investment – 2010 and beyond—cont'd

For smaller recreational and community sport facilities, the amount of public money available to construct these facilities has reduced significant, and has resulted in private building of these types of complexes. However, with the increase in the privatization of sport facilities, the question is whether this will trickle up to the professional level – i.e. fully privatized facilities with no governmental interaction. While the trends show less public involvement (and hence more private involvement), there does not seem to be a time in the near future that public subsidy totally disappears from sport facilities. Municipalities need to show support in their communities for sport – since a large majority of the population has an interest in some aspects of sport, recreation, and/or leisure. Tax dollars need to support the interests of the public who pay those taxes – however it is becoming abundantly clear that there is a cap to the spending recommended.

On the private side, it is possible that we are nearing an economic and financial cap. The money is not endless, and with shifts in the economic and financial climate globally, the amount corporations are willing to spend on naming rights may be reaching a crescendo. They are discovering other sponsorable products that offer the potential of a great return on investment (ROI) and return on objectives (ROO). Hence facilities are trying to meet this shift with offering sponsorships and advertising on everything from turnstiles to steps in the arena, so that they can get more money from more sponsors at a lower cost per sponsor.

## Suggested discussion topics

1. In these trying economic times, how would you justify to a municipality (both the elected officials and the taxpayers) to enter into a public–private partnership for a recreation or community sport facility?
2. Identify 10 sponsorable non-traditional inventories within a professional sport arena or stadium (no naming or traditional signage rights), and explain how you would utilize those areas for a greater return on the infrastructure's investment without turning the facility into a mass of advertisements that distract from the events?

There are numerous projections we can make here, however only time will tell what will come down the road and how the changes will have a direct effect on the financing of sport facilities in the twenty-first century and beyond. However, there are two areas that are projected to have a direct effect on the future of sport facility financing: (1) the emergence of the voluntary sector as an additional niche in the financing of sport facilities; and (2) as a result of the globalization of sports, the effects of currency values as related to international/global investments will be significant.

## The influence of the voluntary sector

In years to come it is our view that the voluntary sector will have an increasingly important role to play in the provision of sports facilities for communities. The voluntary sector already owns and controls many facilities such as clubs, pitches and club houses. Rather than public authorities taking additional risk in trying to provide facilities themselves, there is some logic in the strategy of incentivizing the voluntary sector to open its facilities for the benefit of the wider community. An obvious example is the use of club facilities for after school clubs and as resources for young people to use during school holidays. It is widely accepted that sport and the voluntary sector can be used to help deliver wider government agendas such as health improvements, community cohesion, reductions in delinquency and improvements in educational attainment. It is therefore more cost effective to offer clubs' financial contributions than to provide new facilities from scratch. Not only does this approach make sound commercial sense, but there are also strategic benefits as well. The voluntary sector is more dynamic than government and can react quickly to changes in the external environment as it is not constrained by bureaucracy. The voluntary sector is also able to get closer to the customer than public authorities. Furthermore, the voluntary sector is capable of operating at lower cost than public authorities and is more able to attract funding from charities and lotteries. Thus for these reasons it is a win–win situation for public and voluntary bodies to work together closely. In an era when public money for investment in sports facilities will be increasingly scarce, there will be a strong business and environmental case to make best use of that which already exists before new facilities can be justified. Consequently, at community level the voluntary sector is likely to have an increasingly important role to play in helping to provide new sports facilities and wider community access to existing sports facilities.

## Effect of currency value on international/global investments

The notion that sport is a global business is well illustrated by the fact that many high profile sports facilities are funded by international investors as well as domestic investors. Much of the debt that has been raised to support the development of Wembley Stadium in London is owed to German banks. The United Kingdom uses Sterling as its currency whereas Germany uses the Euro. The net effect of this situation is that if the two currencies fluctuate against each other, then one party will be better off than expected and the other worse off. In 2009 Sterling has fallen from £1 being worth around €1.40–1.10 – a fall of just over 20%. As discussed earlier the owners of Wembley Stadium paid around £45M as interest in 2007. An adverse currency fluctuation of 20% would add around £9M per year to the company's interest charges and could make the difference between the company being viable or being in financial trouble. There are very few sports facilities that could take a financial hit of £9M without it having an adverse effect on the business whether this be cutting cost or having to stage more events to recover the deficit. In real life it is unlikely that such a stark situation would ever materialize. As part of Wembley Stadium's efforts to manage its financial risks it will have negotiated sources of mitigation such as fixed exchange rates or exchange rates that float between two agreed fixed points but not beyond something that would impact too unfavorably on one party. More advanced sources of mitigation might the use of currency hedge funds and options. This is not the time to explain what these financial instruments are. However, their existence and application in the financing of sport facilities serves to illustrate further the broad range of skills and knowledge that sports facility managers may be required to call upon throughout their careers.

## Chapter review

Financing is defined as the act of obtaining or providing money or capital for the purchase of a business enterprise. Developing new sports facilities is a risky process that invariably requires complex financial arrangements, as it is unlikely that any organization from any sector will have the spare cash available to develop and build a sport facility from the outset of a project. It is therefore a current practice that the financing of sports facilities tends to be made with financial contributions from a variety of sources. When borrowed money (or debt) is used to finance a development the stance of those borrowing the money is the belief that they can make sufficient profit to be able to service interest costs and still make a profit. For the providers of loans, the stance taken is that the interest being paid on the loans justifies the risk of lending to the developer. In practice the two parties' fates are inextricably linked – for everyone to get a fair return on their investment, the development has to succeed.

Considerations around financing sports facilities are not confined to how much a building costs to construct in the first instance. For both buildings and equipment due consideration must be given to what are known as 'life cycle costs', which are defined as the maintenance of physical asset cost records over the entire asset lives, so that decisions concerning the acquisition, use, or disposal of the assets can be made in a way that achieves the optimum asset usage at the lowest cost to the entity. The importance of being aware of life cycle costing can be appreciated by the finding that as much as 90% of the lifetime costs attributable to an asset are determined by decisions made in the early part of the asset's life. The evidence that lifecycle costing for an asset is based on can be complicated as indicated in the range of considerations including purchase costs, running costs, maintenance costs, training costs, and decommissioning and disposal costs.

The justification for financing many sport facilities is often based on arguments made about the economic benefits that the development will have on the local community. For sports facilities there are five key areas in which positive economic benefits can be delivered – construction, employment, supply chains, local income, and events. The manner in which potential economic impacts are quantified is by the use of specially commissioned economic impact studies, which attempt to model the future economic impacts of a sports facility or to measure the actual economic impact of a facility or an event.

Financing of sport facilities come in three basic forms – public financing, private funding, and public–private partnerships. Public funding of sport facilities comes from hard taxes, soft taxes, and bonds. Private funding comes from revenue created by sport businesses to enhance the financing efforts for a sport facility. Many times, to effectively finance sport facilities, there is a need for a better relationship between municipalities and private entrepreneurs. The public sector has the authority to implement project funding through the governing process, while the private sector has the ability to contribute financing and management expertise in the area of sport facilities.

Historically, the financing for sport facilities before 1960 was referred to the Period of Antiquity, where the government was the primary source of funding for sport facilities general obligation bonds funded from the general property tax. The Period of Growth in the 1960s saw municipalities build sport facilities that focused on multipurpose use and unique architectural designs – funding through the government still though general obligation bonds, but with the increase in need for funding the government started offering bonds secured through a multitude of hard and soft taxes. The 1970s and early 1980s saw significant public subsidy offerings to sport facilities during the Period of Revitalization in sport facilities, which focused on building sport facilities in conjunction with improving the infrastructure of cities. The Period of Discontinuance hit between 1984 and 1986. This was a significant time of change in the way in which sport facilities would be financed, and there were questions regarding the logic of dumping significant amounts of money into sport facilities when there were bigger economic and financial issues that needed to be addressed with governmental appropriations. As a result, there was a need for change, and hence the period from 1986 to around 1995 is referred to as a Period of Change in sport facility financing. During this time, there was a transition from fully public financing to public–private partnerships, and there was some growth taking place in privatized facilities. Since 1995, sport facility financing has taken another shift into the Period of Partnerships, where the shift has gone to funding being provided by both private and public entities, and has extended into the running of sport facility operations.

So what does the future hold for sport facility financing? Only time will tell. But we can safely project that economic issues affecting both public and private entities will be at the center of the discussion. In addition, the emergence of the voluntary sector as an additional niche in the financing of sport facilities and the effects of currency values as related to international/global investments seem to be significant concerns related to the financing of sport facilities in the future.

# 4 Planning, design, and construction processes

## Chapter outline

## Chapter objectives

The objective of this chapter is to articulate the planning, design, and construction processes that are necessary prior to the management and operation of a sport facility. The four phases to be covered will be (1) preliminary planning; (2) development of design; (3) construction; and (4) preparation for training and management of facility. The planning process will cover how to create a program analysis for a sport facility, and how to conduct feasibility studies including project descriptions, scope and constraints of the project, identification of need for the facility, strategic significant, sport and economic impact, capital costs, revenue projects, and timelines. The second section will describe the basics of the design process, including space allocation, timetables, site selections, and cost estimates. The third section, about the construction process, will encompass the selection process for contractors, the creation process of detailed shop drawings, how to obtain building permits, what is involved with groundbreaking, and the actual construction process in terms of capital improvements, new construction, and technological innovations. Special attention will be given to the importance of the aging of the population, human rights and disability discrimination legislation, and diversity management related to universal design principles and the major dimensions of access (mobility, vision, hearing, cognitive and the sensitivities), as well as to the topics of "greening" and sustainability of sport venues. The conclusion of the chapter will bridge the gap to the next section of the book about the implementation of management and operations in sport facilities, including organizational management, human resource management, financial management, operations management, and legal responsibilities.

# Phase 1 – preliminary planning

In the previous two chapters, the authors describe the various ownerships structures and financing options for sport facilities. These two areas serve as a foundation for the preliminary planning process that eventually leads to the design, construction, and management of sport facilities.

Preliminary planning involves all of the initial tasks that need to be completed in preparation for a specific course of action. A sound preliminary planning process allows the sport facility manager to effectively and efficiently utilize resources to organize, implement, control, and make decisions. Through the preliminary planning process, timelines and standards are established, initial problems are addressed, and strategic, tactical, and operational goals are formalized – working within the philosophy and mission of the organization, and toward end results articulated in the vision.

With regard to sport facilities, there are generally six parts to the preliminary planning process, namely: completing a program analysis, conducting feasibility studies, convening a planning committee, selecting an architect, developing a master plan, and creating a program statement.

## Program analysis

A program analysis focuses on the need for the facility in terms of the programs that are either already established or planned to be established. In order to conduct an appropriate program analysis, a sport facility manager must first have a clear understanding of the organizational PMV (philosophy, mission, and vision). The organizational philosophy focuses on what is important to the sport facility from a business values and beliefs standpoint. The organizational mission focuses on the reason for the sport facility and the guiding managerial principles. These guiding principles are articulated through the organizational goals – the tasks that need to be completed to achieve the mission, and the organizational objectives – the specific methods to be utilized to accomplish those tasks. These organizational goals and objectives are governed by the policies and procedures set forth by the organization – usually articulated through an operations manual, a human resource manual, and standard operating procedures in the industry. The organizational vision focuses on the future and where the sport facility and associated organizations ultimately want to be.

## Feasibility studies

The program analysis is usually articulated through feasibility studies. A feasibility study is an examination of the likelihood that an idea or concept can be transformed into a business entity. Feasibility studies have a number of components including the project description and site selection; the scope and constraints of the project, a needs identification; the strategic significance of the project, the sport, economic, and societal impact; capital costs and revenue projections; and timelines.

| Component | Explanation |
| --- | --- |
| Project description | A general overview of the facility, including square footage, inclusions, and amenities. |
| Site selection | The location of the facility including attractiveness of location, acreage/hectare available, natural and environmental conditions (weather, soil, grading, wetlands, forestry, rocks/minerals), ease of access, and community support. |
| Scope of the project | The processes that are required to define and control the work necessary to complete the project. |
| Constraints of the project | Specific restrictions that may have an adverse affect on the scope of the project and related actions. |
| Needs identification/ assessment | The verification process as to whether the facility is essential. Includes identifying current and future trends, assessing similar facilities/competition, evaluating the relevant social indicators, and determining demand/usage potential. |
| Strategic significance | The potential of having a positive, long-term impact based on the vision of the organization. |
| Sport impact | How the facility will have a direct effect on the future development of sport in the locale? |
| Economic impact | How the facility will directly stimulate the total amount of expenditures in the area? |
| Societal impact | How the facility will directly affect the social fabric and well-being of the community? |
| Capital costs | The expenses incurred on land, buildings, construction, and equipment related to the management and operation of the facility. |
| Revenue projections | The forecasting of sales and other income sources to offset expenses and predict net profit or loss. |
| Timelines | The listing of specific benchmarks, deadlines, and schedules related to effective and efficient management and operation. |

## Planning committee

Once the feasibility study is completed and a decision to move forward is made, a planning committee is convened to move the project forward. The most difficult part of putting together a planning committee is to limit the size so work can be accomplished, but ensuring that all constituencies and key stakeholders are represented. Individuals who may have a role on a planning committee include the following:

- Initial investors/entrepreneurs in the facility (the individual who most likely conducted or commissioned the program analysis and feasibility study).
- Construction company.
- Consultants/experts in the design and construction of sport facilities.
- Bank representatives/financiers.
- Accountants.
- Elected community officials/administration.
- At-large community representative(s).
- Representative(s) from organization(s) who plan to utilize the facility.

The purpose of the planning committee is to shape the design of the sport facility. Major responsibilities include advancing the development of sport facility efficiently and systematically, establishing an information system about the sport facility, and standardizing the processes of facility use. The three initial responsibilities of the planning committee are selecting an architect, developing the master plan, and establishing the program statement.

## Selecting an architect

The main responsibility of an architect is to help design a functional facility. The architect must have a full understanding of the purpose of the facility, be able to visualize the various uses of the facility, and foresee as many issues or problems with the design prior to construction. The communication process between the planning committee and the architect is crucial to the success of the facility – because if the architect does not understand the vision of the planning committee, the appropriate design cannot come to fruition.

In addition to drawing drafts and building scaled models, the architect can serve as a resource when updating site studies, securing zoning and planning approval, obtaining building permits, surveying land, groundbreaking, and any other pre-construction situations that may arise. To that end, there are three key places to look for architects. First would be through the construction company that has been selected. Often, as a result of relationships built during previous projects, the construction company can recommend an architect that would fit best for the project. Another way to find an architect would be to conduct research of similar facilities or projects and collect references about the architects used. A third method is to contact the governing body for architects in your area – in the United States it is the American Institute of Architects – to get a referral list.

The planning committee will publish a request for a proposal from architects, who will then submit their qualifications, references, examples of previous projects, and possibly even a first draft of the project. The planning committee would then review the applications, conduct reference checks and research previous projects, select their top choices, and bring the architect in for a full interview process and presentation. The goal during this interview is to evaluate the knowledge of the architect, assess whether the architect understands the vision of the planning committee, and determine if personalities seem to fit together. The final determination should be made based on this interview process, the price of the bid, and the perceived quality of work expected to be produced by the architect.

## Master plan and program statement development

After the architect is selected, the next step in the planning process is the development of the master plan. The development of a master plan allows the planning committee to take their vision for the sport facility and plot a path for making it a reality. The main purpose of the master plan is to break down the sport facility project into feasible segments based on numerous factors related to priorities, finances, and time. In addition, the master plan allows the planning committee to begin to contemplate the architectural design of the facility in terms of interior and exterior aesthetics – including look, feel, and appropriate fit within the landscape.

While drawings are often the end result of a master plan, the plan also seeks to answer the "who, what, where, when, why, and how much" of the sport facility, including:

- site conditions and environmental/sustainability impact analyses;
- structural, architectural, mechanical, electrical, and plumbing factors;
- space requirements and mapping;
- financial issues;
- legal parameters;
- control and management considerations; and
- provisions for dealing with any potential errors and omissions.

In order to complete an effective master plan, there also need to be facility visits and trend analyses. Facility visits allow the planning committee to look at similar facilities to what they are designing. The function part of the visit involves a features analysis – where the planning committee evaluates the positive and negative aspects of the facilities they visit, and then use that information to incorporate the best functions into their design, while avoiding the pitfalls experienced by that facility. Trend analyses also need to be conducted to determine the changes in social, economic, political, or environmental patterns that may have an effect on the design and function of the sport facility.

*Program statement*

Once the master plan is completed, a program statement is developed to summarize the major components of the master plan. This program statement will ultimately be used to review the major components of the project, market the project to gain financial and general support for the project, and serve as a framework document for the design and construction of the sport facility. Some of the inclusions within a program statement are:

- project goals and objectives;
- basic assumptions about the sport facility – supported through robust research;
- current trends affecting the planning process;
- a listing of the current and future programs to be a part of the facility;
- initial specifications/features, space needs assessment, and space allocations;
- facility usage plans – including auxiliary and service areas;
- supplies needed – including items such as equipment, furniture, and other supplies; and
- environmental and sustainability functions.

# Phase 2 – facility design

Once the master plan and program statement have been developed and agreed upon, it is time to design the sport facility. The architect (in partnership with the planning committee) will create drawings and scaled models of the sport facility. As a part of this process, narratives will be written in support of space allotments and utilization plans, atmospheric conditions, environmental issues, and specification sheets – including the types of materials to be used in the construction of the facility.

## Facility design basics

When designing a new facility, or modifying an existing one, space allocation and management is a crucial part of the process as it focuses on the planning, projection, allocation, evaluation, and use of space. The goals of effective space management are to ensure space is appropriately and fairly distributed based on the needs assessment, provides an avenue to establish standards for allocating space, affords the opportunity to determine needs that can be consolidated into the same space to help reduce other costs (utilities, maintenance, and operations), aids with the construction process by reducing the likelihood of errors and omissions, and allows the planning committee to conduct a final evaluation to determine any shortfalls in space inventories (especially prevalent n the area of storage).

The six step process that serves as the foundation for space management is discussed below.

## Sport facility space allocation and management process

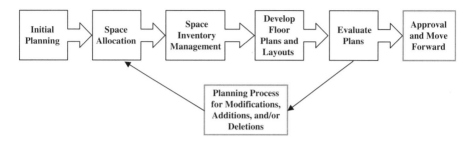

The initial stage is the planning process, where current and future space requirements are addressed in terms of the needs assessment. Included in this planning is the amount and type of space needed; the configuration of the space including dimensions, square footage/metreage, volume, shape, and location; and space utilization in terms of specific activities, support functions, organizational control, and required adjacencies. Next is the process of allocating space – which must be justified in terms of needs, the footprint of the facility, the organization of the facility in terms of similar requirements (e.g. bathrooms and locker rooms in adjacent zones due to similar plumbing needs) and the flow of the facility (ingress/egress/movement in/around facility). Third is space inventory management – which allows for keeping track of the types of sizes of space, an identification system for areas, an information database of key features required in specific spaces (utilities, HVAC, special needs/uses), and a diary identifying the eventual uses for spaces. Once spaces are allocated, floor plans and layouts are developed so that the previous information can be transferred from a written form into a visual form. The plans are then evaluated by all pertinent parties with two results – either a return to the planning process for modifications, additions, or deletions from the plan, or approval to move forward.

During this process, there are a number of considerations that must be taken into account, both internal and external to the facility.

1. When spaces are allocated, errors are often made because the focus is only on the specialized spaces within the facility. Do not forget to spent equal time on shared spaces and flexible-use/multipurpose spaces to ensure those needs are met as well.
2. Storage space always seems to be the last item on the minds of designers/planners. Ensure that the appropriate storage spaces are designed into the building for equipment, maintenance, custodial, and electronics.
3. Security and management control of the facility is crucial to the ongoing safety and operation of space. Ensure your plans take into account appropriate ingress/egress (both general and emergency), sightlines and other observatory features for staff, and flow within the facility to ensure safe passage for users.
4. With regard to atmospherics, a sport facility manager must direct considerable attention to the way in which its atmosphere can promote the desired relationship

with clientele, and the safe and enjoyable participation in specified activities. Atmospherics may include appropriate lighting, flooring, sound/noise levels, temperature, and the general ambiance of the facility.

5. Environmental conditions will have a direct effect on the proper operation of the facility, and need to be taken into account early in the process. Examples include: (1) weather and prevalent wind direction may affect how the building faces or where rooms are placed; (2) wetlands and other environmental issues may affect the placement of the footprint and ancillary areas related to the facility; and (3) surrounding communities and the effect of facilities noise and lighting have on them.

6. Specification sheets (spec sheets) should be created to detail the types of materials to be used in the construction of the facility. This includes construction materials, paints and finishes; mechanical, electrical, plumbing, and other utility systems; doors, windows, floorings, ceilings, and wall coverings; appliances, fixtures, and electronics; and furniture and other pertinent equipments.

## Timetables

Once these basics are confirmed, timetables are created to move the project forward in an effective and efficient manner. Timetables are usually created backwards from the projected opening date of the facility to the date the timetable is created. The timetable is designed not only to keep the progress of the construction within acceptable parameters, but also to provide a framework for the design and implementation of documents related to the management and operations of the sport facility – including the hiring and training of staff, publicity of the facility, and planning for the grand opening. A timetable is a live document – consulted, evaluated, and modified frequently. In general, the architect is responsible for the creation and management of the timetable – but the owners, planning committee, or the architect may "fast track" certain parts of the project based on needs, environmental situations, or delays. While these "fast tracks" may be more expensive initially, they are often needed to speed up the completion time of the facility to ensure other problems or issues do not occur.

## Site selection

As described earlier in this chapter, the site selection is defined as the process of choosing a location for the facility – taking into account such considerations as the attractiveness of location, available acreage/hectare, natural and environmental conditions (weather, soil, grading, wetlands, forestry, rocks/minerals), ease of access, and community support. It is possible at this point in the process that a site has already been selected. If so, the planning committee will confirm if the site is appropriate for the facility designed, and determine if modifications are necessary. However, in some cases, planning committees will wait until this time to select a site based on the facility they have designed. In either scenario, an analysis of the site in terms of numerous factors needs to be conducted at this time, including:

- access;
  - internal – movement within site;
  - external;
    - Ingress/egress;
    - Roads and traffic generation/impact;
    - Forms of public transportation available;
- Utilities;
  - Water;
  - Electric;
  - Sewers/cesspools;
  - Telephone/cable/broadband;
  - Oil/natural gas transmission;
- Availability of space for adequate parking;
- Environmental issues;
  - Atmospherics;
  - Climate;
  - Nuisances (e.g. animals);
  - Natural features (topography, geology, hydrology, pedology);
- Community and political issues;
  - Structural;
  - Support;
  - Easements;
  - Zoning requirements;
- Economic issues;
  - Labor;
  - Demographic trends;
  - Taxes;
  - Utility costs;
  - Competition.

## Cost estimate

There are multiple purposes for creating a cost estimate ranging from determining whether the planning committee can afford the facility they want to build – to secure public and/or private financing.

The first part of the cost estimate is building the cost review. This major expenditure includes general construction costs for materials, personnel, and equipment; site works; fit out (the cost of the shell without adaptations for specific use – partitions, floors, ceilings, walls, mechanical, electrical, environmental); specific activity and ancillary area costs; car parking; contingencies; insurance; security; landscaping; and consultancy/project management fees. Another major cost is land acquisition. Fees over and above the purchase price include potential easements, appraisals, the purchase price, and attorney fees. Other possible fees may be related to zoning requirements, conveyancing, filing of deeds, stamp duties, banking/mortgage loans, and environmental issues. A final major cost is for support needs in the facility including furniture, equipment, communications, and supplies.

# Phase 3 – construction

Once the design phase is completed, it is time to break ground and construct the facility (or in the case of an existing facility, start renovations). In order to initiate this process, a contractor needs to be chosen, detailed shop drawings need to be created, and groundbreaking and actual construction need to be started – including securing necessary building permits. This section of this chapter takes you through this process.

## Contractor selection process

The main responsibility of a contractor is as the main builder for the sport facility. While the overall responsibility of the project falls on the contractor, work is usually completed in coordination with subcontractors for specific tasks.

Many times a contractor will actually be a subcontractor to an architect. In many cases, this is the best scenario for a planning committee, as the contractor knows the work of the architect, and there is usually a more seamless transition through the construction process. While this may seem like the easiest and best route to take for the project, it is integral that the planning committee carry out due diligence and conduct a thorough bid process for the contractor.

As with the architect, the planning committee will publish a request for proposal from contractors, who will then submit their qualifications, references, and examples of previous projects. The planning committee reviews the applications, conduct reference checks, researches previous projects, selects their top choices, and bring the contractors in for a full interview process. The architect should be a part of the interview process to help in evaluating the knowledge of the contractor, assessing if the contractor understands the vision of the planning committee, and determining if they can effectively work together. The final determination should be made based on this interview process, the price of the bid, and the perceived quality of work expected to be produced by the contractor. Once the contractor is selected, contracts are negotiated and the construction process is put into action.

## Creation of detailed shop drawings

One of the first responsibilities of the contractor is to create a detail set of shop drawings from the architect's renderings. The architect needs to work closely with the contractor during this phase to ensure that all essential parts of the facility are included. The shop drawing will address all aspects of the facility including appearance, performance aspects, and governing principles. Also noted on the shop drawings are any modifications, additions, or deletions that have been made based on the recommendations of the architect and/or contractor. This information is extremely detailed to ensure that there is total clarity and completeness about the project, and so the planning committee can get a full visual of what the project will eventually look like. One of the issues a planning committee must look out for with regard to these changes is that they need to ensure that the changes do not represent a compromise that gives up essential aspects that are important as addressed in the original needs assessment. In addition, the planning committee needs to be open-minded to concepts brought forth at this stage, because this is the final change to make any significant changes before ground is broken on the project. This is very important because any changes made once construction has started often will result in delays to the overall project and increased costs.

### Groundbreaking and actual construction

In preparation for groundbreaking, the contractor will secure all building permits. Usually this process involves filing for a building notice with the municipality, having the site approved by the municipality (which may also involve town meetings for the community to speak on the project), plans and detailed shop drawings are evaluated and approved, zoning issues are addressed, and finally the application will be accepted and the permits are issued.

The groundbreaking is an exciting time for all involved because it brings all the hard work through the planning and design process from concept to reality. As such, it is appropriate at this time to celebrate, and hence a groundbreaking ceremony should be scheduled. The first step is to select a date for the groundbreaking – one that can bring together the best audience. This audience usually will include owners, municipality officials, chamber members, and the community. Early afternoons during the week (Monday–Friday) have shown to be the best time for a groundbreaking – and also are a great time to entice the media to cover the event. Also, it is important to make sure that your groundbreaking does not conflict with other activities in the area, as you would like to maximize attendance, and that you plan for inclement weather in your planning process.

Invitations should be sent to all pertinent individuals who were integral to reach the groundbreaking stage. This should include planning committee members, architects, contractors, business associates (bankers, consultants, project managers), local business owners near your construction site, volunteer associations in the area, community leaders, elected officials, and the media.

An emcee should be chosen for the event to welcome guests and introduce dignitaries. In addition, choose appropriate guest speakers for the groundbreaking – given those individuals enough advanced notice about their participation, and how long they will speak (2–3 minutes is the standard).

Groundbreaking ceremonies should between 20–30 minutes. Activities in addition to speeches that may be included during the groundbreaking would include having a plot of dirt with ceremonial shovels to enact the first dig on the site involving all pertinent dignitaries, tours of the site, exhibits of the shop drawings, music and/or entertainment, raffles, and refreshments. It is also important to have literature about the facility available to hand to all that attend.

After the groundbreaking, there are two important steps. First is to contact all pertinent media with a summary of the groundbreaking and pictures from the event. Second is to send out thank you notes to all speakers, sponsors, and other dignitaries.

Once the hoopla from the groundbreaking has died off, the construction process has started. During this phase of the project, it is important that there is open communication among designated planning committee members, owners, architects, and contractors. Depending on the scope of the project, it can take anywhere from 4 to 18 months to fully construct a sport facility.

---

## Online case study – revitalization of sport facilities

In July 2008, Allegheny County (Pennsylvania, USA) administrators announced the donation of 78 acres of land from the Sports Legacy Foundation to develop a world class athletic complex. The donated property, located within the second most populated county in Pennsylvania, was formerly owned and operated by the Pittsburgh and Lake Erie Railroad. The land has been under environmental clean-up for years and ownership of the property will officially be transferred to Allegheny County Department of Parks once the environmental work is completed. The Sports Legacy Foundation stipulated that the land must be transformed into a facility offering nontraditional playing fields including rugby, soccer, and lacrosse.

* For more details about this case, go to the online supplements for this text and get information about justification for the project, the initial planning process, key aspects about the donated land and the geographic region, and suggested discussion topics.

---

## Phase 4 – preparation for training and management of facility

Throughout the construction process, and especially when construction is nearing completion, the focus turns to the management and operation of the sport facility. Included in this process are preparing the facility management infrastructure, attracting events to be staged in the facility, and then preparing an event management infrastructure.

The following chapters in this textbook will take you through a series of concepts that will aid in the preparation for training and management of sport facilities. Each of these areas is crucial to the understanding of global sport facility management, and will serve as a framework for realizing the scope of responsibilities involved in the implementation of management and operations.

- *Organizational management (Chapter 5)* – the processes involved in understanding human and organizational behavior, as well as leadership and governance methodologies used to improve organizational performance and effectiveness within the sport facility.
- *Human resource management (Chapter 6)* – the practices and procedures focused on managing sport facility personnel.
- *Financial management (Chapter 7)* – the basic fiscal and economic skills that are an important part of the sport facility manager's overall portfolio of management skills.
- *Operations management (Chapter 8)* – the general functions that are integral to the production of quality programming and services within a sport facility.
- *Legal concerns (Chapter 9)* – the general principles related to negligence law, contract law, and governmental law that affect the management and operation of sport facilities.
- *Management and operations in action (Chapters 10–13)* – includes the relationship of sport marketing, event planning, risk assessment, and security planning to sport facility operations management.
- *Effectiveness of management and operations (Chapter 14)* – focuses on the importance of benchmarking and performance management to the efficient and effective operation and management of sport facilities.

## Chapter review

The purpose of this chapter was to introduce the planning, design, and construction processes – all of which are integral to the management and operation of a sport facility. The first process is the preliminary planning process, which encompasses the program analysis, a feasibility study, convening of a planning committee, selecting an architect, and development of the master plan and program statement. The program analysis focuses on the need for the facility in terms of the programs that are either already established or are planned to be established. The feasibility study serves to determine the likelihood that the facility concept can be transformed into a reality through creating/ evaluating program descriptions; conducting project scope/constraint, site, and needs, an impact analyses; and forecasting strategic significance, cost and revenue projections, and timelines. The planning committee is convened and represents all key constituencies and stakeholders in the facility project, and will shape the design of the sport facility. A key member that will be added to the committee through a bid, interview, and selection process is the architect, who will be the key individual to design a functional facility. Eventually, the development of the master plan and program statement will serve as the blueprint to take the vision for the sport facility and make it a reality.

The second phase is the actual design of the facility. Facility basics involves implementing a space management plan, which involves ensuring space is appropriately and fairly distributed, establishes standards for allocating space (including consolidation to reduce costs), reducing the likelihood of errors and omissions, and conducting final evaluations to determine any shortfalls in space inventories. As a part of this phase, timetables are created, sites are selected, and costs are estimated.

Phase three is the actual construction process. The initial step in this process is to select a contractor through a bid, interview, and selection process. Many times, the contractor may actually be a subcontractor of the architect to have a more seamless transition from planning and design to construction. Once the contractor is selected, detailed shop drawings are created that address all aspect of the facility including appearance, performance aspects, governing principles, modifications, additions, and deletions. Once these plans are finalized, ground-breaking is scheduled and construction is started.

The final phase is the preparation for training and management of the facility. Although much of the focus is on the actual construction process, which can take anywhere from 4 to 18 months to fully construct a sport facility, it is important that plans are implemented in preparation for the opening of the facility. Organizational structure of the facility must be created, human resource and operation manuals must be designed and implemented, financial plans must be evaluated and finalized, and legal issues and responsibilities must be taken into account. Furthermore, projections need to be made related to how the management and operational structure will look once implemented, and a procedure for evaluating efficiency and effectiveness needs to be established. These concepts are the framework for the rest of this textbook.

# Section Two

## Implementation of Management and Operational Strategies

# 5 Organizational management

## Chapter outline

## Chapter objectives

Organizational behavior is the study of human behavior in the work environment. Understanding the dynamics of organizational behavior is of great significance to a facility manager as it explains employee behavior and performance. In today's sport facilities, where organizations are competing in a global environment, managers must be capable of working effectively in diverse teams with diverse skills and abilities. This in turn improves employee performance, thereby enhancing organizational effectiveness and satisfying key stakeholders. However, the key to ensuring an optimal level of positive organization behavior is through quality organizational management of the sport facility.

The purpose of this chapter is to articulate the important concepts of organization management as related to individual and group behaviors in sport facilities, including a description of the principles of motivation, stress management and well-being, leadership, use of power and authority, politics, conflict management, decision-making, and problem solving. This chapter will also cover various leadership and organizational management concepts that affect international and global sport facility operations, including determinants of organizational culture and change, and the effects of cultural diversity and global organization behavior.

## Introduction to organizational management

The job of a facility manager is best described in terms of management functions and roles. The four major functions of management are planning, organizing, leading, and coordinating (or controlling). Planning involves selecting and prioritizing goals and objectives and the methods to be used to achieve desired results. There are various types of planning, for example, strategic planning, business planning, project planning, and staff planning. Organizing is simply identifying resources and allocating those selected resources to meet specific goals and objectives established during the planning stage. Sport facility managers may organize their staff, teams and events, or sponsoring agencies. Leading entails providing direction for the sport organization and its staff and influencing staff to follow the desired direction. Coordinating or controlling activities include monitoring resources and processes to achieve goals and objectives in an efficient manner.

Management roles can be divided into three categories – interpersonal roles, informational roles, and decision-making roles. Interpersonal roles are social in nature and include serving as a figurehead or "face" of the sport organization. Informational roles include disseminating pertinent information to staff members and acting as a spokesperson to external constituencies. The facility manager also assumes a decision-making role that includes initiating change, resolving disputes, and conducting negotiations with internal and external entities.

## Individual behavior in the workforce

Individual worker differences are based on personal characteristics. Workers may differ regarding demographic factors such as gender, age, socioeconomic background, education level, race, and ethnicity. Additionally, the presence of various levels of abilities and skills has a relationship with job performance. It is the facility manager's job to align a person's abilities and skills to the appropriate job requirements. Job analysis is a common technique used to help a manager match the individual to a specific job. Job analysis involves identifying tasks and behaviors associated with the position, and the responsibilities, education, and training required to successfully perform the job's requirements. Personality characteristics play a major role in job success or failure. Many successful managers are extroverted or outgoing and are social, assertive, and active. Emotional stability also affects job performance. Positive emotional traits include being calm, enthusiastic, courteous, and friendly which is a necessity when dealing with facility patrons. The facility manager must be dependable and responsible, organized, and an effective planner.

Perceptions on the job are significant. Employees who perceive their job to be challenging and interesting have high job satisfaction and motivation, which results in better performance. Attitudes are also determinants of job behavior. An attitude is a mental state of readiness that is learned and organized through experience. Facility managers are sometimes required to change the attitude of workers to enhance job performance. To change a worker's attitude three factors must be considered: trust in the facility manager, the message being communicated, and the situation itself. If the manager is not trustworthy it is highly unlikely that the employee will change his or her attitude. Likewise, if the message being communicated is not convincing it will not be accepted. The facility manager must gain the respect of his or her staff to successfully initiate change in job behavior and performance.

The values and beliefs of employees influence job performance. In an ideal situation, the values of employees match the values of the job and organization, thereby leading to higher job performance. Typical values sought by organizations include respect, uncompromising integrity, trust, credibility, and desire for continuous improvement. Personal ethics (individual beliefs on what constitutes right and wrong, or good and bad) is another key factor for understanding individuals in organizations. The ethical behavior of organization members can have an impact on the public's perception.

## *Motivation*

Two foundational theories of motivation are Maslow's Hierarchy of Needs and Herzberg's Two Factor Theory. Maslow's Hierarchy of Needs model emphasizes five levels of individual needs, starting with basic physiological needs at the bottom and self-actualization needs at the top (see Figure 5.1). Lower order needs such as food, security, and human contact must be satisfied first before progressing to the higher order needs that are concerned with personal development. Physiological needs are the first order of needs and include basic bodily needs, i.e. water, food, rest, and sleep. Once physiological needs are satisfied the individual is concerned with his/her safety needs or obtaining a secure environment. Third, social needs are addressed and this constitutes belonging to a group or affiliation with people. Once social needs are met, esteem needs are addressed with concern for self-respect, prestige, recognition, and appreciation. Lastly, at the pinnacle of the pyramid, self-actualization needs are satisfied through self-fulfillment and reaching one's fullest potential (Figure 5.1).

Herzberg's Two Factor Theory proposes two different sets of job factors: Motivators (motivate and satisfy workers that relate to higher order needs)

Figure 5.1 Maslow's hierarchy of needs.

and hygiene factors (prevent dissatisfaction and relate to lower order needs). Motivator factors are intrinsic and include the work itself, responsibility, recognition, achievement, and job advancement. Hygiene factors are extrinsic and may include pay, status, job security, coworkers, or quality of management. The presence of motivators can help energize a work staff, and the absence of hygiene factors can cause dissatisfaction. This theory helped managers realize that job design was critical to make the job itself more intrinsically satisfying.

Enhancing motivation by job design is possible through job enrichment. Job enrichment refers to adding variety, responsibility, and managerial decision-making to make the job more rewarding. Job enrichment can be achieved by providing direct feedback, new learning opportunities, control over scheduling, unique experience, control over resources, and personal accountability. Direct feedback provides immediate evaluation of the employees' work so necessary changes can be made. An enriched job provides employees the opportunity to acquire new knowledge through job-related experiences or professional training. Employees also prefer to schedule their own workload and working hours. A job can provide unique experiences or qualities that is rewarding and uncommon in other positions, e.g. a sport facility manager may get the chance to meet famous athletes. Another source of job enrichment is having control of resources, such as finances and labor. Finally, personal accountability for job results is essential, meaning the employee accepts credit for a job well done and accepts the consequences of a poor job performance. To ensure the success of job enrichment, managers must know if their employees need or want more responsibility and personal accountability.

### Stress management and well-being

Managers should be concerned with work-related stress as it affects productivity levels. Prolonged exposure to work stress may result in work exhaustion (burnout). Burnout is a pattern of emotional, physical, and mental exhaustion in response to job-related stressors. Sources of job-related stressors include the following: (1) work overload (long hours and less free time), (2) lack of control over one's work schedule, (3) lack of reward for one's contribution (lack of pay and no recognition), (4) breakdown of a work community (lack of connections among people), and (5) lack of fair treatment.

Individual consequences of stress include psychological, emotional, and behavioral reactions. Psychological symptoms include increased heart rate, blood pressure, or perspiration. Emotional symptoms may include anxiety, frustration, low self-esteem, depression, poor concentration, or mental blocks. Behavioral effects may be accident proneness, impulsive behavior, or alcohol abuse. Work-related stress has financial implications on the organization because of reductions in operational effectiveness. There is also a cost associated with mental and physical health problems related to stress, such as medical bills, absenteeism, workplace accidents, or turnover.

Individual approaches to stress management fall into three categories: control, symptom management, and escape. Control simply means being in control of one's work life, such as practicing good work habits and time management, i.e. establishing daily priorities and minimizing procrastination. Physical exercise can manage symptoms of work-related stress. Exercise combats stress by releasing endorphins in the body that act like antidepressants. Escaping from the stressor is another stress management technique; however, eliminating the stressor is the most effective method (i.e. hiring additional event staff if the facility team is understaffed).

The sport organization can address employee stress management by providing an employee assistance (support) program (EAP) and/or establishing a wellness. Employee assistance programs are designed to deal with both work- and non-work-related stress, such as emotional difficulties or substance abuse. It is also important for employees to stay in good physical and mental shape. An organization sponsored wellness and fitness program can educate workers on maintaining a healthy lifestyle. These types of programs can offer medical examinations and stress management seminars. Some organizations have supported on-site massages and "nap time" during the workday.

## Group behavior and teamwork

Two commonly formed types of groups are formal groups and informal groups. Formal groups include command, task, and team groups. Command groups are specified in organizational charts and include employees reporting to a supervisor or manager. A task group is formed to complete a particular task or project, for example, a task force is assigned to develop a facility risk management plan. Teams are comprised of a group of people who work closely together and share a common vision or goal.

Informal groups include interest groups and friendship groups. Interest groups are formed to achieve a mutual objective among the group, not related to objectives of the organization. For example, certain interest groups may form to present a unified front to management for more pay or benefits. Friendship groups form because employees have something in common, such as age, ethnic background, or even similar sporting interests. Groups form for several reasons. Group members have social needs (enjoy interacting with others), esteem needs (belonging to a high status or prestige group), group goals (similar objectives), and economic benefits (when the productivity level of a group affects individual wages).

### Leadership

Leadership is the process of influencing followers (employees) to attain organizational goals. Leaders provide direction, generate trust, take risks, and reinforce the belief that success will be attained. Leadership traits and personal characteristics have been researched since the early 1900s. Specific traits and characteristics of effective leaders include self-confidence, trustworthiness, emotional intelligence, desire for power and achievement, and a sense of humor. A self-confident leader has the potential to instill confidence among his or her staff. Trustworthiness is critical to leadership effectiveness and is exhibited through behavioral consistency (being reliable and predictable) and integrity (telling the truth and keeping promises). Having a passion for the work and the people is an important aspect of emotional intelligence in order to inspire others about their work duties. Furthermore, a strong power motive encourages the leader to influence others, and the need for achievement propels a sense of urgency to act efficiently.

Studies conducted at The Ohio State University and University of Michigan originated much of the theory underlying leadership styles. The Ohio State researchers concluded that employees conceptualized their leaders' behavior on two leadership dimensions – consideration and initiating structure. Consideration is concerned with the degree to which a leader creates an environment of warmth, friendliness, trust, and support through leader behaviors such as being friendly, being concerned about the personal welfare of employees and informing staff of new developments. Initiating structure describes the degree to which the leader establishes structure for staff members through activities such as assigning specific tasks, establishing procedures and protocols, scheduling workloads, and clarifying expectations. The Ohio Studies found that employee turnover was lowest and job satisfaction highest under leaders rating high in consideration.

The University of Michigan researchers studied the differences in employee-centered and production (job)-centered leaders. Employee-centered leaders focus on employees by delegating decision-making and creating a supportive work environment. They are concerned with employees' personal advancement, growth, and achievement. Production-centered leaders focus on completing tasks and closely supervise employees to ensure that work is completed using stated procedures. They use coercion, rewards, and positional power to influence behavior and performance. It has been reported that most productive work teams had leaders who spend time planning, are employee-centered, and not engaged in close supervision of employees.

## Contingency theories of leadership

After the behavioral theories of leadership, researchers attempted to identify which leadership style would produce the best results. The contingency theory of leadership explains that the most effective style of leadership is dependent on factors relating to employees' and the work environment itself. The two contingency theories of leadership that we will discuss are the Path-Goal Theory of Leadership and the Situational Leadership Model.

The Path-Goal contingency theory focuses on how leaders influence employee perceptions of work goals, self-development goals, and paths to goal attainment.

The model explains what effects different types of leader behavior will have on employee morale (satisfaction) and productivity (performance). The four primary types of leader behavior are directive leadership, supportive leadership, participative leadership, and achievement-oriented leadership. Directive leadership involves setting standards and communicating expectations to workers. Supportive leadership emphasizes concern for the well-being of the workers and developing mutually satisfying relationships by treating workers as equals. Participative leadership involves consulting with workers to solicit suggestions and including them in the decision-making process. The achievement-oriented leader sets challenging goals, expects high performance levels, and expects workers to assume responsibility.

Contingency variables considered in this theory are personal characteristics of workers and environmental pressures and demands that the worker must cope with to accomplish goals and satisfaction. Personal characteristics include a person's locus of control, experience, and ability and skill level. Environmental factors are not within the control of the worker and may include work tasks, authority system of the organization, or the workgroup itself. Any of these variables can motivate or constrain the worker.

Individuals with a highly perceived level of ability to perform task demands would not be suitable for a directive style of leadership. Additionally, individuals with an internal locus of control (believe rewards are contingent on their efforts) are more satisfied with a participative style of leadership. Individuals with an external locus of control (believe rewards are beyond their control) are more satisfied with a directive leadership style. Table 5.1 highlights the leadership style most appropriate in a given situation.

Paul Hersey and Kenneth Blanchard developed the Situational Leadership Model (SLM) to assist leaders in selecting their leadership styles based on the readiness of employees. The SLT is based on two types of leader behavior: task behavior (similar to initiating structure) and relationship behavior (similar to consideration). The situational variable between the task and relationship behaviors and leadership effectiveness is the worker's maturity level (or readiness). Readiness is defined as the ability and willingness or confidence of the worker to accomplish a specific task. Two dimensions measure worker readiness – job maturity (technical ability) and physiological maturity (level of self-confidence and self-respect). Hersey and Blanchard developed four styles of leadership styles for managers to utilize depending on the readiness level of the employee:

1. Telling: the leader defines roles and tells employees what, where, how, and when to perform specific tasks.
2. Selling: the leader provides employees with instructions and is supportive.
3. Participating: the leader and employees share in the decision-making process to complete a quality job.
4. Delegating: the leader provides little instruction, direction, or personal support to employees.

**Table 5.1** Path-goal leadership styles and contingency relationships

| Leadership style | Situation |
| --- | --- |
| Directive | Positively affects morale (satisfaction) and productivity (performance) on workers completing ambiguous and complex tasks with little or no experience in doing the tasks, and no formalized procedures to help them accomplish their tasks. However, this style of leadership will negatively affect satisfaction of workers completing clearly defined tasks. |
| Supportive | Positively affects the satisfaction and efforts of workers completing stressful, tedious, and frustrating tasks. This style of leadership enhances the intrinsic value of tasks, increases workers' self-confidence, and lowers anxiety so tasks can be successfully completed. |
| Participative | Positively affects satisfaction and effort when work tasks are unstructured. This style of leadership increases workers' understanding of the relationship between their efforts and goal attainment. It helps workers select their own goals resulting in increased motivation as they have control over their own work. |
| Achievement-oriented | Positively affects satisfaction and productivity when tasks are ambiguous and nonrepetitive. This style of leadership will cause workers to strive for higher standards of performance and have more self-confidence in their ability. |

Source: DuBrin, A.J., 2002. The Winning Edge: How to Motivate, Influence, & Manage Your Company's Human Resources. South-Western College Publishing, Cincinnati, OH; Slack, T., Parent, M.M., 2006. Understanding Sport Organizations: The Application of Organization Theory, second ed. Human Kinetics, Champaign, IL.

The key point to situational leadership is as the employee's readiness level increases, the leader should focus more on relationship behavior and less on task-oriented behavior. As an individual matures (becomes more skilled) he/she needs less direction, although he/she may still need some motivation and encouragement. When an employee becomes self-sufficient, a minimum of task and relationship behavior is needed. Suppose that a sport facility manager determines that his or her new employee has low self-confidence and is insecure about performing job duties. The sport facility manager would exercise a "Telling" style of leadership to provide specific instructions and closely monitor performance. However, as the employee grows personally and professionally in their job role, the leadership style may be adapted to meet their current needs. Employees who are considered self-sufficient or provide an area of expertise, the sport facility manager would exercise a delegating style of leadership.

## Transformational and charismatic leadership

Leaders are continuously forced to make changes in their organizations to address the evolving and highly competitive global nature of the business world. Transformational leaders are capable of influencing major changes in the organizations objectives, strategies, culture, or philosophy. Transformational leaders go beyond the routine transactional leader who is concerned with only exchanges between the leader and employee to achieve a set of goals. The transformational leader can develop new visions for the organization and inspire followers to attain these new visions. Transformational leaders exhibit several key characteristics. They have the ability to clearly communicate a positive vision of the future. They support and encourage staff development and treat employees as individuals. They provide encouragement and recognition to employees and empower their staff by fostering trust and involvement in decisions. Furthermore, they encourage innovative thinking, lead by example, and exude charisma to inspire staff to be highly competent.

Charisma is a major contributing factor to transformational leadership. Charismatic leaders possess several key characteristics. Charismatic leaders provide vision to the organization that extends beyond organizational goals. They are effective communicators and formulate achievable dreams and vision for the future. Inspiring trust is also critical in order to get followers to share their vision, and make sacrifices upfront with the potential for future success. Charismatic leaders are also very energetic, action-oriented, and serve as a model for getting tasks completed on time. Additionally, they are able to manage their impression well through physical appearance.

## Dysfunctional aspects of leadership

Effective leadership is an extremely important asset to the sport organization. However, it can also be its worst liability. We have previously discussed the characteristics of successful leadership and the required traits and behaviors; it is now critical to highlight the dysfunctional patterns in leadership which may result in bad leadership and subsequently a dysfunctional organization. The Plochg Business Psychology Consulting Group highlighted dysfunctional leadership symptoms and common reasons leaders fail:

- Conflict avoidance: some managers need to be liked; therefore, they are unable or unwilling to make difficult decisions in case it threatens their acceptance.
- Micromanagement: managers may become so detail-oriented that they can't let go of control. A lack of trust in the capabilities of others has a negative effect on performance and ruins morale.
- Manic executives: are possessed with boundless energy and push themselves and others to the limit. They are so hyperactive they don't know what they are doing wrong.
- Inaccessibility of leadership: some managers have no time for others, are unapproachable, or may hide behind assistants and closed-door policies.

- Game players: can only talk and think about themselves, and lose attention when others talk. They refuse to let subordinates shine and use and abuse them rather than helping them grow and develop. Game players experience high turnover among their employees.
- No 360 degrees feedback: there is limited or no leadership performance feedback.
- Personal agendas: some managers recruit and award promotions based on internal politics, e.g. hiring friends to guarantee personal loyalty at the expense of more qualified candidates.
- Inefficient use of resources: budgets are allocated based on favoritism rather than business needs.

## The influence of power and politics

Power is the ability to influence decisions and control resources and is obtained in a variety of ways. Interpersonal sources of power are legitimate, reward, coercive, expert, and referent. Legitimate power refers to the individual's ability to influence others based on his or her position within the organization. The position gives the individual the right to influence or command others. Reward power is the individual's ability to reward an employee for compliance and is normally used as a follow-up to legitimate power. Coercive power is the power to punish and employees tend to comply out of fear, i.e. fear of being blocked for a promotion. Expert power is exerted when the individual possesses a special expertise that is highly valued. The more difficult it is to replace the expert, the more power they possess. Referent power is based on an individual's personality or behavioral style. A person's charisma is an indication of their referent power to influence others. Structural power involves resources, decision-making, and information power. Power may stem from access to resources such as money, labor, or technology. Additionally, the extent to which individuals can affect decision-making and their accessibility to pertinent information affects power levels.

Organizational politics is the use of informal strategies and tactics to gain power. Political tactics involve developing power contacts and establishing alliances. Power contacts can help support proposals and recommendations for promotion. Controlling vital information and keeping informed of organizational developments is another key factor. Also, being courteous, pleasant, and using sincere flattery can influence people.

## Managing conflict

Intergroup conflict can be either functional or dysfunctional. Functional conflict enhances the organization's performance. Employee disagreements may occur on the correct method to achieve project goals but this type of conflict leads to innovative solutions. Dysfunctional conflict hinders the organization's performance as employees' waste time disagreeing and placing personal interests above the interests of the organization. Three main causes of group conflict are work interdependence, goal differences, and perceptual differences. Work interdependence occurs when organizational groups depend on one another to complete tasks. Depending on the level of interdependence, the conflict level potential ranges from low to high. When organizational groups have mutually exclusive goals problems may arise. Perceptual differences in what constitutes importance and priorities can also cause group conflict.

The need to exercise conflict management is inevitable in any organization. There are five different styles to handle conflict resolution; these include competitive, accommodative, sharing, collaborative, and avoidant. A competitive (dominating) style is one in which the person wants to win at the expense of another's concerns. Accommodative (appeasement) style is more concerned with taking care of another's concerns before one's own concerns. Sharing (compromise) style is in the middle between competitive and accommodative. This style results in moderate or incomplete satisfaction for both parties involved. Collaborative (integration) is concerned with a win-win situation for both parties; therefore both parties are fully satisfied with the outcome. Avoidant (neglect) style is when the person is indifferent to the concerns of either party and may withdraw from the conflict.

The most common method of managing conflict is the use of formal authority. The manager has the ultimate power to resolve disputes. Conflict avoidance is commonly used by ignoring the conflict; however, this is considered as a short-term solution. Another way to manage conflict is to remove the interdependence between groups to complete tasks, or merge groups together to reduce conflict. Confrontation and negotiation require a level of maturity for groups to sit down and acknowledge the conflict and search for a solution. When conflicts are drawn out, a third party may be used to resolve the issue. Finally, job rotation is a method utilized to prevent or manage conflict. Through this practice the individual is exposed to job roles and responsibilities within other units. They acquire an understanding of situations and needs in other units and are able to relay information about their home units.

### Decision-making and problem solving

Managers make decisions on a daily basis. Decisions are either programmed or nonprogrammed. Programmed decisions are repetitive and routine, and are made on the basis of policies and past experiences. An example of a programmed decision for a facility manager is whether to increase the number of crowd management staff as the number of spectators increases. Nonprogrammed decisions are new and unique, and have no pre-established guidelines to aid decision-making. An example of a nonprogrammed decision for a facility manager is whether to relocate a sport facility to a new site. Managers make decisions under three types of conditions: certainty, risk, and uncertainty. A decision made under a condition of certainty means the manager is aware of all the alternatives and the costs and benefits of each alternative. Sometimes decisions are made under conditions of risk. Managers may know the alternatives but are not exactly sure of all the benefits or costs associated with their options. Finally, a decision made under a condition of uncertainty is when the manager knows very little about the alternatives or their potential outcomes.

An individual's propensity for risk may influence decisions. Managers with high aversion to risk establish different objectives and alternatives than a manager with a low risk aversion. After a decision is made, managers may experience cognitive dissonance (or post-decision anxiety). There may be a conflict between what the decision-maker knows and believes and the decision made, thereby resulting in second thoughts or doubts. The manager may also experience an escalation of commitment or increasing commitment to a previous decision when it would be better to withdraw (i.e. turn a poor decision into a good decision). The decision-making process involves several key elements: (1) establish specific goals, objectives, and measurable results, (2) identify and define the problem, (3) establish priorities, (4) consider causes of the problem identified, (5) develop alternative solutions, (6) evaluate alternative solutions, (7) select best solution, (8) implement, and (9) follow-up.

In most organizations decisions are made through some sort of group (e.g. teams, task forces). Nonprogrammed decisions normally require pooled talent as a greater amount of knowledge helps reach the best solution. Specific techniques used by managers to gain the input of a group include brainstorming, idea quotas (i.e. management requires two ideas per month from workers), forming heterogeneous groups (diverse groups may bring various viewpoints), offering financial incentives (paying employees for useful suggestions), and designing a creative space within the building (creating the opportunity for physical interaction facilitates the flow of ideas).

## Organizational culture and change

Organizational culture is a system of shared values, beliefs, assumptions, and understandings that influence worker behavior. A strong (thick) organizational culture is characterized by employees sharing the same core values. A weak (thin) organizational culture is one in which employees do not possess common values. Organizational culture has the potential to affect organizational effectiveness. Managers can create an appropriate organizational culture by setting a vision and getting employees excited about the fundamental purpose of the organization. Second, they can help develop the culture by taking action, for example, the NFL's partnership with United Way promotes to all NFL stakeholders their goal of assisting youth development and giving back to the community. Once a culture is created it must be maintained (or changed if it's not working). Ways to manage an organization's culture include the following: (1) what leaders pay attention to, measure, and control through comments or rewards, (2) their reaction to critical incidents and how they handle organizational crises (such as firing an employee for unethical conduct), (3) deliberate role modeling, teaching, and coaching by leaders as they set an example for the rest of the organization, (4) linking behavior to rewards and punishments, and (5) criteria for recruitment, selection, promotion, and retirement.

If the current culture is not appropriate then the manager is faced with the task of changing the culture. First, the manager must gain support for this change. Methods to gain support for change include education and communication. This allows for discussion and negotiation of aspects involved in the change process. Participation and involvement of employees provides an opportunity to have a say in the change that affects them, this also helps increase compliance. Financial benefits of the change should be openly communicated. An increase in salary could be an advantage. The change process should not be too overwhelming at first. Avoid change overload and try to make small changes over a period of time instead of sweeping changes overnight.

### Cultural diversity and global organizational behavior

Cultural diversity in the workforce is important in today's global economy. To value diversity one must value a wide range of cultural and individual

## Organizational healing

Different methodologies in leadership. Changes in the political and power structure. More conflicts as a result of change, especially if there is a perception that the removal of previous management/leadership was unwarranted. New tactics employed in decision-making and problem solving. All of these – and more – are evident during a shift in organizational structure and changes within the organization. And while these organizational modifications may be necessary to help with the survival of the organization – i.e. keep the doors of the business open – many of the employees and management structure may not agree with, understanding, or believe in the changes. These issues, if not dealt with, can erode the organization from the inside out.

Organizational healing is defined as the efforts related to repairing the social aspects of the organization, including issues related to continuity, vision, and broken self-concepts, that are needed if an organization is to operate in a strong, fit, and well manner after an actual or other perceived negative situation. This is not the process of surviving a negative situation – it is dealing with the after-effects of the negative situation. While in general this is a group-oriented process that looks at all parts of the organization as one interacting unit, actions and beliefs of individuals still need to be taken into account.

*Continued*

## Organizational healing—cont'd

One of the best methods to implement a process of organization healing in a sport facility is to stop all operations, close the doors, and focus solely on healing. This may be accomplished through in-service programs, retreats, team building activities, and any activities that open the lines of communication across the organization. This should not be a judging process – rather a time to discuss, reflect, explain, and create an atmosphere of understanding and openness. The overall goals of this process are:

- To reinforce the importance of each individual and an integral part of the overall organization;
- To create and maintain a process of open communication and connection;
- To enhance and strengthen the organizational culture; and
- To develop new organizational bonding methods that create new unity, sense of stability, and believe in the organization.

### Suggested discussion topics

1. As stated in the case, organizational healing is a collective and individual process. In many cases, the collective organization may be healed, but there may be individuals and small groups of individuals who do not "buy-in". Explain in detail how would you deal with those individuals? What could happen to the organization if their lack of "buy-in" is not dealt with?
2. Sport organizations are renowned for creating ceremonies, rituals, or other activities that embrace bonding within the organization. You are the new owner of a sport facility where you have kept most of the previous staff because of their expertise, however, many do not believe in you because you bought out the very popular previous owner. Explain how you would go about implementing a program of organization healing, including the development of a ceremony/ritual/activity, that will bond the organization.

differences. A truly diverse organization is one where all employees, regardless of cultural backgrounds, achieve their full potential. Diverse organizations have a competitive advantage potential and offer benefits in various ways. A multicultural workforce enhances the ability to reach a multicultural client base and this marketing advantage leads to increased sales and profits. Effectively managing a diverse workgroup can prevent turnover and absenteeism. Furthermore, it reduces the likelihood of discrimination lawsuits, thereby reducing costs. Organizations with a history of employing and effectively managing a diverse workforce have an advantage in recruiting top talent from minority groups. Workforce heterogeneity also offers the organization a creativity advantage. Diverse groups are more likely to develop creative solutions to problems. To understand how to work well with diverse groups one must first examine different cultural values (see Table 5.2).

## Table 5.2 Cross-cultural values

*Individualism vs. collectivism*
Individualistic cultures are made up of people who are concerned for their own interests first. They tend to be more concerned with their own careers than the good of the organization (e.g. United States, Canada, United Kingdom, and Australia). Collectivism is a feeling that the group or organization receives priority over individual interests (e.g. Japan, Mexico, Greece, and Hong Kong).

*High-power distance vs. low-power distance*
Power distance is the extent employees accept the idea that members of the organizations have different levels of power. In a high-power distance culture, employees willingly comply because they have a positive orientation toward authority (e.g. France, Spain, Japan, Mexico, and Brazil). In a low-power distance culture, employees only accept directions when they feel the superior is correct. They do not willingly recognize a power hierarchy (e.g. United States, Ireland, Germany, and Israel).

*High uncertainly avoidance vs. low uncertainty avoidance*
High uncertainty avoidance cultures contain a majority of people who do not tolerate risk and want predictable and certain futures (e.g. Japan, Italy, Argentina, and Israel). Low uncertainty avoidance cultures contain people who are willing to take risk and accept the unknown (e.g. United States, Canada, Australia, and Singapore).

*Materialism vs. concern for others*
Materialism refers to the acquisition of money and material objects and a de-emphasis on the caring for others (e.g. Japan, Austria, and Italy). A concern of others means building personal relationships and having a concern for the welfare of all (e.g. Scandinavian countries).

*Long-term orientation vs. short-term orientation*
Employees from a long-term orientation culture believe in planning for the long term and not demanding immediate returns on investments (e.g. Pacific Rim Countries). Short-term orientation cultures demand immediate results and have a propensity not to save (e.g. United States and Canada).

*Formality vs. informality*
Cultures high on formality respect traditions, rituals, and ceremonies (e.g. Latin American countries). Informality cultures have a casual attitude toward tradition, social rules, and rank (United States, Canada, and Scandinavian countries).

*Urgent time orientation vs. casual time orientation*
Some cultures perceive time as a scare resource and are impatient; they tend to have an urgent time orientation (e.g. United States). Other cultures tend to view time as an unlimited resource and are more patient and have a casual time orientation (e.g. Asians and Middle Easterners).

*Source: DuBrin, A.J., 2002. The Winning Edge: How to Motivate, Influence, & Manage Your Company's Human Resources. South-Western College Publishing, Cincinnati, OH, pp. 282–285.*

Culture also impacts management and leadership style in an organization. Research conducted by Geert Hofstede revealed national stereotypes of management styles. German managers are technical experts who assign tasks and solve problems and are primarily authoritarian. Japanese managers tend to rely on group consensus for decision-making. French managers of major corporations are considered part of an elite class and exhibit superior and authoritarian characteristics. Dutch managers believe in quality and group problem solving and do not expect to impress employees with their status. Chinese managers maintain a low profile and major decisions in Chinese organizations are made by one dominant person who is often over the age of 65.

## Chapter review

Organizational behavior is the study of human behavior in the work environment. A key difference between managers and leaders is that managers preserve order and consistency, whereas leaders deal with change in a rapidly changing competitive environment. Four types of leader behaviors are directive leadership, supportive leadership, participative leadership, and achievement-oriented leadership. Hersey and Blanchard (1988) developed four styles of leadership for managers to use depending on the maturity level of the follower: Telling, Selling, Participating, and Delegating. Transformational leaders influence major changes in the attitudes and assumptions of staff members and are capable of building commitment for major changes in the organization's objectives and strategies. Charismatic leaders exude several key characteristics, these include their ability to establish an organizational vision (or lofty goal), are masterful communicators, inspire trust, are energetic, and are adept at impression management. Dysfunctional leadership symptoms may include conflict avoidance, micromanagement, inefficient use of resources, and no 360 degrees feedback.

Organizational culture is a system of shared values, beliefs, assumptions, and understandings that influence worker behavior. Diverse organizations have a competitive advantage potential and offer benefits in various ways, e.g. marketing advantage over a multicultural client base, lower turnover and absenteeism, reduces likelihood of discrimination lawsuits, advantages in recruiting top talent from minority groups, and possess a creativity advantage. To understand how to work well with diverse groups one must first examine different cultural values.

# 6 Human resource management

## Chapter outline

## Chapter objectives

This chapter takes a look at the increased growth, interest, and complexity in human resource management in sport facilities, with significant emphasis on managerial competencies, the strategic importance of human resource management, and the implications of legislative, governance and ethical issues in terms of employees, volunteers, and customers of sport facilities. This emphasis will be accomplished by understanding individual differences in abilities, personalities, values and motivations inherent in each group, and how to manage those groups strategically through managing human resources (including human capital management and leadership); the integration of strategic human resource management, with special focus on knowledge management; employment of personnel practices including job analysis and design, recruitment and selection of personnel, and orientation, training, and development of new personnel; and performance management focusing on appraisal systems; reward systems, promotions/succession management, and termination processes. The end of this chapter will focus on the development of and inclusions for a sport facility human resources manual.

## Human resources in sport facilities

While the infrastructure of a sport facility is certainly important, without people working in and using the facility the infrastructure is useless. Hence it is safe to say that the most important resource for a sport facility is the human resource. Human resource management is the function within an organization that is responsible for the recruitment, training, and retention of personnel, but goes much more in depth in an effort to strategically move the organization forward toward a vision.

However, prior to analyzing these human resource practices, it is important to recognize who the major human resources are in a sport facility. For the purpose of this section, we will break down these human resources into three categories – professional staff, volunteers, and clients.

## Professional staff

Professional staff are the employees of a sport organization who are hired to perform specific jobs/tasks in exchange for some form of remuneration. Within sport facilities, there are usually four levels of professional staff – executive, administrative, supervisory, and general.

The executive level has the most power and authority, and is made up of senior or top managers within the sport facility, and are usually responsible for the majority of the management and operations of the overall sport facility. Typical titles of professional staff at the executive level include Presidents, Chief Executive Officers (CEO), Vice Presidents of various operations, and General Managers.

Administrative level professional staff, also known as middle managers, are accountable for the day-to-day operations of specific departments or operations within a sport facility. These staff members have a unique position within the organization since they connect both the upper and lower levels of management within the sport facility, hence must have a balance leadership of lower professional staff with managing the tasks set forth by upper management. In sport facilities, these individuals are usually directors or coordinators of various departments such as marketing, facility operations, business operations, sport programs, and food and beverage services.

Supervisory level professional staff are responsible for the day-to-day operations within a specific unit in a department. These assistant or associate level managers are responsible to ensure that the specific tasks within their unit are completed based on the directives from their middle manager, and are the connection between the specialists working in each unit. For example, within the department of sport programs, there may be assistant directors for boys/men's programs, girls/women's programs, kids programs, and camps/clinics. These managers have little authority in the grand scheme of the overall sport facility, but are the ultimate authority general staff answer to.

General staff are the specialists within individual units who complete the tasks as assigned by the management structure within a sport facility. These professional staff are specialists in their area of employment – such as coaches, custodial staff, front office staff, security, and officials.

It is important to remember that the professional staff at the top levels are mostly responsible for the conceptual management of a sport facility, the general staff is in charge of conducting the technical aspect of running a sport facility, and the middle managers are accountable for the highest levels of interpersonal skills – are they must ensure concepts are communicated to general staff, and technical issues are articulated to upper management. Regardless of the level of professional staff, ultimately each is responsible for ensuring that the planning, organizing, and controlling of the sport facility is appropriately administered through proper direction and adequate staffing.

## Volunteers

However, one of the challenges in sport facilities, especially as related to many of the events that take place in them, is the cost of staffing those events appropriately. Sport facility managers need to ensure that all internal and external laws and regulations are followed, especially as related to the number of staff members that need to be present in various areas to ensure the safe and enjoyable experience of guests. However, the costs to staff the required number of people would cripple most events – especially at the hallmark (Super Bowl, World Cups, etc.) and regional (marathons, triathlons, bike tours, etc.) levels. In addition, organizations without a large budget (especially non-profits such as Special Olympics) could not even dream of holding events. This would be devastating to sport facilities, because if there are no events, then there is no need for a facility. This has led to the significant growth of another major human resource that work in a sport facility – volunteers.

A volunteer is a non-employee who willingly becomes involved with an organization or event for no compensation to assist with a need that could not otherwise be offered. This definition is generic in nature, as there is truly no universally agreed upon description. This is because it depends on the viewpoint – those who volunteer looks at volunteerism as giving time, effort, and expertise to an organization with a need for either socially responsible or altruist reasons; those who take on volunteers look to accomplish the goals and mission of the organization by securing individuals who have expertise to meet the need without having to put them on the payroll.

---

## Volunteerism around the world

Sports, no matter what the event, always are in need for volunteers, and hence sport facility professional staff member must recognize the importance. Volunteers are imperative to the success or failure of an event, and hence to the positive or negative image of a sport facility. Sport facilities that hold events ranging from the small local recreation basketball tournament to the Olympics need volunteers to succeed. These organizations usually will consider any volunteers they can get their hands on, regardless of their professional background.

* As the volunteer concept has many definitions globally, it is important to understand the various volunteer concepts from around the world. For more details about these volunteer concepts, go to the online supplements for this text to get information about volunteerism in Australia, Canada, and England, with suggested discussion topics to consider.

## Customers and clients

Customers and clients are a unique human resource for sport facilities because of the service orientation involved. These individuals are often participants and/or have some involvement with sport events that take place in sport facilities. Sport in general is in the position of producing services and consuming services simultaneously. Therefore, the customer or client of a sport facility provide both inputs and outputs – and hence must be considered a human resource.

Similar to the volunteer, the customer/client as a human resource does provide the opportunity for a sport facility to offer a service through the events it hosts, while at the same time lowering the expense of paid staff by having customers and clients help staff the events. Examples might include scorekeepers and secondary officials for games, completing registration and waiver forms on behalf of the facility, as greeters to give directions to other guests and customers to the sport facility, and as extra security to help control crowds.

## Individual differences in human resources

Regardless of the type of human resources, it is important to recognize the individual differences between people. Individual differences are usually affected by factors including personality, motivation, attitudes, and perceptions.

Personality is defined as the unique and personal psychological characteristic of an individual which reflects how they respond to their social environment. An individual's personality reflects their individual differences. While personality can change, it is generally permanent and consistent. Sport facility managers must be able to manage human resources in term of their self-concept and their stage in the life cycle. Self-concept goes beyond self-image; it includes recognizing who the human resource wants to be (ideal self), how the human resource believes they are viewed by others (perceived self), and how the human resource interacts with their reference group (reference group self). As far as the stage in the life cycle, sport facility managers must recognize that human resources are different as they transit through life, which in turn modifies their individual attitudes, values, and identities.

Motivation is the influence that initiates the drive to satisfy wants and needs. For human resources in sport facilities, this may be achieved through motives such as accomplishment, fun, improvement of skill, health and fitness, or the desire for affiliation. Motives are emotional or psychological needs that act to stimulate an action. Emotional motives involve the selection of goals according to individual or subjective criterion. Rational motives entail selecting goals based on objective criterion. In general, motives will never fully satisfy needs, because new needs develop as a result of the satisfaction of old needs. Therefore, to motivate human resources, sport facility managers need to focus on three specific needs: power, affiliation, and achievement. Power is where the human resource wants to have control over their environment.

Affiliation is the most basic concept of social interaction, and some human resources need interaction with other human beings and to be in an atmosphere of connectedness and belonging. Achievement involves the need for personal accomplishment through being self-fulfilled or having high self esteem and/or prestige.

An attitude is a state of mind or behavioral predisposition that is consistently favorable or unfavorable with respect to a product or situation. Attitudes are formed in many different ways, but most often they are formed either from personality factors or are learned from environmental influences. Sport facility managers are constantly trying to influence the attitudes of their human resources. Some of the strategies employed include changing the basic motivational function of the human resource, associating their involvement as a human resource with a respected group or sport event; and working out conflicts between two attitudes, preferably moving from negative to positive.

Perceptions involve gaining an understanding of the individual values, attitudes, needs and expectations of an individual by scanning, gathering, assessing, and interpreting those insights. For human resources, perception involves the process of interpreting the world around them (in this case the sport facility) through sensations, images, and affections. Sensations are the most basic element of perception as they are the immediate and direct responses from the sensory organs. Images are the pictures that are formed in the mind to differentiate what is perceived. Affections are the actual emotions emitted as a result of the perception. The perceptions of human resources can easily be transmitted to other human resources, customers, clients, and the general public, hence it is important for the sport facility manager to ensure that the sport facility is perceived in a positive light as often as possible.

## Human resource practices in sport facilities

As stated earlier in the chapter, human resource management is the function within an organization that is responsible for the recruitment, training, and retention of personnel, but goes much more in depth in an effort to strategically move the organization forward toward a vision. With this in mind, the sport facility manager has a number of responsibilities inherent in this area. These include developing the values and principles for leading and managing people in the sport facility, defining the strategies to the utilized, developing the policies to guide all human resources, and implement the procedures and methods to apply those policies – thus creating a human resource management structure for the sport facility.

This section of this book will cover the major human resource management practices for sport facilities. First will be an explanation of managing human resources for sport facilities, followed by an analysis of the various functions innate to strategic human resource management. This information will then be applied to the two most important concepts in human resource management as related to sport facilities – employment of personnel, and performance management.

## Managing human resources

The most important function within human resource management in sport facilities, and most likely in any organization, is to understand the best way to manage people. Management is the process of planning, organizing, directing, and controlling tasks to accomplish goals, meet the mission of the organization, and work toward a vision. As such, human resource management focuses on planning, organizing, directing, and controlling people within the organization. In human resource management, employees/personnel are looked at as assets – just like a piece of equipment or the infrastructure of the sport facility. Human resources have significant costs to the sport facility in the forms of outlays of payroll, benefits, and other perks. They also have significant costs as their actions (or lack thereof) as service providers could lead to additional expenses or reductions of revenues.

This leads to two questions. First is "should human resources simply be looked at as another asset for a sport facility?" After all, these are human beings, not inanimate objects, and their knowledge and skills are a unique benefit to a sport facility. The second question is "do all people want to be managed?" This is a deeper question that looks into the individual differences of people. It is true that many people prefer to just be told what to do, and they will accomplish the tasks. However, there are those who believe they are an asset that brings great value to the sport facility, and have a desire to grow both personally and in concert with the organization. As a result, this bring forward two additional concepts to consider in the managing of human resources – human capital management, and leadership of human resources.

### Human capital management

Human capital management is defined as the management of the most important asset within an organization – the people. This is a slightly different concept than human resource management, where many times the people are looked at as costs to the organization. However, it seems that more and more sport organizations – especially as the service-based economy become more prevalent in the sport industry – are injecting human capital management concepts into their human resource practices. The reason is the realization that human resources are more than just a necessity as a support service to a sport facility. Human resources add value to the overall organization, because of their training, expertise, adaptability, commitment, and loyalty. Their individual training and expertise determine the skills and services available within the sport facility. Adaptability to change provides strategic flexibility for the sport facility. Commitment and loyalty of human resources – because of the ownership they feel in being an integral asset to the organization – often equates to the ability to maintain competitive advantage.

## Leadership

As a result of this shift toward implementing human capital management philosophies into the human resource management process, the other issue to evaluate is the how the concept of leadership become part of managing human resources. Leadership is a very different concept than management, but is often improperly used interchangeable. Leadership is the process of guiding and inspiring people. Leadership is not straight forward, as people have difference preferences in the way in which they want to be lead, and leaders will utilize different styles of leadership based on the situation at hand.

While there are numerous different models of leadership, generally there are three basic styles of leadership – autocratic, democratic, and laissez-faire. Autocratic leadership is more of a dictatorial style of leadership where the leader tells the human resources what to do, and limits discussion about alternative courses of action. While this does not promote a sense of teamwork in the organization, it is an important style to utilizing when time is limited, there is a lack of skill or knowledge amongst the human resources (as in the case with entry-level employees), or when new groups of people have not worked together in the past (as in the case of a group of new employees).

Democratic leadership is a participative style of leadership when human resources are involved with the decision making and problem solving processes related to the operation of the sport facility. This style of leadership recognizes the importance of teamwork, and takes into account the individual skills and knowledge of the human resources. This style of leadership is effective when there is time to make decisions and the human resources are motivated to be involved. This style of leadership is highly ineffective when there is a high level of conflict within a human resource group.

Laissez-faire (the French word for "hands-off") leadership is where the leaders defer decision making and problem solving to the human resources because of their extensive experience, skill, and knowledge about a given process. This is an especially powerful style of leadership with long-time employees who are familiar with the routines and services within a sport facility. It is also very powerful when there is good communication and cooperation between human resources within the sport facility.

Managers manage tasks – leaders lead people. So as we look at the evolution of human resource management, it is important to recognize the shift in looking at human resources as costs necessary to complete tasks within a sport facility. Human resources are assets to the sport facility, and they may work more effectively by being influenced and inspired rather than by being told what to do. As this shift becomes more prevalent across human resource practice, it will have a direct effect on the process of strategic human resource management.

## Strategic human resource management

Strategic human resource management for sport facilities involve an integrative approach to creating human resource strategies that seeks to accomplish goals based on the desired outcomes for the sport facility. There are numerous elements to having a strategic outlook for human resources in a sport facility, including the strategic intentions of the ownership structure; the availability and allocation of resources to meet the opportunities and needs of the sport facility; attain a competitive advantage over similar sport facilities; and the strategic capabilities of the overall organizational structure of the sport facility. In order to attain these strategic outcomes, sport facility managers must be able to efficiently plan, organize, and control knowledge.

## Knowledge management

Knowledge management is the acquisition, sharing, and use of intelligence, understanding, and expertise within a sport organization to aid in the accomplishment of tasks, processes, and operations. This is a crucial part of human resource management in a sport facility as the knowledge of personnel, and the sharing of knowledge throughout the organization, allows the operation of the sport facility to be more efficient and effective.

Knowledge within a sport facility usually falls under four categories:

- *Embedded knowledge* – the information which is articulated within rules and regulations, and organizational policies and procedures;
- *Embodied knowledge* – the practical skills, understandings, and applications of concepts exhibited by employees and management;
- *Embraced knowledge* – the theoretical/conceptual/cognitive skills exhibited by employees and management; and
- *Encultured knowledge* – the collective intelligence, values, and beliefs of the entire organization.

In order to most effectively manage knowledge, sport facility managers seek to utilize all existing intelligence in the best possible manner. In some cases, this may involve choosing specific individuals to work on tasks where their expertise lie – in other cases it may entail documenting and storing information for referral by others in the future. The goal is to ensure productivity in all processes and procedures on a continuous basis. However, it is important to recognize that all knowledge may not exist internal to the organization. This is why recognizing the importance of professional development to renew the knowledge of personnel, as well as to bring in outside knowledge when necessary to accomplish tasks that cannot be completed by those in the organization, is crucial to knowledge management. Those organizations that do not stay ahead of change or their competition are setting themselves up for reduced success.

While it is important to know how to acquire the knowledge necessary to successfully operate a sport facility, this is not enough. Knowledge is only useful if it can be transformed into usable outputs. This is where understanding the structural capital and business strategy of a sport facility is crucial to success. Structural capital is the understanding of the organizational structure and how information and knowledge moves horizontally and vertically through that structure to accomplish tasks that meet the needs and desires of customers. Business strategy involves understanding the management practices of top managers and ownership, and how the competencies and capabilities of personnel are most effectively managed to accomplish the mission and goals set forth by them to move the sport facility forward as a business.

Knowledge management is crucial to the success of human resource management. However, knowledge is only as good as the people who own that knowledge, and the organization is set up to effectively utilize those individuals. Hence, the way in which jobs are designed, personnel is selected, and employees are integrated into the organization is essential to quality human resource management.

## Employment of personnel

Employment is the process of making a living through work or conducting business. Managers seek to employ the most knowledgeable individuals to efficiently and effectively run the operations of sport facilities, especially because of the intricate designs, skills, and knowledge necessary based on the wide variety of facilities. In order to most effectively hire the best and brightest, job tasks need to be analyzed and appropriate positions should be designed. This also requires quality recruiting and selecting of personnel, followed by the implementation of an orientation, training, and development program for new personnel.

### Job analysis and design

Job analysis is the process of examining and evaluating the specific tasks to be completed within an organization and determining the best way to design a method for completing them in the most timely and relevant way. Usually, job analysis for a sport facility requires understanding the current organizational structure of the sport facility, the work activities that need to be accomplished, and the knowledge and informational content present within the organization at present. Once this information is compiled, tasks are grouped, positions are determined, job titles are assigned, and organizational charts are modified as necessary.

This is followed by the process of designing a job description. The main purpose of the job description is to articulate the job responsibilities of the position opening and the expected competencies of candidates for the position. The following are usual inclusions within a job description:

- Job Title;
- Commitment Required;
  - Usually articulated in hours per week;

- Salary;
  - With notation of rewards and incentives available over and above the salary;
- Summary of the Job;
  - Duties and responsibilities;
  - Authority and reporting structure;
  - Performance standards;
- Knowledge;
  - Education requirements;
  - Experience requirements;
  - Skills and abilities desired (including qualifications);
- Contact Information;
- Application Deadlines;
- General Information about the Sport Organization/Facility;
- Any Required Legal or Governmental Statements;
  - Equal employment opportunity statements;
  - Background/criminal checks (especially when working with children in sport facilities).

The job description is used to standardize the information about a specific task or group of tasks, including the essential duties of personnel working under that description. This is important in standardizing and balancing the work assignments between employees in the organization, and can be effectively used to stylize the training and quality assessment programs within a sport facility, as well as to assure compliance with industry standards and legal responsibilities. Another major use of job descriptions is in the creation of job announcements to recruit new personnel – as the job description provides parameters for managers to do quality searching for employees, can be used to formulate questions during the interviewing process, and provides the most important information to potential job candidates.

## Recruiting and selection personnel

Recruiting and selecting of personnel occurs for one of two reasons – a new position has been created, or an individual has left a position either because of termination, temporary leave, or job change. Regardless of the reason, the sport facility manager must engage in the recruitment and selection process, which involves submitting recruiting documents, engaging in the actual selection process, empowering a search committee, conducting interviews, carrying out reference checks, making the hiring decision, and documenting the entire process.

The recruitment and selection process starts by submitting recruiting documents, which usually included a request for hire memorandum explaining the need for the hire, and an updated position description. Once approved, a job posting is created to be published in newspapers, websites, and other job listing services.

As application come in, a major tasks is to go through all the applications to select the most qualified candidates for the position. It is important to review the position description point-by-point to ensure your understanding of all requirements, and then develop a plan to most effectively identify and assess the candidates. As a part of the selection process, depending on the number of applicants, there may be multiple levels of assessment. For example, assume there is a pool of 100 applicants, and eight are deemed to be most qualified. Phone interviews may be the appropriate next step to further assess the candidates and determine the most appropriate candidates to bring in for face-to-face interviews.

Applicant pools may be only assessed by the direct supervisor who is conducting the hiring process, but it is recommended that applicant assessments be conducted by a search committee. A search committee is a group of individuals who evaluate, screen, and interview individuals seeking employment. This often is a mix of direct supervisors, potential co-workers, and outside of department employees, and can give additional perspectives into the selection process of employees for the sport facility.

Once the applicant pool is reduced to the final candidates, interviews take place. The purpose of an interview is to elicit information from an applicant to determine their ability to perform the job. Successful interviewers learn how to ask the right kind questions, how to keep the applicant talking about relevant information, and how to listen – because much of what is learned about applicants in an interview is based on their past experience, and past performance is one of the best indicators of future performance.

When conducting interviews, there are two types of questions – non-directive and directive. Non-directive questions do not give the applicant any indication of the desired answer, are usually phrased in the news reporter's style of who, what, when, where and how, and often they begin with the words "describe" or "explain". Examples of non-directive questions include:

- Describe your experiences working as a scheduling manager for sport facilities?
- Explain what you consider to be the most important responsibilities of a sport facility manager?
- Why does this position interest you?
- How has your background prepared you for this position?

It is also important ask follow-up questions if the response is unclear or incomplete. Clarify and verify any piece of information by asking the candidate to explain their answer again or to elaborate on the given answer.

Directive questions are useful for drawing out specific information. In direct questioning, the interviewer asks, directs, or guides the applicant to specifics. Often, these questions result in a "yes"; or "no" response. Examples of directive questions include:

- Do you have experience running a specific type of scheduling software?
- Are you still employed at your current job?
- Do you have certifications in pool and spa operations?

In addition to non-directive and directive questions, interviewers often develop special questions that are unique to the specific candidate either because of the education or experience, or as a result of a previous answer during the interview. One type of question format would be using self-evaluation – where the interviewee is asked to provide their perceptions and beliefs. Many times, this type of question focuses on asking about an applicant's likes and dislikes, or strength and weaknesses.

Another type of question may be behavioral and/or experience-focused. This type of question asks the applicant to describe as closely as possible the actual behavior that went on in a particular situation. The use of superlative adjectives such as most/least, best/worst, and toughest/easiest tend to stimulate specific events in the mind of the interviewee and therefore make it easier to respond. An example would be:

• On your resume you noted that you were the Director of Scheduling at ABC Facility. Can you share with the committee a time where you had a double-booking scenario and how you dealt with the situation?

Another method for developing special questions is by using a problem solving/judgment type question that involves a scenario that might be common on the job. An example would be:

• You are the facility supervisor on a Saturday evening when you are called to the basketball court where a person is lying on the ground under the basket unconscious. You hear from the other individuals on the court that the player went up for a dunk, got undercut by another player, and came down back and head first on the floor. How would you handle this situation?

Once all candidates have been interviewed and evaluations collected from all members of the committee, usually candidates are rank ordered in preference of selection. At that point, the top candidate is pursued. The first step in this process is to conduct reference checks. It is important to remember that information received in an interview is biased and typically includes only what the applicant want to share. A thorough reference check may produce additional information to help insure that the most suitable candidate is hired. It is a way to clarify, verify and add data to what has been learned in the interview and from other portions of the selection process. The best source of information on any candidate is a current or former employer, especially the direct supervisor if possible. On-the-job performance is the most useful predictor of future success. The supervisor can specify the quality and quantity of work, reliability, potential problem areas and job behaviors. It is better to do phone reference checks rather than utilize written references provided by candidates – the validity of written references cannot often be verified.

It is also important to contact multiple references (usually three minimum is a good standard) to verify that the information about the candidate is consistent.

Assuming all reference checks go well, it is time to offer the position. However, this is not the end of the recruiting and selection process. Many things can happen at this point...

• The person is offered the position and after negotiation they accept the position.
• The person is offered the position and after negotiation they decline the position.
• You offer the person the position, and they turn down your offer.

If they turn down your offer, you need to start the reference check process on your next choice, and depending on the results...

- The individual(s) are offered the position and they either accept or decline the offer.
- The individual(s) are deemed not appropriate for the position.

Should the latter happen, the following processes will take place:

- Re-review of applicants not offered interviews in the first round to determine if any of them are qualified for an interview.
- If so, the interview process starts again. If not, they either:
  - Re-post the position for new applicants;
  - Re-evaluate the need within the sport facility to see if current employees might be able to cover the responsibilities in-house, and hence adjust their positions.

If a person is selected for a position, they often need to come into the human resource office to complete paperwork. This may include:

- Contracts;
- Personal demographic data;
- Tax and work verification paperwork;
- Payroll and benefits paperwork;
- Verification of receipt of human resource and operations manuals.

They may also need to bring in updated or additional paperwork such as updated resumes, education transcripts, and medical clearance forms. In some cases, this paperwork process is conducted in coordination with orientation for the new employee...

## Orientation, training, and development of new personnel

Orientation involves introducing new employees to the organization; training is the education of the employee in their job tasks; and development is the further education of the employee to further their skills, and value to the sport facility. Each of these processes is integral to the proper management of human resources, and hence the effective and efficient operation of a sport facility.

New employee orientation is the first step in integrating personnel into the sport facility. Effectively orienting new employees to the sport facility and to their positions is critical to establish successful, productive working relationships. The employee's first interactions with you should create a positive impression of the sport facility. The time you spend planning for the new person's first days and weeks on the job will greatly increase the chance for a successful start. An effective orientation program will:

- Foster an understanding of the organization culture.
- Help the new employee make a successful adjustment to the new job.
- Help the new employee understand their role and how they fits into the total sport facility operation.
- Help the new employee achieve objectives and shorten the learning curve.

- Help the new employee develop a positive working relationship by building a foundation of knowledge about facility philosophy, mission, objectives, policies and
  procedures, rules and regulations organizational structure, and vision.

Depending on the education and experience of the new employee, training
may be extensive or specialized. Extensive training may be for new employee
with little education or experience, or has shifted into a new area of responsibility. Specialized training may be given to a new employee with many years of
experience in the field, but is in need of specific knowledge individual to the sport
facility. Training should be an ongoing process to help employees advance their
knowledge and skills, and therefore advance the operation of the sport facility.
Some of this training may be in the form of development and certification
programs. These may include attending seminars, trainings, conferences, or even
classes offered at a local educational service or college/university.

## Performance management

Performance management is the process of evaluating the past and current
performance of employees. This evaluation is usually conducted by the immediate supervisor of the employee, and is kept on file by the human resource
coordinator. The process of performance management usually involves three
ongoing stages. First is the planning of performance and development metrics,
where goals are set and measurement parameters are agreed upon. Second is the
managing of performance throughout the employment process, where the
supervisor and the employee gauge the successful attainment of goals. The final
stage is a performance review, where the supervisor (at a predetermined time –
can be 90 days, 6 months, or annually) assesses progress and accomplishments to
determine exceptional, acceptable, or non-acceptable performance. These
performance reviews are governed by the appraisal system set forth by the
individual sport facility.

## Appraisal systems

Employee performance appraisal systems are crucial to the successful administration of a sport facility. It is an important tool for making decisions about
employee advancement, retention, and termination; salary increases; and
employee improvement. Appraisal systems usually include three basic steps –
collecting data, evaluating performance based on the data, and documenting the
evaluation in writing. In collecting the data, immediate supervisors should assess
behaviors of the employee, and avoid personality issues and differences unless
they impact performance. The evaluation is about the employee's performance
and not their personality. Once the data is collected, it can then be used measure
performance and appraise the employee's value to the sport facility.

A performance appraisal should be seen as a way to maximize performance
for the employees and the overall organization in the future instead of focusing
on what has happened in the past. The ultimate goal of performance appraisals is

to enhance the career building of the employee and advance the operation of the sport facility. At times, this is not possible, which may result in the termination or voluntary separation of the employee from the organization. All performance appraisals should be done in writing and verbally reviewed with the employee. Employees should be given advanced warning when the evaluation meeting will occur. It is a good practice to have the employee do a self-evaluation prior to the meeting so that discussion points can be created.

Appraisal processes can be both very exiting yet stressful time for an employee, as there is always fear that the employee's belief of their performance is not the same as the supervisor's. However, if there has been regular discussion and evaluation throughout the year, rewards have been provided when attaining a certain level of performance, resources have been provided to the employee to succeed such as proper training and development to do their job, and clear organizational and personal goals have been articulate and agreed upon, there should be no surprises during the appraisal process. Therefore, a well-prepared appraisal system explores the past, accurately examines the present, and creates a plan for the future – hence enhancing retention and personnel relations.

## Reward systems

Reward systems are the policies and strategies of a sport facility that focus on compensating employees in a fair, equitable, consistent, and transparent manner. There are numerous reasons for rewarding employees, including:

- the added value they create for the sport facility;
- the exhibition of exhibiting the appropriate behaviors, or meeting the desired outcomes;
- the development a performance-based organizational culture where accomplishment is rewarded;
- the motivation of people to be committed and engaged with the organization;
- the retention of high-quality employees;
- the development of positive employment relationships.

The total reward an individual may receive financial and non-financial in nature. The most basic of rewards is a raise in base salary or basic pay. Other monetary rewards may include bonuses/additional commissions, long-term incentives (such as pensions), shares in the organization, profit sharing, and other incentives such as company cars and use of company-owned property/ equipment. Non-financial rewards may include flex time (partial days off), holidays, and memberships (such as country clubs or sport facility). One of the most significant non-financial rewards is earning a promotion, and is an element of succession management.

## Promotions and succession management

Succession management is the process of making provisions for the develop-ment, replacement and strategic application of key people over time. It is inevitable that people will retire, leave an organization, or be promoted to another position, hence a succession plan must be in place. In some cases, succession will come from within via a promotion. In other cases, it requires hiring a new employee. Regardless, succession management requires the identification of the organization's values, mission, and strategic plans in a proactive manner that ensures there is continuing leadership within the sport facility by cultivating talent, preferably from within the organization, through planned development activities.

## Termination processes

While the overriding goal of sport facility managers is to hire, cultivate, and retain the best employees, it is probable that a sport facility manager will have to terminate an employee at some point in their career. The process starts by documenting all the reasons for terminating the employee, and then set up a meeting with that employee to discuss the following:

- Explain to the employee how and why they are no longer working at the company. It is important to tell the truth, including facts such as the employee's poor performance, regardless of how uncomfortable it is. It is also crucial that the discussion be based solely on the performance – do not make remarks about an employee's personal character.
- Let the employee know that the decision is final and when the termination will be effective.
    - If for poor performance – normally immediate.
    - If as a result of a layoff – the date in the near future.
- Inform the employee about benefits available to them, if any. This may include unemployment, health insurance, and severance pay. Each municipality has laws that govern how and when final pay and vacation pay is handled.
- Provide the employee a written termination notice. If the employees does not show up for the meeting, or are being terminated because they failed to show up for work, send the termination notice via certified mail.
- Collect any keys, access cards, uniforms, equipment, and/or any other property that is owned by the sport facility.

With regard to the last bullet point, certain employees may have access to confidential material such as access codes and computer files, that need to have access denied prior to the termination meeting. In some cases, this confidential material may go with the employee and be used against your facility when they go and work for a competitor or another company where their knowledge of your company may put you in a competitive disadvantage. To prevent such a problem, there are two courses of action: (1) after the termination meeting, have a company employee accompany the terminated employee to observe them "cleaning out their desk" and then escort them off the premises; and (2) have an employee signed agreement when they were hired (usually found in the human resource manual) that seeks to ensure the preservation, protection and continuity of the confidential business information, trade secrets and goodwill of the sport facility.

## Creating human resource manuals for sport facilities

The purpose for creating a human resource manual is to have a central document that articulates accurate and current information regarding the policies and procedures of the sport facility as they relate to employees/personnel/volunteers/ other associated human resources. The information provided usually includes, but is not limited to, employment and employee relations, benefits and compensation, general information about the sport facility, and policies/procedures of the sport facility.

There are usually three sections to a human resources manual for a sport facility. The first section is the philosophy and expectations of human resources, which is a compilation of information to introduce the sport facility to the employee. This usually starts with a welcome to the employee and an articulation of the sport facility's philosophy, mission, and goals. This is followed by an explanation of the purpose of the manual – which usually focuses on the manual as an operational and reference guide for the employee. The rest of this section usually focuses on general statements deemed important by the ownership of the sport facility. These statements may include general information about ethics and conduct, pride of ownership, owner expectations, daily routines, attendance, scheduling, job descriptions, and contact information.

The policies and benefits section is the meat of the human resource manual. This section itemizes each of the human resource policies that should be understood by an individual working with or in a sport facility. The following would be a sample of the inclusions within a human resource manual:

1. A general statement about the human resource manual being a live document, that changes will be made as needed, and that notification will be provided within a reasonable amount of time.
2. Policies whose offenses may result in sanction or termination – including equal employment opportunities, sexual harassment, and smoking/substance abuse.
3. Employment policies including types of documentation needed, and confidentiality and privacy statements.
4. Employee compensation and work information such as anniversary dates, evaluations, workday, pay information, overtime, and gratuity allowances.
5. Benefits information related to payroll deductions, insurance, retirement plans, reimbursements, and leave allowances (holiday, vacation, illness, medical, funeral, jury duty and other legal obligations, personal time, and leave of absence).
6. Performance-related policies including performance reviews, merit increases, performance improvements, separations, and severance.
7. General sport facility policies as related to dress code, upkeep of facility and offices (including common areas, infrastructure, equipment, and appliances), and use of facility-issued utilities (electronic communication, keys, lockers, computers, phones).

8. An employee agreement form that seeks to ensure the preservation, protection and continuity of the confidential business information, trade secrets and goodwill of the sport facility. Concepts included in this agreement may include employment issues, no solicitation obligations with respect to employees and customers, nondisclosure obligations, possession of company information and materials, absence of conflict agreement statements, remedies should there be a breach of the agreement, and any additional miscellaneous information deemed important to the sport facility.

The final section is the operations manual, which builds on the concepts embedded in the human resource manual to articulate how the sport facility has to be managed. This section will be covered in more detail later in this book (Chapter 8). A sample of the first two sections of a human resource manual as described above can be found in the appendix of this book.

## Chapter review

Human resource management is the function within a sport facility that is responsible for the recruitment, training, and retention of personnel, but goes much more in depth in an effort to strategically move the organization forward toward a vision. Typically in a sport facility, there are three types of human resources. First are professional staff, who are the employees of a sport organization who are hired to perform specific jobs/tasks in exchange for some form of remuneration. Within sport facilities, there are usually four levels of professional staff: executives have the most power and authority, is made up of senior or top managers within the sport facility, and are usually responsible for the majority of the overall sport facility; administrators are accountable for the day-to-day operations of specific departments or operations; supervisors are responsible for the day-to-day operations within a specific unit in a department; and specialists/general staff complete the tasks as assigned by the management structure within a sport facility. Second are volunteers, who are non-employees willingly involved with an organization or event for no compensation to assist with a need that could not otherwise be offered. Last are customers and clients, who are often participants and/or have some involvement with sport events that take place in sport facilities, hence provide both the inputs and outputs of the sport facility.

Regardless of the type of human resources, it is important to recognize the individual differences between people. Individual differences are usually affected by factors including personality, motivation, attitudes, and perceptions. Personality is defined as the unique and personal psychological characteristics of an individual which reflects how they respond to their social environment. Motivation is the influence that initiates the drive to satisfy wants and needs. For human resources in sport facilities, this may be achieved through motives such as accomplishment, fun, improvement of skill, health and fitness, or the desire for affiliation. Attitudes are states of mind or behavioral predisposition that is consistently favorable or unfavorable with respect to a product or situation.

Perceptions involve gaining an understanding of the individual values, attitudes, needs and expectations of the sport consumer by scanning, gathering, assessing, and interpreting those insights.

The most important function within human resource management in sport facilities, and most likely in any organization, is to understand the best way to manage people. Management is the process of planning, organizing, directing, and controlling tasks to accomplish goals, meet the mission of the organization, and work toward a vision. As such, human resource management focuses on planning, organizing, directing, and controlling people within the organization. However, there is more than just managing the people to maximize value and minimize costs to the sport facility operation. Effective human resource management also requires sport facility managers to understand human capital management – the concept that people are the most important asset to an organization and should be treated as such. This then results in the transformation of the management process more toward leadership – where employees are guided and influenced to the benefit of their individual growth and that of the sport facility.

To move a sport facility forward, the process of strategic human resource management must be implemented, which is an integrative approach to creating human resource strategies that seek to accomplish goals based on the desired outcomes for the sport facility. This is most effectively implemented through the appropriate managing of knowledge, or the acquisition, sharing, and use of intelligence, understanding, and expertise within a sport facility to aid in the accomplishment of tasks, processes, and operations.

In order to guarantee the sport facility has the optimal level of knowledge, sport facility owners and managers must employ the best and brightest to effectively and efficiently run the operations of sport facilities, especially because of the intricate designs, skills, and necessary knowledge based on the wide variety of facilities. The stages involved with employing a personnel starts with an analysis of the job to be filled by examining and evaluating the specific tasks to be completed within an organization and determining the best way to design a method for completing them in the most timely and relevant way. Then a job description is created to articulate the job responsibilities of the position opening and the expected competencies of candidates for the position. Next is the recruitment and selection of employees, accomplished through a process of submitting recruiting documents, engaging in the actual selection process, empowering a search committee, conducting interviews, carrying out reference checks, making the hiring decision, and completing contracts and other pertinent documentations. This is then followed by employee orientation (introducing the job and the sport facility to the new employees), training (the education of the employee in their job tasks), and development (furthering the education of the employee to improve their skills and value to the sport facility).

Performance management is the process of evaluating the past and current performance of employees. Performance is evaluated through appraisal systems to make decisions about employee advancement, retention, and termination;

salary increases; and employee improvement. The ultimate goal of performance appraisals is to enhance the career building of the employee and advance the operation of the sport facility. Reward systems are often put into place to provide extra compensation (financial and non-financial) for employees who have been deemed worthy. A succession management process takes rewards a step further by making provisions for the development, replacement and strategic application of key people over time. This process also helps to hire new employees when the termination process is implemented because of poor performance or layoffs.

All the information about human resources is usually documented in a human resource manual. Its purpose is to have a central document that articulates accurate and current information regarding the policies and procedures of the sport facility as they relate to employees, personnel, volunteers, and other associated human resources. The information provided usually includes, but is not limited to, employment and employee relations, benefits and compensation, general information about the sport facility, and policies/procedures of the sport facility. The manual usually has three sections: (1) the philosophy and expectations of human resources, which is a compilation of information to introduce the sport facility to the employee; (2) the policies and benefits section, which itemizes each of the human resource policies that should be understood by an individual working with or in a sport facility; and (3) the operation manual, which builds on the concepts embedded in the human resource manual to articulate how the sport facility has to be managed.

# 7 Financial management

## Chapter outline

## Chapter objectives

This chapter is concerned with giving readers an overview of why financial skills are an important part of the sport facility manager's overall portfolio of management skills. Finance has often been described as the 'language' of business. People who wish to progress their careers need to be fluent in this language both in terms of understanding it and being able to communicate in it. You will not become fluent in finance by reading one chapter of a book. However, having read this chapter we hope that you feel you have been pointed in the right direction and will have the enthusiasm to develop your financial skills further.

## Introduction to sport facility financial management

For all sport facilities, whether they be iconic stadiums played in by professional teams, municipal facilities for public use, or a local recreational rugby club, it is essential that the overall governance of the organization be under-pinned by sound financial management. Without needing to be an accountant and having a specific training in finance, there are two key questions that all senior managers should be able to respond to in the context of their business.

First, 'is the selling price higher than the cost?' In other words, is the organization making a profit? For non-profit-making organizations, such as members' sports clubs and municipal facilities, we can modify the first question to: 'is the organization operating within the resources allocated to it?' If facilities are not profitable or do not operate within their resources, then problems will follow. In the context of our own lives if we live beyond our means, then varying degrees of problems will occur. Initially, we may experience a cash-flow problem such that there is 'a lot of month left at the end of our money'. Next we might incur interest payments we are unable to meet; and finally, we end up being declared 'bankrupt'. The same analysis is applicable to sport facilities that do not operate within their resources. How many 'one man band' gyms have you seen that have been opened by a bodybuilding enthusiast that are here today and gone tomorrow? Why do these businesses fail? The simple answer is that selling price is not higher than the cost; the business gets into financial difficulty and dies. By contrast, why do the iconic sports stadiums survive? The simple answer is that they are profitable or the selling price is higher than the cost. When profits are made they can be reinvested in the business to improve it, to develop new products, and to keep ahead of the game.

The second question all businesses must answer is, 'is the business well set to continue trading?' In financial terms, the second question is a reference to an organization's ability to pay its creditors as they fall due and having the freedom to pursue strategies of its own unfettered by external influences. Many business failures are not because there is limited demand for the product or that the selling price is too low. The principal cause of business failure is that despite buoyant demand for a product, the organization runs out of cash and is unable to meet its own obligations. In some cases, despite being profitable, a business may be 'highly geared'; that is, it has a high level of borrowing and therefore has to pay regular sums out to service interest and debt charges. When a business cannot service its loans, the providers of debt finance become nervous and may call in their loans and a situation can arise whereby the providers of loans have more control over a business than those charged with the day-to-day running of the business. Under these conditions, it is unlikely that a business would be well set to continue trading. In many respects, success or failure in business generally and sport facility management specifically hinges crucially on the ability to be profitable, to be able to pay bills as they fall due, and to be able to service debts. Hopefully, having read the above you have thought to yourself 'this is little more than common sense really' and 'you don't need to be trained in finance to understand the significance of the two questions'. If you are with us so far, please carry on. If not, please re-read the above and make sure you understand the two questions and why they are important for budding sport facility managers.

In the remainder of the Chapter we will demonstrate how the two questions underpin an understanding of finance in a more formal way by looking at operational finance issues such as financial reporting and budgeting.

## Learning the language

In this section, we cover two key points of terminology that help to illustrate how finance is the language of business. We start by looking at the definitions of 'financial accounting' and 'management accounting', which are the two types of accounting techniques used in all businesses.

## Financial accounting

Financial accounting is defined as the classification and recording of monetary transactions of an entity in accordance with established concepts, principles, accounting standards and legal requirements, and their presentation, by means of profit and loss accounts, balance sheets, and cash-flow statements during and at the end of an accounting period. There are three points to note concerning the above definition of financial accounting. First, financial accounting is concerned with the relatively passive activity of recording and classifying financial transactions. Second, financial accounting is governed by a series of prescribed procedures ranging from 'established concepts' through to 'legal requirements'. Third, the presentation of the results of financial accounting is in a specified form, i.e. profit and loss account, balance sheet, and cash-flow statement (known collectively as financial statements). It is a legal requirement for businesses to carry out financial accounting and in many countries companies are required to file their accounts with public bodies. The significance of public filing of accounts is that often the published accounts of an entity will be the only financial information available in the public domain about the entity.

## Management accounting

Management accounting is defined as the process of identification, measurement, accumulation, analysis, preparation, interpretation, and communication of information used by management to plan, evaluate, and control within an entity and to assure appropriate use of and accountability for its resources. There are three points to note concerning the above definition of management accounting. First, compared with financial accounting, management accounting involves being proactive, that is, the information generated by management accounting is used for planning, decision-making, and control, whereas financial accounting data are used for reporting on a historical basis. Second, management accounting is compiled and reported in a way which best suits the needs of an organization, rather than in the prescribed formats used in financial accounting. Third, management accounting is concerned with the efficient and effective use of resources. It therefore follows that meaningful assessments of whether the management of a sport facility has been efficient and effective are most likely to be determined using management accounting techniques. There are no legal requirements to give external users access to management accounting data.

In reality, perceptive managers should acknowledge that financial accounting and management accounting are two sides of the same coin. We are required by law to record our financial transactions, according to the rules of financial accounting. However, no professional manager will plan to record financial transactions and wait to see what happens after a year. In practice, good managers plan their operations so as to achieve a desired outcome. The only way to achieve a desired outcome is to plan and control your business. Planning and control disciplines are achieved by techniques such as budgeting, break-even analysis, and capital investment appraisal. These techniques are some of the key disciplines found within management accounting.

Thus, there is a direct link between financial accounting and management accounting. The term 'financial management' could quite legitimately be defined as 'the application of financial accounting and management accounting techniques to the management of an organization'. It is in this sense that the term 'financial management' is used throughout this chapter.

*Activity*: obtain the published accounts or financial statements of a sport facility business in which you are interested. It could be a stadium, arena, municipal swimming pool, or a local community club. Use these financial statements to test whether you understand the points being made throughout this chapter. Use a spreadsheet package, such as Excel, to replicate the analysis shown in this chapter on the financial statements you have obtained.

## Finance fundamentals

Financial accounting uses a combination of concepts and rules to produce financial statements in a standardized form. These 'statements' are the profit and loss account (also known as the income and expenditure account for non-profit organizations); the balance sheet which is a statement of the assets, liabilities, and a valuation of the net worth of a business (capital); and the cash-flow statement which explains how much cash a business has generated and how it has used such cash. There are two common uses of financial accounting data that managers of sport facilities are likely to encounter. First, financial statements can be used to explain in-house financial performance. For example, the manager of a stadium could use his or her financial statements as evidence of the organization's overall financial performance and health in a meeting with shareholders or the providers of loans. Second, financial statements are often the only publicly available information from which a diagnosis of the financial health of other organizations is made, for example other businesses that you might consider trading with. Would you extend credit to a business that was not profitable and therefore might have problems paying your bills? The logic behind the practice of presenting and analyzing financial statements is that it is considered possible to make a diagnosis about an organization's financial health from its profit and loss account, balance sheet, and cash-flow statement.

Typical questions might include:

- Can it afford to pay its bills?
- Does it have sufficient financial resources to be able to borrow funds to invest in new equipment?
- Is it worth investing in?

Careful use of financial accounting data can be used to report internal performance and to make diagnoses of external organizations. How a manager might set about answering these questions is best illustrated using a practical example.

The profit and loss account is an analysis of how the capital or net worth of an organization has changed over a given period. If a concessionaire at a sport facility buys in popcorn at 50 cents per portion and sells it for $5, then he has made a profit of $4.50; or in other words, the concessionaire's net worth has increased by $4.50. This increase in net worth can then be used to pay towards the running costs of the concession such as rental, staff wages, and electricity as well as (hopefully) resulting in some profit for the owner.

The same thinking can be applied to a facility as a whole, as shown in Figure 7.1. In the year 201Z, the sport facility generated $5.40 M worth of income (turnover) of which $3.90 M was used on the direct costs of providing the service (cost of sales) leaving a gross profit of $1.50 M. A further $1.14 M worth of other expenses was offset against the gross profit, leaving a pre-tax profit of $0.36 M. The organization is required to pay tax on its profits of 30% or $0.108 M and therefore the retained profit for the year was $0.252 M. To illustrate how the profit and loss account is an analysis of how the organization's capital has changed, the bottom line of the profit and loss account in Figure 7.1 can be summarized as meaning: 'at the end of year 201Z the organization had $0.252 M of extra resources available to it compared with the same time last year'.

The facility featured in Figure 7.1 has clearly demonstrated a positive answer to our first key question 'is the selling price higher than the cost?' It is customary for financial statements to contain the data for 2 years worth of trading activity, that is, the year in question and the comparative figures for the previous year. Therefore a follow up question might be, 'how does this year's performance

|  | Year 201Z | Year 201Y |
|---|---|---|
| Turnover | 5,400,000 | 5,100,000 |
| Cost of Sales | 3,900,000 | 3,828,000 |
| Gross Profit | 1,500,000 | 1,272,000 |
| Other Expenses | 1,140,000 | 1,110,000 |
| Pretax profit for year | 360,000 | 162,000 |
| Taxation | 108,000 | 48,600 |
| Retained profit for year | 252,000 | 113,400 |

Figure 7.1 Sample sport facility profit and loss account

compare with last year?' In Figure 7.1, the current year 201Z shows a profit of $0.252 M, whereas in the previous year 201Y the profit was $0.113 M. In simple terms, it can be concluded that this year's performance has been an improvement on the previous year's performance.

Another important question to ask is 'how does this year's actual performance compare with planned performance?' If the organization concerned had planned to make a profit of $0.20 M, then clearly a surplus of $0.252 M demonstrates that not only has the organization operated within its resources, but also in financial terms it has been more effective than expected because the actual surplus was $52,000 better than planned. Equally, had the profit target been $0.3 M then despite making a profit, the organization would have been relatively ineffective because actual performance was $48,000 less than planned performance. Financial statements tend not to reveal planned performance to the outside world and therefore without management accounting data, financial statements should be used cautiously and with a realization of their limitations.

All businesses need to grow. It is a harsh fact of life that costs escalate every year and staff need pay rises for their incomes to offset the effects of inflation. In this respect, it is necessary for businesses to grow simply to standstill. Thus if a business wishes to deliver on the first question 'is the selling price higher than the cost?', it has to grow so as to keep pace with its increased costs. On a positive note businesses also need to grow in order to invest in product development, maintenance, marketing and ensuring that key personnel's skill levels are fit for purpose. Measuring growth is achieved by using horizontal or year-on-year analysis. Figure 7.2 shows the data from Figure 7.1 subjected to horizontal (year-on-year) analysis.

The growth calculation involves two parts: firstly, calculating the change in each component of the profit and loss account (this year minus last year); and, secondly, expressing the change as a percentage of last year. Thus in Figure 7.2, the absolute increase in turnover is $300,000 which in turn is a 6% increase on

| | Year 201Z | Year 201Y | Change | %Change |
|---|---|---|---|---|
| Turnover | 5,400,000 | 5,100,000 | 300,000 | 6% |
| Cost of Sales | 3,900,000 | 3,828,000 | 72,000 | 2% |
| Gross Profit | 1,500,000 | 1,272,000 | 228,000 | 18% |
| Other Expenses | 1,140,000 | 1,110,000 | 30,000 | 3% |
| Pretax profit for year | 360,000 | 162,000 | 198,000 | 122% |
| Taxation | 108,000 | 48,600 | 59,400 | 122% |
| Retained profit for year | 252,000 | 113,400 | 138,600 | 122% |

Figure 7.2 Profit and loss account horizontal analysis

the previous year. Signs of successful growth are an increase in turnover and an increase in profit. In the case of Figure 7.2, turnover increased by 6% and profits increased by 122%, which is clearly a sign of successful growth.

A second way of analyzing financial statements is using common size or vertical analysis, where a key variable (usually turnover on the profit and loss account) is given a value of 100% and all other lines on the profit and loss account are expressed as a percentage of this key variable. A fully worked example can be seen in Figure 7.3.

In Figure 7.3, in 201Z for every $1 of turnover, 28 cents was left over as gross profit, whereas in 201Y for every £1 of turnover 25 cents was left over as gross profit. Efficiency can be defined as the relationship between inputs and outputs, in this case turnover and gross profit respectively. Thus in the case of Figure 7.3, we can conclude that because there is more output for each unit of input, the facility has improved its efficiency. The same logic holds true for the bottom line, 'retained profit for the year'. For every $1 of turnover 5 cents is left over as retained profit, whereas in the previous year, 201Y, retained profit was only 2 cents per $1 of turnover. Thus at the retained profit level, the organization has also become more efficient. Bringing Figures 7.2 and 7.3 together, it can be concluded that the organization has become more efficient because as turnover has increased (6%) costs (cost of sales and other expenses) have increased at a lower rate (2% and 3% respectively). Thus in simple, common sense terms and in the absence of any other data such as an organization's business plan, it is proven possible to obtain useful information about an organization's financial performance from its published profit and loss account.

The second question, 'is the business well set to continue trading', can in part be obtained from analysis of the balance sheet. Reading, interpreting, and explaining a balance sheet is not solely the domain of trained accountants. Any manager

|  | Year 201Z | Common Size | Year 201Y | Common Size |
|---|---|---|---|---|
| Turnover | 5,400,000 | 100% | 5,100,000 | 100% |
| Cost of Sales | 3,900,000 | 72% | 3,828,000 | 75% |
| Gross Profit | 1,500,000 | 28% | 1,272,000 | 25% |
| Other Expenses | 1,140,000 | 21% | 1,110,000 | 22% |
| Pretax profit for year | 360,000 | 7% | 162,000 | 3% |
| Taxation | 108,000 | 2% | 48,600 | 1% |
| Retained profit for year | 252,000 | 5% | 113,400 | 2% |

**Figure 7.3** Profit and loss account vertical analysis

with a basic understanding of logic should be able to identify and articulate the meaning of a balance sheet. The purpose of a balance sheet is to put a value on the net worth of an organization. Doing this requires a list of those things of value (assets) that the organization owns such as buildings and cash; and a list of those things the organization owes to others (liabilities or creditors). The difference between these two figures is the capital, net worth, or equity of the business. As an example, if you have a stadium worth $100 M and your mortgage is $60 M, then your capital (net worth) is $40 M (i.e. $100 M minus $60 M). To illustrate the point, imagine that Figure 7.4 is the balance sheet for the same sport facility whose profit and loss account was featured in Figures 7.1, 7.2, and 7.3 above.

A balance sheet is no more than a listing of the assets and liabilities of a business and a valuation of its net worth. However, there is a little terminology

| | 201Z | 201Y |
|---|---|---|
| FIXED ASSETS | | |
| Buildings | 2,000,000 | 1,980,000 |
| Equipment | 470,000 | 260,000 |
| Total fixed assets | 2,470,000 | 2,240,000 |
| CURRENT ASSETS | | |
| Stock | 30,000 | 24,000 |
| Debtors | 15,000 | 9,000 |
| Cash | 217,000 | 123,000 |
| Total current assets | 262,000 | 156,000 |
| CURRENT CREDITORS | | |
| Creditors payable within 1 year | 228,000 | 144,000 |
| NET CURRENT ASSETS | 34,000 | 12,000 |
| *NET ASSETS* | *2,504,000* | *2,252,000* |
| CAPITAL | | |
| Ordinary Shares $1 | 500,000 | 500,000 |
| Profit and loss account | 2,004,000 | 1,752,000 |
| *TOTAL CAPITAL* | *2,504,000* | *2,252,000* |

**Figure 7.4** Sport facility balance sheet

that needs to be learnt to understand fully what a balance sheet represents. First, on a balance sheet 'fixed' means of long-term value to an organization (i.e. 2 years or more), part of the business infrastructure and not regularly traded on a day-to-day basis. Sport facilities hope to use gym equipment, as an example, for more than 2 years and the purchase and sale of gym equipments is not a regular part of the business' activities, therefore gym equipment is described as a fixed asset. By contrast, businesses hope to convert stock of say food and drink for resale and debtors (people who owe the business money) into cash within a year and certain creditors need to be paid within a year. Anything which is planned to be converted into cash or paid within 1 year is said to be 'current'. Thus in Figure 7.4 for the year ended 201Z, assets minus creditors equals $2.504m which in turn is the net worth of the business. Also in Figure 7.4 the closing capital for 201Y was $2.252m, that is, the net worth of the business at the date of the balance sheet. The difference in capital between 201Z and 201Y is $2.504m minus $2.252m which is equal to $0.252m. The figure of $0.252m is not a coincidence. The organisation's profit and loss account in Figures 7.1, 7.2, and 7.3, details a profit of $0.252m and the definition of the profit and loss account is an analysis of how capital has changed. Therefore, there is a direct link between the balance sheet and the profit and loss account i.e. the profit and loss account 'explains' how the balance sheet or the value of the business has changed. If the selling price is higher than the cost, then the balance sheet will increase in value.

Two of the determinants of whether a business is well set to continue trading are the ability to pay its bills and the degree of control it has over its assets. The ability to read and articulate the meaning of a balance sheet is an important skill for the financial manager. One of the ways in which professionals read a balance sheet is to examine the relationship between important figures on the balance sheet. For example, the ability to pay debts as they fall due is called 'liquidity' and is measured by liquidity ratios. Liquidity ratios compare the amount of current assets available to pay current creditors. The first of these is called the current ratio and simply compares total current assets with total current creditors as shown in Figure 7.5.

|                    | 201Z       | 201Y     |
|--------------------|------------|----------|
| Current assets     | 262,000    | 156,000  |
| Current creditors  | 228,000    | 144,000  |
| Current Ratio      | 1.15:1[1]  | 1.08:1   |

[1] (262,000 / 228,000):1

Figure 7.5 Current ratio calculation

The current ratio calculation shows that in 201Z, for every $1 of current creditors, the organization had $1.15 in current assets. This finding suggests that the organization can meet its bills. Furthermore, comparison with 201Y indicates that there has been a marginal improvement in liquidity from 1.08:1 to 1.15:1. It is sometimes the case that businesses are unable to sell their stock as quickly as they would like. As a result, a second liquidity ratio, the quick ratio, also known as the acid test, can be calculated. This is very similar to the current ratio but excludes stock from the calculation as shown in Figure 7.6.

|                    | 201Z      | 201Y      |
|--------------------|-----------|-----------|
| Current assets     | 262,000   | 156,000   |
| Minus stock        | (30,000)  | (24,000)  |
| Equals             | 232,000   | 132,000   |
| Current creditors  | 228,000   | 144,000   |
| Quick Ratio[1]     | 1.02:1    | 0.92:1    |

[1](232,000 / 228,000): 1

**Figure 7.6** Quick ratio (or acid test) calculation

The acid test ratio reveals that in 201Z the organization still had sufficient resources to meet current creditors, whereas in 201Y, once stock is taken out of the equation there is only 92 cents available to meet every $1 of current creditors. As a basic principle, liquidity ratios of at least 1:1 would be regarded as being a prudent level of liquidity. Once a liquidity ratio falls below 1:1, further clarification might be necessary from an organization's management concerning their strategy for being able to settle debts as they fall due.

Liquidity tests are one of the ways in which managers can assess the credit worthiness of potential business contacts. For example, a sport facility manager might consider hiring out a venue for an exhibition or conference. Whether agreeing to hire out a venue proves to be a good or bad decision depends in part on whether or not full payment is received for the services offered. Credit terms might be offered to an organization with a strong balance sheet and acceptable liquidity levels, whereas a hirer without such credentials might be required to pay in advance or indeed be declined.

The extent to which a business is in control of its assets can be measured by the 'debt ratio', which is a measure of the extent to which an organization's assets are funded by creditors. The point can be illustrated using an everyday example of two home owners who both have houses worth $500,000. Owner A has a mortgage for $100,000 and Owner B has a mortgage for $250,000. Common sense tells us that Owner A is in a better position than Owner B, but how can the relationship be quantified to demonstrate the point?

|                      | Owner A | Owner B |
|----------------------|---------|---------|
| House (asset)        | 500,000 | 500,000 |
| Mortgage (creditor)  | 100,000 | 250,000 |
| Net worth (equity)   | 400,000 | 250,000 |

The debt ratio measures the extent to which assets are funded by debts, so the debt ratio for each owner would be:

|                      | Owner A | Owner B |
|----------------------|---------|---------|
| House (asset)        | 500,000 | 500,000 |
| Mortgage (creditor)  | 100,000 | 250,000 |
| Debt ratio[1]        | 20%     | 50%     |

[1]Debt ratio = (creditors/assets) × 100.

Applying the same logic to Figure 7.4, the debt ratio for each year would be:

|                  | 201Z      | 201Y      |
|------------------|-----------|-----------|
| Fixed assets     | 2,470,000 | 2,240,000 |
| Current assets   | 262,000   | 156,000   |
| Total assets     | 2,272,000 | 2,396,000 |
| Total creditors  | 228,000   | 144,000   |
| Debt ratio[1]    | 10%       | 6%        |

[1]Debt ratio = (creditors/assets) × 100.

The debt ratios of 10% for 201Z and 6% for 201Y reveal that the sport facility has very low levels of debt and therefore is in control of the vast majority of its assets. Organizations with high debt ratios can, to all intents and purposes, be controlled by their creditors. For example, if a balance sheet reveals very high levels of borrowings, it may well be that the banks and other providers of funds are the real controllers of the business rather than the owners. In the case of a sport facility, this situation may manifest itself in the bank determining opening hours or influencing programming in return for continued financing or not calling in loans. Any business that struggles to pay its bills because of an adverse liquidity position or that is not necessarily in control of assets can reasonably be described as not being well set to continue trading. By contrast, if these indicators are positive, it enables those with a business relationship with an organization to be confident that they are dealing with a financially sound enterprise.

The measures of financial performance we have examined thus far have been confined to data from the profit and loss account in isolation (is the selling price higher than the cost?) and the balance sheet in isolation (is the business well set to continue trading?). It is however possible to combine measures from both the profit and loss account and the balance sheet to gain further insights into business performance. An important relationship to consider in this regard is the trading performance of a business and the owners. In Figure 7.4, it can be seen that the net worth or value of the sport facility is $2.5 M. A sobering question for the owners to ponder is whether the $2.5 M is best kept in the business or invested elsewhere. In economics this is known as the 'opportunity cost'; or in other words, what is the best option foregone as a result of having $2.5 M tied up in a sport facility? To answer this question we can use the measure of retained profit for the year ($252,000) from the profit and loss account and link it to the value of the business, or total capital, from the balance sheet ($2.5 M). As with the other ratios illustrated above, it is worth making the calculation for both years so that changes over time can be assessed.

|                                | 201Z      | 201Y      |
| ------------------------------ | --------- | --------- |
| Retained profit                | 252,000   | 113,400   |
| Total capital                  | 2,504,000 | 2,252,000 |
| Return on shareholders' funds  | 10%       | 5%        |

For the year 201Z, the return on shareholders' funds is 10% and compares favorably with the return that might be achieved if you invested the same amount of money in a deposit account. This finding suggests that it is worthwhile running the business rather than settling for a lower return on investment from a 'safe' option such as having money on deposit. Furthermore, in the year 201Z the business has doubled its return on shareholders' funds from 5% in 201Y to 10%, which indicates a very positive direction of travel. In short, the owners of the business can be satisfied with the business performance of the facility.

In the commercial sector, people invest in businesses by purchasing shares in a business. A share is a quantified stake in a business that gives the owner a right to a 'share' in the profits (or, losses) made by that business. We can see in Figure 7.4 that the balance sheet, for our example sport facility, states that there are 500,000 $1 shares. Linking this to the profit figure from the profit and loss account ($252,000) enables us to calculate that each share earned 50 cents in the year 201Z. Again, making the comparison with the year 201Y in which earnings per share were 23 cents, we can confirm from yet another angle that the business has improved over the last year.

There are many more ratios and analysis techniques that can be used to assess the financial statements of business organizations. However, this section of the chapter has focused on the basic common sense areas that sport facility managers should investigate. What you have seen thus far is a cursory overview. If you can understand the basics such as the two key questions and how you might provide answers, this will be a good start. Like any language, fluency comes with practice, experience, and immersion in the culture.

# Financial planning

For managers of sport facilities the most likely way in which you will experience the pressures of financial management is through the process of compiling and being held accountable to the budget. What you have seen so far has been an indication of the financial position and financial health of a business. The financial statement you saw in Figure 7.1 was the summary of a sport facility's performance for 1 year and the balance sheet in Figure 7.4 was a snapshot of the business' financial position at a point in time. Businesses do not lurch from year-to-year and hope that their financial statements show a favorable outcome. Well-managed facilities are continually monitoring their performance on a daily, weekly, monthly, and quarterly basis. Questions we need answering include:

- How many admissions did we achieve today?
- How does this compare with target?
- How much did we sell to our customers when they were on site?
- How does this compare with target?
- How many staff hours did we use?
- How did this compare with target?

Financial performance needs to be managed so that you achieve what you set out to achieve. In this regard, the budget can be said to be the objectives of an organization expressed in financial terms. The budgeting process helps us to address questions such as:

- Where are we now in financial terms?
- What are we trying to achieve in financial terms? and,
- How are we going to achieve it?

If you work in sport facility management, you will rapidly find that one of the differences between a job and a career is that those people who have careers have responsibility for budgets and are successful in achieving them. In the remainder of this section we will look at the budgeting process, the format for an operating budget, and how budgets can be used to monitor performance.

## The budgeting process

The most frequently used budgeting process is 'continuation' budgeting which refers to situations whereby the business objectives of an organization do not change significantly from one financial period to the next. Under these conditions, it is sensible to continue with the same approach to budgeting. An example of a continuation budget might be a health and fitness club whose main aim is to make a profit for the owners of the business who will pursue the same approach for running their business as they have in the past. If the club's basic operations lead to a situation whereby the selling price is higher than the cost, then besides increasing the number of members of the club or how much they are charged for their memberships, there is no point wasting time and resources on a more complicated approach to the club's finances.

An important point about budgeting, when it is done well, is that it is an ongoing process rather than a time limited one-off event. The actual mechanics of collating the numbers involved in a budget is a small part of the overall budgeting process. By bearing in mind that budgeting is designed to help an organization with planning, decision-making and control, it is possible to appreciate that budgeting is a continuous part of business life. This point can be reinforced by viewing budgeting as steps in a logically sequenced planning process as shown in Figure 7.7 with each stage discussed in turn afterwards.

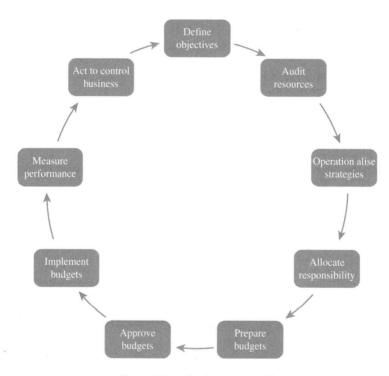

**Figure 7.7** A budgeting model

### Define objectives

The first question to ask when involved with any financial business planning is 'in monetary terms, what are we trying to achieve?' This question should provide a clue that most sane business people would not answer by saying 'making a loss'. Losses are made in business but it is inconceivable to imagine that managers set out deliberately to make losses. Losses normally occur when there is a mismatch between what was planned and what happened in reality. Organizational objectives will vary according to the nature of the business. A community sports club, which exists for the benefit of the members, may desire nothing more than to break even or to make a small surplus to maintain its existing facilities. A more complex organization, such as the New York Giants, needs to balance the requirements of producing a successful team on the pitch (utility maximization) with the requirements of being a commercial franchise (profit maximization).

## Audit resources

The audit of resources is a 'reality check' on the objectives. Its purpose is to ensure that the objectives and the resources required to achieve them are internally consistent. As an example, Sheffield United Football Club needs around 15,000 spectators per home match to break even. With a stadium capacity of nearly 31,000, it is clear that 15,000 people can be accommodated at a home match so long as they can be attracted to the match in the first place. The term 'resources' should be used in the widest sense to include personnel and the skills required to ensure that those running the business are 'fit for purpose'.

Where there is a discrepancy between the objectives and the resources available to achieve them, two courses of action are possible. First, the objectives can be changed so that they are compatible with the resources. Second, the gap between the resources available and the resources required can form the basis for prioritizing capital investment such as increasing the capacity of a stadium, or identifying training and development needs to ensure that staff have the skills to deliver what is required of them.

## Operationalize strategies

Having defined objectives and confirmed that you have the resources to deliver them, the model proceeds to consider the day-to-day actions to be used to deliver the required performance. In a health and fitness club, these might include the marketing plans, pricing policies, customer care protocols, and opening hours. If organizational objectives can be regarded as 'what' we wish to achieve, then operational strategies can be regarded as 'how' we plan to achieve the objectives. For example, a swimming pool manager aiming to achieve a turnover of $1 M per annum from an annual throughput of 100,000 admissions needs to think carefully about how he or she can convert every click on the turnstile into an average of $10. This will probably be via a combination of parking fees, admission costs, secondary spend on food and drink, locker hire, use of drying machines, and the sale of items such as goggles and arm bands.

## Allocate responsibility

The successful delivery of financial objectives does not happen by accident, or as the result of compiling a spreadsheet. Facility management in sport is primarily a service industry and the key people who determine the extent to which objectives are delivered are the facility's staff. So that people can see where their efforts and talents fit in into a business' overall plan, it is good practice for staff to have agreed responsibility for their particular areas of work. Agreed responsibility is particularly important in situations where staff can be rewarded, or indeed punished, on the basis of their performance. For example, basic performance for a fitness consultant in a health club might be 20 new peak-time members per month, with financial incentives on offer if the agreed target is exceeded. If it is known and clearly stated 'who is going to do what and by when?', then there is the basis for a meaningful comparison of actual performance compared with planned (or expected) performance.

## Prepare budgets

It is worth noting that the actual preparation of budgets, that is the 'mechanics', does not occur until the mid point of the budgeting model shown above. This is important because it makes the point that budgeting is not some isolated or abstract process but is actually integral to the way an organization approaches business planning. When preparing a budget there are two important considerations to address, namely: 'how much' income or expenditure will there be? and 'when' will the expected income or expenditure occur? To illustrate the point, if a swimming pool is expecting 100,000 admissions per year at an average admission price of $7.50, then the answer to 'how much income will be generated?' is $750,000. However, it is unlikely that a pool will average nearly 2000 admissions per week for 52 weeks of the year. There will be peak times such as during school holidays and half terms and off peak times such as during the winter when it is cold. Hence, to make sure that the appropriate level of resource, such as staff, is in the right place and at the right time, it is necessary to plan the predicted level of activity on a week-by-week or month-by-month basis. Conducting such an exercise enables managers to plan ahead for situations where expenditure may be greater than income and there is insufficient cash to meet the shortfall. Having identified situations that require management action, strategies can be put in place to deal with them such as negotiating an overdraft facility at the bank, rescheduling capital expenditure, or imposing an expenditure embargo on non-essential revenue items. The important point to note is that the process of budgeting identifies potential problems in advance so that appropriate action can be taken to avoid such problems or to mitigate their consequences.

It is more likely to be good fortune rather than good planning that the first draft results of the budget will deliver the financial outcomes required. As a result managers may need to revise their budgets so that the desired outcomes are achieved. In practice, there are five ways in which a budget can be revised.

1. Increase revenue whilst keeping costs constant, for example by increasing prices, increasing throughput or a combination of the two methods. Note the assumptions that underpin the thinking here. In the case of deciding to increase prices to balance

the budget, there is the assumption that the market will bear such an increase and that revenue will increase despite the likelihood that some people may either stop participating or take their business elsewhere.

2. Decrease expenditure whilst keeping income constant, for example by making savings on expenditure or reducing the amount of the service on offer (e.g. reducing opening hours).

3. Increasing income whilst decreasing costs, as 1 and 2 above are not mutually exclusive.

4. Alter the financial outcome required. It may be that it is not possible to bring the required outcomes and the budget into line by using 1, 2, and 3 above. Rather than altering income and expenditure, management may decide to alter the financial outcome required. This approach can work both positively and negatively. If staff provide managers with a budget that exceeds the required bottom line and the assumptions underpinning the budget are correct, then it would make sense to increase the overall budget target accordingly. Alternatively, imagine that the targeted outcome cannot be met by revisions to income and expenditure as a competitor has recently opened a new facility nearby and is poaching some of your customers. Under these conditions, managers might agree to settle for a reduced financial outcome, for example an annual profit of $0.45 M rather than $0.50 M, which in turn would require a reworking of the budget.

5. Alter the overall business objectives. It may be the case that it is impossible to arrive at an acceptable solution to a budget using steps 1–4 above. Under these conditions, it may be that the required outcomes and the organization's capabilities are not compatible. The only remaining alternative is to change the organization's objectives. As an example, it is often the case that municipal sport facilities are required to meet social as well as financial objectives. On occasion, pursuit of these differing aims may be incompatible in the sense that programming activities for target groups prevent revenue maximization. Every use of resource has an opportunity cost, that is the price of the best alternative foregone. In order to make the budget balanced, it may be that some priorities that are no doubt desirable have to be sacrificed to protect more important business interests.

The relevance of preparing a budget, comparing it with business objectives, and taking corrective action where appropriate indicates the importance of achieving 'internal consistency'. Using the budgeting model shown in Figure 7.7 helps to ensure that what an organization wishes to achieve in overall terms and the financial consequences of doing so are consistent. If potential problems can be identified at the planning stage, appropriate action can be taken by devising strategies to deal with adverse circumstances. This type of approach has a far greater chance of success and is more desirable than trying to deal with situations reactively as they occur without prior warning.

### Approve budgets

When an acceptable balance has been achieved between an organization's business objectives and the subsequent financial consequences, then the preparation of budgets is complete. From this point the budget should be approved formally. It is recognized good practice for the approval of a budget to be formalized in the official records of a business such as the minutes of a board or committee meeting. In an ideal world, budgets should be approved in advance of the financial period to which they relate. The importance of a budget being approved formally is that those who have compiled it and those people whose performance will be judged by it, have a clear picture of what their responsibilities are. This clarity has two benefits. First, if you know what is expected of you, then evaluation of your performance can be based on hard facts rather than personal opinions. Second, expectation creates accountability, which provides managers with the focus to concentrate their efforts on those things which are important to meet the key business objectives.

### Implement budgets

Once a budget has been approved, it can be implemented with effect from the date to which it applies. For example, if an organization's financial year operates from 1st April to 31st March, then it would be a reasonable expectation for the budget to be approved at least a month before the start of the new financial year. A less than ideal situation would be an organization entering a new financial year without an approved budget, as this would in effect be an admission that the business had no direction in financial terms.

### Measure performance

To reinforce the point that budgeting is integral to overall business planning, it is important to realize that the budgeting process does not end once the process of getting a budget to the implementation phase is complete. Once a budget is operational it is good practice that periodically, a check is made between how the business is actually performing compared with how it was planned to perform. For operational issues, such as admissions and staff hours used, this might be a daily or weekly check, whereas for overall business performance monthly and quarterly checks are the conventional norms. Measurement of performance is not an end in itself and is only valuable if it is used to add value to the process of management in a business by being the basis for action where necessary.

### Act to control business

Decision-making should be made on the basis of the best information available to help those making the decisions. It is rare that there will be a perfect match between budget and actual comparisons; so, the first decision to make is whether or not variances are within a tolerable range. If variances are tolerable, then major changes in policy will not be necessary. By contrast, if variances are considered to be so large that proactive management action is needed, then this is the time when good managers show their worth. Variances can of course be positive, for example when a business is considerably ahead of target. The only management action required here might be to continue with the same policies to revise targets upwards. By contrast, if actual figures compared with budgeted figures reveal a significant shortfall in performance, then more proactive corrective action may be needed. Such action might include extra marketing effort to increase sales, reducing price to stimulate sales, or reducing costs in an attempt to maintain profit margins.

In concluding this section it is worth reiterating two key points about budgeting being a logically sequenced planning process.

1. Budgeting is a process designed to help managers make sensible decisions about running and controlling their businesses. The ability to contribute fully to the budgeting process and to be held accountable to it is one of the key differences between managers and the staff who they manage.
2. Compiling a budget is an iterative process. It is unlikely that the first draft of a budget will produce an acceptable result. Various scenarios will be modeled and differing assumptions will be tested until an acceptable solution is found. Figure 7.7 is a simple model of an ideal process. The basic point is that each step of the model is a reality check on the previous step. The end game is to ensure that an organization's overall plans and the financial consequences of those plans are internally consistent.

## Compiling a simple operational budget and monitoring performance

To help bring the points made in the budgeting model outlined above to life, in this section we present a case scenario examining the basics of compiling a budget, the assumptions that are used to derive the figures used, and how those figures are used to monitor performance. It is for this type of work that the ability to use a spreadsheet, such as Microsoft Excel, is an important skill to acquire and to be able to demonstrate to prospective employers.

The scenario, which can be found in the online supplements for this text, focuses on membership, budgeting, and financial performance for a health and fitness club. As the manager of the new health and fitness club, you will be required to set a target of annual memberships in response to senior management's belief that the level of sales equates to the ability to meet its running costs and deliver a given profit. You will be provided figures for various costs including staffing, marketing, premises, office, cleaning/maintenance, and miscellaneous. You will use the data given to you in the scenario to compile a monthly budget to illustrate this information and to test whether the profit forecast is justified. You will also be provided examples that illustrate the data given in the scenario in a structured way that models the expected income, expenditure, and monthly profit.

## Chapter review

The key point arising from this chapter is that sport facility managers require well-developed financial skills in order to be effective in their jobs and to develop their careers. Sadly a 9000-word chapter will not achieve this for you, but hopefully it will point in the right direction in terms of the knowledge you require to make a genuine career in this business. Finance does seem to have its own language and like all languages, fluency comes with practice. Readers should not be intimidated by finance or finance professionals who seem to wield a disproportionate amount of power in some businesses. The vast majority of finance is little more than addition, subtraction, multiplication, and division plus the ability to use spreadsheets (which of course will do all of the 'number crunching' for you). Furthermore, finance is intuitively logical and once you understand the logic there will be no more smoke and mirrors to confuse you. However, you do not need to go to the other extreme and become an accountant so long as you can communicate confidently with accountants and colleagues who are in charge of a business' finances. What this chapter has shown is that even for simple day-to-day operations, finance and financial skills are an important part of the knowledge base of a sport facility manager. If you wish to work at an even higher level such as managing the development and construction of new sport facilities, then you will require even more financial skills such as capital investment appraisal and negotiating leverage (or borrowings) to finance your ambitions. These are some of the more exciting aspects of sport facility management and it is well worth acquiring the skills and experience to be able to operate at this higher level. With a bit of luck, this chapter will have given you the confidence to realize that the first steps of acquiring skills in finance are not too difficult.

# 8 Operations management

## Chapter outline

## Chapter objectives

Operations management for a sport facility is defined as the maintenance, control, and improvement of organizational activities that are required to produce products and services for consumers of the sport facility. In order to effectively manage operations, a sport facility manager must understand how the operational structure integrates with the operation of the sport facility. As a result, knowledge about the concept of total quality management (TQM) is crucial. TQM is a comprehensive, structured approach to operations management that seeks to improve the quality of facility services through constant refinements in response to feedback from users and staff.

This chapter will also focus on general sport facility operating procedures, and the importance of managing them within governmental guidelines and budget parameters. A general overview of facility operations, facility services, event management, and risk management concepts will be discussed. The conclusion of the chapter will provide information about the development of a sport facility operations manual, and how it builds on the human resources manual.

## Operational structure

Chapter 2 on ownership structures covered the various legal business structures of a sport facility and the operational framework each allows is crucial to the operations and management of a sport facility from a legal and functional standpoint. In addition, there was an explanation that to appropriately govern a sport facility, a manager must have a clear understanding of the concept of organizational effectiveness, which is the concept of how efficient a business is in achieving the outcomes set forth in the planning processes. Chapter 5 introduces the concept of organizational behavior as the study of human behavior in the work environment, and how the concepts leadership and organizational culture are crucial to the management of sport organizations. Chapter 6 on human resource management explored the recruitment, training, and retention of personnel, and their role of strategically moving sport facilities forward towards a vision. This includes how the organizational chart is utilized to integrate operations in the sport facility, and the job descriptions that articulate the responsibilities of personnel. The financial management chapter (Chapter 7) focused on why financial skills are an important part of the sport facility manager's overall portfolio of management of skills. Understanding each of these areas in detail serves as a framework for developing the operational structure of a sport facility. However, there are two additional concepts that must be understood before engaging in operations management – history and philosophy.

From a historical perspective, by knowing about what has happened in the past with regard to a sport facility, a manager can see why things are the way they are as of now, what potential there is in the future, and how the organization has functioned. It is important to know about history because you can then educate others who do not know as much. Without knowing what has happened in the past, a sport facility manager cannot truly understand the organization, and how the operation of the sport facility came to its current situation. In addition, by understanding what happened in the past and the current situation of today, the sport facility manager can better understand what can happen in the future because they can understand what should be avoided and what can be accomplished to move the sport facility forward towards a higher level of success.

From a philosophical standpoint, understanding the values and beliefs of the sport facility organizational structure provides a framework and reasoning for why operations are conducted. The philosophy also serves as a framework for the mission of the sport facility (the purpose of the organization), the vision (where the organization wants to be in the future), and the action plan (what the organization wants to accomplish – articulated through goals, objectives, and strategies; and within the parameters of policies and procedures).

The integration of all of these concepts serves as a framework for operations management. However, there is a need to have a complete and organized approach to operations management in order to succeed. This is where total quality management (TQM) can be a significant asset to the sport facility manager.

## Total quality management (TQM)

TQM is a comprehensive, structured approach to operations management that seeks to improve the quality of facility services through constant refinements in response to feedback from users and staff. The main purpose for implementing a quality TQM program for a sport facility is for controlling operational and service quality with the end result being the improvement of all aspects of activity implementation.

TQM processes are divided into four sequential categories: plan, do, check, and act (the PDCA cycle). The planning involves defining the problem to be addressed, collecting relevant data, and determining the main cause of the problem. The doing phase entails implementing a solution and choosing the best measurement to gauge its effectiveness. The checking phase is an evaluation of the results to confirm success or failure. The acting phase is the documentation of results, articulation of process changes to the entire organization, and making recommendations for the problem to be addressed in the next PDCA cycle.

There are four key reasons for a sport facility manager to implement a TQM process: (1) measure and analyze how tasks are being accomplished, (2) eliminate procedures that are not working, (3) allow for input from all employees within the sport facility based on their areas of expertise, and (4) eliminate stereotypical thinking and replacing it with visionary thought processes. This measurement and analysis process is most often implemented through the process of benchmarking. Benchmarks are individual management tools used by a sport organization to plan for evaluation, measurement, and improvement. Benchmarking is an important concept to sport facility managers to implement for three key reasons. First, they help facility managers to achieve better results by enabling them to understand the drivers of performance and how to influence them. This is achieved by both data benchmarking (comparing statistical performance with others) and process benchmarking (comparing the key decisions made to achieve good performance). Second, benchmarks provide much more authoritative reporting of performance than an organization's performance reported in isolation. Third, when benchmarking techniques become established as part of organizational culture, they provide the basis for a clear focus on the business essentials as well as the direction for continuous improvement. We will revisit this concept in the capstone chapter of this book (Chapter 14), where we will bring together various concepts from the entire book , and show how all aspects of sport facility management effectively interact with each other.

However, focusing specifically on operations management, their major goal is to ensure quality control through TQM. One of the most widely used models of quality control to measure business effectiveness in sport facility management is Deming's 14 Key Principles of Points for Management. In brief, the principles are:

1. Create constancy of purpose towards improvement of product and service.
2. Adopt the new philosophy.
3. Eliminate dependence on mass inspection and require statistical evidence that quality is built in.
4. Do not award business on the basis of price – quality is much more important.
5. Find problems and continually improve the quality control system.
6. Institute the most current methods of on-the-job training.
7. Implement the most current methods of supervision of employees to ensure maximum quality of operation and services provided.

8. Eliminate fear to increase the level of employee effectiveness.
9. Breakdown barriers between departments/work areas.
10. Get rid of numerical goals and replace them with quality goals.
11. Eliminate work standards and quotas.
12. Remove barriers that prevent part-time, hourly, and volunteer workers from having pride of ownership in the work produced for the sport facility.
13. Institute an efficient and effective program of education and retraining.
14. Create an operational structure in top management that forces implementation of the above principles on a regular basis.

*Adapted from*: TQM: A snapshot of the experts. (2002). Measuring Business Excellence, 6(3), 54–57. Retrieved June 7, 2009, from ABI/INFORM Global database.

For a sport facility, there are four major areas of TQM that managers should be concerned with: (1) customer service, (2) empowering employees, (3) human resource management, and (4) media and public relations. Probably the most important is customer service, because without customers, there would be no purpose for the sport facility. There are five pillars of quality that are integral to customer service and the TQM process:

1. Quality services start with customer service, because only the customer can define whether the right service is being offered, and the quality of its offering.
2. There must be a commitment to continuous improvement.
3. There must be the ability and a willingness to be measured and evaluated.
4. Employee and staff must be empowered, be held responsible for their actions, and view themselves and their jobs as an integral part of a quality sport facility operation.
5. Quality service should be both recognized and marketed inside and outside the company.

*Adapted from*: Friday, S. & Cotts, D. G. (1994). Quality facility management: A marketing and customer service approach. New York: Wiley.

As related to the empowerment of employees and overall human resource management, it is important to remember that the job of all within a sport facility is ultimately to sell its image. Therefore, employees must do their job in line with the guidelines of the human resource and operations manual, and other duties as assigned by supervisors and ownership. However, to most effectively sell the image, empowering employees with authority and power is integral to the process. Employees need to have an active role in the administration of the sport facility, because employee brings to the table a unique set of qualities that will allow any sport facility to operate at an optimal quality level. Management provides training, resources, and a safe work environment for employees; employees work together with management to control processes, identify problems, and be a part of the solution to improve performance with the ultimate goal of effectively and efficiently serving customers.

Media and public relations is one of the foremost means by which a sport facility seeks to control public opinion regarding its products and services. At times, information will need to be released to the customers, the media, and the general public regarding situations, problem, opportunities, and event results at a sport facility. The release of this information needs to be controlled; therefore, unless specifically authorized by the operational structure of a sport facility, employees should never release information about the operations, policies, procedures, and actions associated with a sport facility to the public (customers, the press, or the general public). Quality control also involves the proper release of information by the proper authorities within a sport facility, and in a voice shared by all members of the sport facility's organization. From a TQM standpoint, if unsure what to say – say nothing, 'no comment', or direct the individual to the person within the organization authorized to speak.

## General facility operating procedures

General sport facility operating procedures are put into place to provide a safe, efficient, and equitable functioning of a sport facility through a commitment to the provision and maintenance of appropriate physical facilities that contribute to a comfortable and conducive sporting and work environment. In sport facilities, there are numerous general operating procedures – examples of some of the major operating procedures include:

- *Hours of operation*: the times that the facility will be open for business.
- *User categories*: individual and family members, daily users, guests, participants and spectators, licensees, employees, and management.
- *Fees and rates*: the cost for use of the facility through various memberships, daily fees, admission fees, guest passes, and rentals.
- *Reservation procedures and space allocation*: methods for scheduling facility usage.
- *Outsourced services*: examples include camps, clinics, merchandise, food service, security, and parking.
- *Procurement practices*: procedures for securing needed inventory, supplies, and equipment.

Probably, the most complex of these operating procedures is the reservation and space allocation process, which includes programming, scheduling, and prioritizations of both the use of the facility and maintenance of the facility. It is important to remember that when implementing a reservation and space allocation process to keep the following in mind:

- Strive to do what is best for the greatest number of users.
- Be consistent with all user groups.
- Continually evaluate the scheduling process and constantly improve the process.
- Take into account activities that are consistent with the mission of the sport facility.

Each sport facility will have a different scheduling and prioritization process based on the type of users, the programs that utilize the facility, the different facility spaces, and the day/time activities take place. The latter two are areas many forget about, as it is entirely feasible to have multiple prioritization schedules based on each part of the sport facility, and different days and times. For example, let us assume ourselves as the assistant director of facility scheduling for a university sports complex. The program that uses the facility includes physical education classes, university-sponsored sport teams, campus recreation/ intramurals program, student-sponsored sport clubs, open recreation time (time for people to walk in and use facilities), and special events. A typical Monday– Friday 8 a.m.–3 p.m. prioritization schedule for a gymnasium might look like the list, in order as above. However, from 3–8 p.m. Monday–Friday, since many classes are completed by then, the prioritization schedule might change to the following:

1. University-sponsored sport teams.
2. Campus recreation/intramurals program.
3. Student-sponsored sport clubs.
4. Open recreation time.
5. Special events.
6. Physical education classes.

From 8–12 p.m., it may change to:

1. Campus recreation/intramurals program.
2. Student-sponsored sport clubs.
3. Open recreation time.
4. Physical education classes.
5. University-sponsored sport teams.
6. Special events.

On weekends, it may change again to:

1. Open recreation time.
2. Special events.
3. Campus recreation/intramurals program.
4. Student-sponsored sport clubs.
5. University-sponsored sport teams.
6. Physical education classes.

With regard to the scheduling and organizing of maintenance, the general premise is to attempt to conduct as much of this work during off-hours; especially overnight, between activities, or after major events. In general, the day shift usually handles the majority of the important work, while second and third shifts take care of janitorial and painting tasks.

In addition to space allocation, scheduling, and prioritization, governmental guidelines and budget management play an integral role to the effective and efficient implementation of operating procedures. Governmental guidelines include those policies and procedures set by federal/parliamentary, state/ provincial/regional, and local/municipality authorities. More detail about the legal responsibilities related to sport facilities will be provided in the next chapter (Chapter 9). Budget management (covered in the previous chapter on financial management – Chapter 7) also plays a critical role in operating procedures, as annual and capital budgeting directly affect what sport facility managers can implement. Without money through the budgeting process and the planning that goes with that process, facility managers cannot hire staff, maintain facilities, implement change, purchase equipment and inventory, and keep the facility operating.

# Facility operations

Now that we have a basis overview of operating procedures, it would be important to recognize the various areas of operation within a sport facility. Sport facility operations can be divided into many different ways, based on the operational structure of the individual organization. For the purpose of this chapter, we will divide facility operating into the following categories: plant and field operations; maintenance and repair; alterations management; inventory management; energy management; waste management and recycling; and environmental management, greening, and sustainability.

## Plant and field operations

Plant and field operations include managing the physical plant, including natural and artificial surfaces. Plant operations are the necessary infrastructure used in the support of facility operations and maintenance. While there are numerous types of specific plant infrastructure for specialized facilities – such as refrigeration and ice systems for ice arenas, filtration and chemical systems for swimming pool facilities, and watering systems for outdoor fields and artificial surfaces – generally the plant operations for a sport facility fall under five systems: (1) heating, ventilation, and air-conditioning (HVAC); (2) mechanical and electrical transportation (elevators); (3) major electrical systems; (4) plumbing; and (5) emergency power/generators. Today, the expectation of facility managers in their role as plant operators is to be a technician with mechanical competence. This expectation is verified by the numerous examinations and certifications that test for technical knowledge and interpersonal skills that most sport facility plant operations require. The reason for this necessary competence is that the facility manager is responsible for expensive equipment, proper operating conditions, quality control and improvement, profits and losses, problem solving, community involvement, and the environment, among many other things. The sport facility cannot survive without quality management of plant operations, because lack of skills operating these functions will result in significant risk, damage, and costs to the sport facility. Therefore, facility managers must understand the unique plant within their sport facility, secure and keep up-to-date about the technical skills and knowledge related to the sport facility, operate in a safe manner with quality consciousness, and possess the effective communications skills required to ensure proper operations by all staff.

## Maintenance and repair

All infrastructural problems and damages to facilities and equipment are detrimental to the continued operation of a sport facility. Shutting down facilities disrupts customers' use and can be perceived as incompetence on the part of those running the sport facility. Hence, proper coordination of maintenance and repair is crucial to operation success.

In general, all maintenance and repair needs that are discovered by staff should be communicated to the facility or operations manager responsible for this area, and be documented on a maintenance form. In addition to reported maintenance and repair, managing staff should, on a regular basis, conduct an evaluation of all infrastructure and equipment to determine the status of its condition, and organize and coordinate appropriate remedies. Based on the severity of the problem or damage, the remedy will take one of the three ways:

- *Maintenance*: this refers to the work necessary to maintain the facilities and equipment. Maintenance includes periodic or occasional inspection, adjustment, lubrication, cleaning (non-janitorial), painting, replacement of parts, minor repairs, and other actions to prolong service and prevent unscheduled breakdown.
- *Repair*: this refers to restoring damaged or worn-out facilities and equipment, or to a normal operating condition. Repairs are curative, whereas maintenance is preventive. Repairs can be classified as minor or major. Minor repairs are those associated with maintenance activities that do not exceed 1–2 workdays per task. Major repairs are those that exceed 2 workdays per task, or are beyond the capability of existing maintenance personnel.
- *Replacement*: this refers to facility and equipment components or systems need to be replaced. It is the exchange or substitution of one fixed asset for another having the capacity to perform the same function. Replacement arises from an asset becoming obsolete, having excessive wear and tear, or being damaged beyond repair.

## Alterations management

While all sport facilities are designed with space and needs in mind, it is inevitable that certain alterations need to take place. Many times these alterations are needed for three main reasons in a sport facility: (1) the need for additional storage, (2) the need for modified spaces for new programming, and (3) the need for additional office space for expanding staff. These alterations can be infrastructural (examples: building new spaces, splitting spaces by adding walls) and/or operational (examples include need for additional electrical outlets, plumbing, or communications). Many sport facilities are designed with the potential for alterations in the future, which in the long run reduces the costs of alterations. Alterations that are unplanned usually have a higher cost – as much as two to three times more than if they were planned for in the design of the sport facility. In some cases, alterations are temporary – usually as a result of a special event. In any case, to ensure that alterations are an appropriate outlay of money, sport facility managers should engage in a cost-benefit analysis for determining whether the benefit of the alteration is worth the money being spent.

## Inventory management

Traditionally, we think of inventory management in terms of having the availability of the products that customers desire, such as with merchandise, food service, and concessions. While these are each concerns of the sport facility manager, those individual tasks fall under the management of those ancillary areas, and will be discussed later in this chapter. Inventory management as related to facility operations involves two distinct areas. First is the inventory of available spaces in the facility, and how those spaces are reserved, scheduled, and allocated (as discussed earlier in this chapter). Second is the procurement process related to the inventory of equipment and supplies used in the various areas of the facility. Some of this inventory includes light bulbs for a gymnasium or arena, tools and supplies for conducting maintenance, cleaning supplies for custodial crews, and tables/chairs/and barricades for event set-up.

## Energy management

Energy management is not a separate function but rather an activity that spans all aspects of a sport facility. Some of the traditional energy management measures include thermostat regulation and investing in energy-efficient capital equipment. However, electrical consumption control is the responsibility of all the employees of a sport facility. Examples include lighting in offices being turned off when not in use; lighting in courts, spectator areas, and other activity areas being dimmed or turned off when not in use; thermostats being lowered during down times and closed times (turn down 1 h before closing and turn up to 2 h before opening); and computers and other electronics being turned off when not in use. Energy costs are among the biggest expenses for a sport facility (usually second to staffing). Taking steps to reduce these costs can significantly improve the operation of a sport facility by increasing the financial resources available for other areas.

## Waste management and recycling

One of the most overlooked costs of a sport facility is the result of the trash that it puts out. While a sport facility's main objective for reducing contribution to the local landfill is to cut costs, the social importance of environmentally friendly business operations cannot be understated. Recycling mandates seem to be a trend that is starting to affect sport businesses everywhere. Some mandates are coming from city governments while others come from within the sport business itself. In addition to typical waste, sport facilities, as a result of general operations, often have a multitude of recyclables that includes paper (newspaper, white paper, all other); aluminum cans; glass bottles and jars (clear, green, brown); scrap metal; Styrofoam; and cardboard. To deal with this, many sport facilities have segregated recycling bins at the rear of the complex.

The only way to reduce costs related to waste management is to reduce the amount of trash going to landfills, since landfill costs are determined by quantity.

One of the biggest problems in trying to implement recycling as part of a waste management reduction programs is getting customers to recycle. Having recyclables mixed in with the trash results in additional costs for the facility. Although the sport facility managers and staff are not in direct control, there are a number of things that a sport facility can do to influence visitors to recycle by raising their awareness. The first way to raise awareness of recycling is through video messages that are displayed during an event. Another important part of recycling awareness has to do with both the visual appeal and the prominence of the recycling bins that are located in the facility. Improving that ratio of bins to seats would make it much easier for people to recycle.

## Environmental management, greening, and sustainability

The concept of recycling and reducing the amount of waste goes directly into the concepts of environmental management. Environmental management is the process of managing the interaction between the human environment and the physical environment/habitats. Globally, ISO 14000 (International Organization for Standardization) guidelines provide requirements for environmental management systems and specified its relevance for organizations wishing to operate in an environmentally sustainable manner. In general, the purpose of the standard is to reduce the environmental footprint of a business and to decrease the pollution and waste a business produces. In sport facility management, this has become an important marketing function more than an operations function. Sport facilities that have the initiative to be more socially responsible are publicly being recognized for their efforts, and while a direct correlation may not be visible in any accounting documents, the cost of environmental awareness is at least partially justified in the positive effect it has on the image of the facility, which is a large component of public relations.

Two of the most relevant environmental management concepts crucial to sport facility operations management are greening and sustainability. Greening is the process of transforming a space into a more environmentally friendly area. Sustainability is the process of being renewable for an indefinite period without damaging the environment. In energy management, we discussed some of the way to be more environmentally friendly (e.g. energy-saving bulbs, as well as in waste management (e.g. recycling). However, one of the biggest issues is the disturbance and reduction of plant life, trees, grasses, and other natural environments due to the construction of sport stadiums and arenas (and associated ancillary areas), artificial surface fields, and sport environments in the natural environment (ski resorts, golf courses, etc.). In response, the below list is just a small example of what some organizations are doing to 'go green' and be more sustainable:

- According to research from 20 studies conducted across the United States, Canada, and Europe, both in cold-weather and hot/humid-weather environments, there are significant drainage and water storage possibilities from run-off on artificial turf fields. Storm water collection and collection and reuse of water from watering are gathered through the drain system under the fields, and then tied into large water retention pipes to allow the rainwater to return to aquifers underground.

- The National Ski Areas Association (NSAA) has implemented an 'environmental charter for ski areas' (http://www.nsaa.org/nsaa/environment/sustainable_slopes) that provides voluntary environmental principles for ski area planning, operations, and outreach.
- The United States Green Building Council (USGBC) has developed leadership in energy and environmental design (LEED) standards for sporting arenas and stadiums (http://www.usgbc.org).

# Facility services

All sport facilities are engaged in the service industry. As such, there is a need to provide a number of facility services over and above the general operating procedures of the sport facility. While the purpose of this section is not to delve into every aspect of facility services in detail, it is to provide information about the major facility services provided in sport facilities. Again, as with operations, there will be specialized services unique to specialized facilities, but the focus for this chapter will be on security, ticketing, parking, custodial/housekeeping, concessions, customer service, and event management.

Regardless of facility service, there are general rules and regulations followed by most, including standards of conduct, general guidelines, and appearance. Standards of conduct focus on providing users of the sport facility (members, guest, visitors, spectators) the best possible examples of conduct, decorum, and good citizenship. The behavior of employees sets the example for all to follow. The care, safety, and welfare of all are paramount, and it is important that any situations that may endanger the health, safety, or well-being of people be dealt with immediately.

An example of general guidelines within a sport facility may include some of the following:

- Treat members with respect and dignity. This is especially important when they are not treating you with respect.
- Be dependable, be on time, and keep promises.
- Use positive guidance techniques including redirection, encouragement, and positive reinforcement. Set appropriate expectations and create program environments that minimize the need for discipline.
- Report any member's or guest's health issues, accidents, or other concerns which you feel need further attention to your immediate supervisor.
- Respect each member's and guest's right not to be touched in ways that make them feel uncomfortable. Respect their right to say no.
- Profanity, inappropriate jokes, sharing intimate details of one's personal life, and any kind of harassment in the presence of our members or guests are unacceptable.
- Information regarding organization members, guests, paid staff and volunteers, both verbal and written, is often privileged and confidential. Personal information is not to be released without written consent of the individual involved.

- A specialized guideline is appearance. A sport facility should expect all of its employees to represent the organization in a professional manner by being neat, clean, and dressed professional attire that is consistent with their job responsibilities in the building.

## Security

Security in a sport facility can range from in-house staff at a small recreational facility, to professional staff from global companies (Contemporary Services Corporation – CSC), local companies (Sentry Event Services in Florida), or league/event based (SAFE Management – the NFL's security company). Regardless of the level of security, there are some important features that all sport facility managers must recognize when working with security. While a more detailed look at security planning and management will be provided later in this book (Chapter 13), we will introduce some basic concepts important to facility operations and providing service here.

The director of security (or the authorized management member overseeing security) is the point person who is directly responsible for security procedures and systems. The head of security also provides liaison between the sport facility and the appropriate local law enforcement authorities. The head of security and other security personnel are not sworn peace officers or law enforcement officers and are not authorized to carry firearms in most cases, but are authorized by the ownership of the sport facility to fully enforce all rules and regulations.

While there are specific staff members hired to work as security, generally all employees of a sport facility act as members of the security team. Employees are the eyes and ears of a sport facility, and should report criminal activities or rule violations occurring as soon as possible to security, who then will respond as required. This response can range from internal disciplinary action to notification to the proper local law enforcement authorities.

## Ticketing

The ticketing operation at a sport facility can range from a small box office of one person selling tickets for general admission to an event (such as a secondary school basketball tournament) to a full-service box office with a separate manager, paid staff, and relationships with secondary and tertiary ticketing services. Ultimately, whether it is the facility manager at a facility holding a small sporting event, or a full-time box office manager, both have the role of selling tickets and controlling admissions to events.

In order to effectively conduct a ticketing operation, the facility manager/box office manager must know their inventory – or the number of seats available to a specific event. Seating capacities vary based on the type of event. For example, certain shows may only require 180-degree seating, such as a concert; others require 260-degree seating, such as a World Wrestling Entertainment event; while others need full-facility seating (most sporting events). This information is then put into a manifest, which gives every seat in the facility a section/row/seat number and attaches the price of the ticket. This pricing can range from one price for all tickets (general admission or festival seating for all) to multiple pricing levels based on closeness to field of play, location in proximity to the center of the field of play, amenities offered in conjunction with the seat, among others.

Full-service ticket offices (such as for large stadiums and arenas) have extra responsibilities as a result of hosting larger events. In addition to overseeing general operations, hiring staff, training staff, and operating computer systems where manifests are stored for issuing tickets, the box office has to initiate on-sales events (first day tickets are on sale), and operate a will call window (a place when tickets purchased in advance can be picked up by attendees to events). In addition, box office managers need to coordinate operation with secondary and tertiary box offices. An example of a secondary box office would be individual teams who sell tickets in addition to the box office. The box office is the place that issues these tickets to the teams, usually through secure access to the manifest in the box office's computer system. Similar processes are utilized for tertiary box offices, which would include online ticketing companies such as Ticketmaster, Ticketek, StubHub, and RazorGator.

## Parking

A sport facility should offer enough parking for spectators, members, guest, employees, and management. The usual standard for a sport stadium or arena is one parking spot for every four seats if there is no mass transit to the facility, and a smaller if there is mass transit available (dependent on quantity of transit and location). For a smaller facility, it really depends on projected usage. For example, a recreational facility with a fitness center and four basketball/volleyball courts may only need 30–40 spots, but if they plan on holding weekend tournaments, the need probably will blossom to 200 spots. Therefore, a parking plan integrated into the entire facility and event-planning process is crucial for offering this service.

Sport facilities have a choice to keep parking services in-house, outsourced, or not offered. In-house ownership of parking services offers the opportunity for maximum financial revenue (if the facility charges for parking), security, and service. Especially for larger events, parking revenues can be significant. In addition, by owning the parking, the sport facility is providing a direct service to their customers. However, by retaining responsibility, the sport facility operator also incurred the responsibility for security. The cost associated with staffing and securing a parking area, along with the responsibility, sometimes outweighs the revenues that can be earned. In these cases, parking services are outsourced to parking-management companies – where the sport facility received a very small percentage of parking revenue but transfers all risks associated with security to the parking management company. Another type of outsourcing is related to offering limited or no parking services. This often takes place in larger cities where there is ample public parking. The sport facility receives no revenue from parking, but does not have to worry about this service because the municipality covers it. For example, Standard Parking Management Company manages all the city parking in New York for the new Yankee Stadium. In Manchester, New Hampshire, other than handicap and a few specialized parking spots, the majority of parking is provided through city-owned parking garages and metered street parking.

## Custodial/housekeeping

Another important service in a sport facility is to ensure that it is clean and functional. This is where custodial and housekeeping services come in. Patrons do not want to come to a facility that is dirty or where simple items such as soap, paper towel, and toilet paper are not readily available. As with almost any other service, custodial and housekeeping can be outsourced or kept in-house. In-house offers more control over keeping the facility clean; however, depending on the size of the facility and the scope of the events, outsourcing may be inevitable. Ultimately, the goal is to provide responsive service to meet the needs of the visitors and the facility, and to enhance the quality of the experience of facility users.

## Concessions

Concessions are defined as a secondary business under contract or license from a primary business to exclusively operate and provide a specialized service. In sport facilities, the main two concession areas are merchandising and food service. As with any other services, concessions can be outsourced or kept in-house. Most often, merchandising is an in-house function, where a majority of food service is outsourced – mainly because of the significant liability.

The major goals of both merchandising and food service are to create a market demand for the products and services offered, and to increase the profitability and financial health of the entire sport facility. The major duties of a concessions manager are:

- Inventory control including turnover, inventory management, shrinkage, and point-of-sales systems.
- Creating effective displays and offering diverse product offerings.
- Marketing and promotion of the merchandise (often in conjunction with the facility marketing manager).
- Determine appropriate pricing points.
- Manage inventory including variation of sizes, inventory on hand, variation of hard and soft goods, management of exclusive brands, and offering a variety of accessories.
- Manage an effective website to promote merchandise and entice additional purchase online.
- In coordination with human resources hire and fire staff, as well as train the staff in the procedures of running the operation and offering high-quality customer service.
- Secure the appropriate licenses and municipal approvals to operate a concessions operation.

- Complete all associated accounting, billing, payments, bookkeeping, and payroll for the concessions operation; and
- Maintain all equipment including displays, kiosks, computer systems, and appliances.

Food and beverage services offer some additional challenges, which often involve implementing an additional planning process for safety. The purpose of this plan is to identify and prevent possible food safety problems in order to enhance food safety. The problems may relate to the purchase, receiving, storage, preparation, cooking, packaging, transport, or display of food. Especially important for ensuring food safety and management is the concept of cleanliness and sanitation. Food preparation areas, facilities, equipment, and all food contact surfaces should always be kept clean because food residues and dirt may contaminate food resulting in food poisoning. A cleaning program should be developed to ensure that cleaning and sanitizing be carried out in a systematic, regular, and effective manner. In addition, good personal hygiene is essential to ensure food safety. Food poisoning bacteria may be present on the skin and in the nose of healthy people. All food handlers should therefore maintain a high standard of personal hygiene and cleanliness in order to avoid transferring food poisoning microorganisms to food.

## Customer service desk

The kiosk at the entrance to the facility. The customer service desk. The main office. These areas, and almost everything implemented at a sport facility, need to have customer service in mind at all times. However, the areas listed above are possibly the most important – as this is where the first impression, members and guests have of the sport facility. The employees working in these areas have an important responsibility to project a positive image for the sport facility, to help maintain security of the sport facility by controlling ingress and egress, and truly set the tone for each person's visit to the sport facility.

Each individual facility will have their own policies and procedures for managing the customer service desk, however most will incorporate the following five policies:

- Every individual who comes in the door must have proof of admission. For larger events such as concerts and professional sport games, this is either in the form of a ticket or a credential. For a facility such as a recreational facility, it may be a card. If there is an allowance for non-members and guests, there should be a policy for signing in, completing appropriate paperwork, and/or paying a fee.
- Individuals restricted from entry to the sport facility should never be allowed to enter without the expressed permission of management or ownership.
- The front desk area (desk, office, and lobby) is kept clean at all times. There is no trash visible anywhere. Countertop is cleaned as needed.
- The only people behind the desk are paid and authorized employees. Members and guests are not allowed behind the desk.
- Customer service desk employees are readily accessible and willing to help members and guests.

## Event management

While all of the previous services described are important to the operation of a sport facility, the single most important is event management. Without events, there would be no need for a sport facility. There are two categories of events in a sport facility – events that are offered through and by the sport facility, and those offered by outside entities that rent or lease the facility. In both cases, coordination between facility managers and event managers is crucial to success on both sides. However, there are usually issues between the managers, because the event manager is mainly concerned about a successful event, and the facility manager is concerned with operating the facility in a safe manner with no damage. These missions often clash, and compromise and teamwork often need to be implemented.

Chapter 11 of this text will discuss in some greater detail about event planning and management from a facility end. It is important to recognize at this point that the role of facility operations is not to run an event; hence, there will be little discussion about actual event management. From a facility operations' standpoint, there are three major service roles:

- Coordination of event ingress and set-up.
- Support during the event.
- Coordination of event breakdown and egress.

# Risk management

Risk management is the process of attempting to prevent the possibility of loss from a hazard such as personal injury, property damage, or economic loss. Risk cannot be eliminated from the environment, but with careful planning it can be managed. Appropriate risk management practices are crucial to reduce legal exposure, prevent financial and human loss, protect facility assets, ensure business continuity, and minimize damage to the sport facility's reputation. All members of the sport facility management team – from ownership to hourly staff and volunteers – have a duty to act in a prudent manner and a duty of care to provide a reasonably safe environment for users of the sport facility.

While this topic will be covered in more detail in Chapter 12 (Risk assessment and management), it is important to recognize that from an operational standpoint, the major areas of concern within risk management involve dealing with the following:

- Non-critical injury/illness.
- Critical injury/illness (requiring emergency medical personnel).
- Appropriate use of alarms and warning signals.
- General emergency evacuation procedures.
- Evacuation of physically challenged persons.
- Dealing with:
  - Electrical power failure;
  - Elevator entrapment;

- Fire;
- Other natural disasters;
- Other facility disasters.

## Creating facility operations manual for sport facilities

The purpose for creating a facility operations manual is to have a central document that articulates accurate and current information regarding the operational policies and procedures of the sport facility. The information provided usually includes the majority of the concepts provided in this chapter, and often more. The operations manual is often connected to the human resource manual (Chapter 6), because it builds on the concepts embedded in the human resource manual, including how operations interact with employment and employee relations, and connects operations with the general information and policies/procedures of the sport facility. A sample of a sport facility operations manual as described above can be found in the appendix of this book.

---

### The Manchester Coliseum

You have just been hired as the facility manager for Manchester Coliseum, a new 47,000-seat stadium that will be the new home of the expansion Manchester Marauders football club. The Chief Executive Officer (CEO) of the Coliseum wants you to create an operations manual that will help the building run efficiently while making your job easier to perform. The following is a list of priorities given to you by the CEO of the Coliseum:

1. *Operations management*: the CEO wants you to describe and diagram the optimal organizational structure, and position descriptions with projected salaries.
2. *Risk management*: the CEO is very concerned with this area. Describe the overall function of risk management within the facility for both football games and other potential events.
3. *Marketing*: the CEO wants a marketing plan developed for the facility that will attract clients and customers.
4. *Event management*: describe this process in your facility, including a chain of command for personnel (parking, security, ticket takers, ushers, etc.).
5. *Concessions/food service*: describe the function of concessions (food service and merchandising) in your facility. Give reasons why you would or would not own the concessions, have an agreement to get a percentage of concessions, or simply lease the space for concessions.

---

*Continued*

---

## The Manchester Coliseum—cont'd

### Suggested discussion topics

1. Where would you start with this operations plan? Identify the steps you will take to create a comprehensive, functional operations plan.
2. What special operational needs will be necessary as a result of the first-ever football game played in the facility (Opening Night for the Manchester Marauders)?

---

## Chapter review

The role of sport facility operations is to consistently maintain quality visitor experiences without the depletion of resources. Good sport facility operations start with a functional organizational structure that allows for quality legal and financial management of the sport facility; understands the importance of operational effectiveness; recognizes the role of organizational behavior and culture as an operational function; and recruits, trains, and retains personnel who strive to strategically move a sport facility forward towards a vision. The implementation of these concepts in the operation of a sport facility can be best articulated through a process of total quality management (TQM) – a comprehensive, structured approach to operations management that seeks to improve the quality of facility services through constant refinements through the PDCA cycle. The TQM process works well for sport facilities because it measures and analyzes how tasks are being accomplished, eliminates procedures that are not working, allows for input from all employees within the sport facility based on their areas of expertise, and eliminates stereotypical thinking and replacing it with visionary thought processes. Sport facility managers are most concerned with the TQM process as it relates to customer service, employee and human resource management, and media/public relations.

Operation management starts with the implementation of general sport facility operating procedures. These are put into place to provide a safe, efficient, and equitable functioning of a sport facility through a commitment to the provision and maintenance of appropriate physical facilities that contribute to a comfortable and conducive sporting and work environment. While there are numerous categories of operating procedures, among the most important is how space is reserved and allocated, and what the user prioritization process is.

Operating procedures may differ based on the various operations and services provided within a sport facility. Major facility operations inherent in most sport facilities include plant operations; maintenance and repair; alterations management; inventory management; energy management; waste management and recycling; and environmental management, greening, and sustainability. Facility services, which may be outsourced or kept in-house, include security, ticketing, parking, custodial/housekeeping, concessions, customer service, communications/electronic management/information security, and event management. Each of these services will have their own general rules and regulations followed by most, including standards of conduct, general guidelines, and appearance.

One of the major concerns in facility operations is risk management, which is the process of attempting to prevent the possibility of loss from a hazard such as personal injury, property damage, or economic loss. Risk cannot be eliminated from the environment, but with careful planning it can be managed. The best way to reduce the amount of risk is to articulate all policies and procedures, rules and regulations, and philosophies and missions in one document. The facility operations manual is the central document that articulates accurate and current information regarding these areas. The operations manual is often connected to the human resource manual (Chapter 6), because it builds on the concepts embedded in the human resource manual, including how operations interact with employment and employee relations, and connects operations with the general information and policies/procedures of the sport facility.

# 9 Legal concerns for owners and managers

## Chapter outline

## Chapter objectives

The purpose of this chapter is to explore the relationship between legal issues and sport facility operations. This chapter is not intended to provide someone with in-depth legal expertise. It is also not intended to provide specific laws that are pertinent to sport facility management, as the global objective of the book would make much of that information useless to the reader based on their location. However, it is intended to articulate the effects of the legal environment on sport facilities. One of the major misconceptions in sport facilities is that risk management and sport law are the same. This is untrue, especially as related to the focus of this section of the text – the implementation of management and operations (risk management is action item, and will be covered in depth in the next section of the book in Chapter 12). This chapter will provide an overview of the major legal principles and standards related to the management and operations of sport facilities including negligence/unintentional torts, criminal law/intentional torts, contract law, and marketing-based legislative issues including intellectual properties and ambush marketing. The chapter will conclude with a brief discussion about the level of legal expertise a sport facility owner and manager should have, and when they should defer to individuals with a higher level of proficiency in the law.

## The relationship between legal concerns and sport facilities

Sport law and sport facility management have a significant relationship, including some of the issues already discussed in this book:

- Laws of ownership structures and governance of sport facilities (Chapter 2).
- Laws governing financing sport facilities (Chapter 3).

- Legal issues related to design and construction of sport facilities (Chapter 4).
- Lawsuit potentials as related to organizational management (Chapter 5).
- Internal and external laws that are regulated in human resource management (Chapter 6).
- Accounting, tax, and financial laws that are a part of financial management (Chapter 7).
- Legal aspects tied to risk management in operations (Chapter 8).
- Legal issues will also be embedded in the upcoming chapters (Chapter 10–13) on marketing management, event planning, risk management, and security management.

As you can see, the law permeates all aspects of sport facility operations management. And while we cannot articulate all the laws and legal concerns that may affect a sport facility manager or owner (especially with the global differences in laws based on individual countries), we can communicate the effect the law has on the operation and management of a sport facility, and the major legal principles that are prevalent globally.

## Effects of the legal environment on sport facility operations

Laws are a body of rules that govern individual or collective actions and conduct as defined by an authorized governing body and having binding legal force. Laws provide accountability and justice for citizens, and in the case of this text, the users and related constituencies of a sport facility. However, the challenge is that laws are constantly evolving through modifications and change, and that evolution has a direct effect on the daily conduct of the management and operation of a sport facility.

A great majority of laws are created by the governments of the world and their designees. These laws may be created at the highest level – usually federal or parliamentary; at regional levels – state and provinces; or at the local level by municipalities. In addition, there are laws that are administrative in nature, and are set by governing bodies such as the International Olympic Committee, and the various sport leagues and tournaments around the world. In an attempt to generalize the categories of law, we present the following four categories:

- *Constitutional Law*: laws embedded in the constitution or charter of a country or region.
- *Statutory Law*: laws created and affirmed by sanctioned legislative bodies.
- *Common Law*: laws that are created based on past legal decisions (precedence).
- *Administrative Law*: rules and regulations created, implemented, and enforced by a specifically authorized agency.

While it would be impossible for a sport facility manager or owner to know every law that will have a direct effect on the management and operation of the sport facility, they do have a duty of care to their users and associated constituents to act in a legal manner. As such, sport facility managers and owners must have a basic understanding of the legal principles and standards that will directly affect them.

## Legal principles and standards related to facility management

Managers and owners should have a basic understanding of the legal principles and standards that are inherent to proper sport facility management and operations. Tort laws are the most significant set of laws that sport facilities encounter. Unintentional torts fall under the category of negligence, and intentional torts fall under the realm of criminal law. Managers and owners also deal with legal ramifications of their management and operations of a sport facility as related to contract laws. In addition, two of the most prevalent legislative issues to impact sport facilities globally in the twenty-first century relate to intellectual properties and ambush marketing.

### Negligence law and unintentional torts

An unintentional tort, more commonly known as negligence, is a failure to act in a manner equal to how a reasonable person would act under the same circumstances. As related to sport facilities, for there to be negligence, four elements must be proven: (1) duty, (2) the act itself, (3) proximate cause, and (4) damages. First is whether the designees of the facility had a duty of care or a duty to act. This duty can arise from an inherent relationship between the personnel or ownership of the sport facility and a user, or from duties that are required as a result of legal standing (employment laws, supervisory obligations, or administration of first aid are three examples). Second, the act, almost always relates to foreseeing risks and preventing harm. Ultimately, all actions should meet a standard of care that limits inherent risks of activities in the sport facility, and prevents negligence behavior by those engage in activities within the sport facility. Third is proximate cause, which means for a charge of negligence to be valid, the action of negligence causes a loss or injury. Fourth are damages, or that there was an actual injury, loss, or emotional harm.

Any party associated with a sport facility can be liable for negligence, ranging from individual employees to administrative staff to ownership. There are a variety of ways to protect against negligence – the most widely used one in sport facilities are waivers, in which the users contractually release the facility and their agents from liability. There is also assumption of risk statutes that protects sport facility against negligence claims for injuries suffered from acts that are inherent and known to be the part of an activity. Other ways to limit negligence liability are through the use of independent contractors for events – in essence transferring the risk of negligence to the contractor;

and purchasing insurance to protect the entire operation in case of any negligent act.

## Criminal law and intentional torts

An intentional tort is a civil wrong based on an intentional act. These types of torts fall under criminal law, and the purpose of these laws is to protect the general health, safety, and welfare of the public. As a result of the inherent activities in sports, there are times, both on the field/court and off, that disagreements and actions may go beyond the realm of what is acceptable in society and cross over to a criminal act. In addition, because of potential interactions between staff and uncooperative patrons, there must be an understanding of crossing the line from what is a duty of care or action, and a criminal act.

The major intentional torts that may take place in sport facilities are:

- *Assault*: when one individual tries to physically harm another in a way that makes the second person under attack feel immediately threatened; there does not need to be actual physical contact – threats, gestures, and other actions that would raise the suspicions of a reasonable person can constitute an assault.
- *Battery*: the unlawful and unwanted physical contact by one person to a second person with the intention to harm.
- *Defamation*: is a written (libel) or verbal (slander) communication of non-factual information with the intent to create a negative image.
- *Invasion of privacy*: interference with the right to be left alone – most often challenges in sport facilities as related to memberships and having a personal locker with a lock on it.

## Contract law

Contracts are a major part of facility management. Other than employment contracts (see Human resource management – Chapter 6), the largest and most significant contracts are those with events that wish to utilize the sport facility, and sponsorship contracts. No matter the type, there are five elements that are part of any contract: (1) the offer, (2) the acceptance, (3) consideration, (4) legality, and (5) capacity. The offer and acceptance is when one party tenders the contract, and a second party agrees to the terms. Consideration involves the exchange of value between the two parties, hence there must be a benefit of some type to both the parties – in an event contract, it is usually a fee to the sport facility and the event acquires a place for it to take place. Legality is simply the contract must not be against the law, and capacity is that both parties entering into the agreement have the authority to do so. Within all contracts, there is additional language covering a multitude of issues. Some of the most common are terms and cancellation clauses with remedies, confidentiality statements, and damages should a breach of contract occur.

Event contracts are usually more detailed because there are a number of specialized elements that need to be included. First, the event itself is only a small part of the contract – there is also the pre-event set-up and post-event breakdown that must be detailed. In addition, any specialized lease agreements for facilities, equipments, and rentals must be spelled out and are often added as an addendum. There must also be an articulation of other ancillary benefits and options, including marketing and sponsorship efforts, concessions and merchandising offerings, and personnel inclusions (examples include set-up/breakdown staff, security, ushers, contractors, and site managers).

A facility sponsorship contract could be for naming rights on the entire complex, or for a specific part of the facility (a court, field, or room). Depending on the size of the facility and the location, these agreements can net up to US$40 M per year over 50 years (example – the current deal between Citi and the New York Mets). In England, the Football Association (FA) will offer advertising rights to Wembley Stadium (i.e. Wembley Stadium 'sponsored by' or 'in association with'), which they anticipate will bring in an additional £5 M per year. In addition to advertising and promotion specifications, the contracts may also include statements of exclusivity (prevents other sponsors in the same industry to enter into agreement with the facility) or non-exclusivity, options to renew, rights of first refusal for renewal, and any intellectual property rights concerns.

### Marketing-based legislative issues

Upcoming in Chapter 10 will be a discussion of marketing management for sport facilities, including issues related to understanding the sport facility consumer from a marketing standpoint, marketing logistics in sport facility marketing, and the relationship between promotions and sport facilities. From a legislative point of view, there are two current issues that are significantly prevalent in sport facility management. The first was mentioned in the previous section – the relationship between intellectual property rights and sport facility management. The second is the effect of ambush marketing legislation on sport facilities.

### Intellectual properties

With the continued growth of sponsorship and advertising agreements in sport facilities of all sizes, sport facility owners and managers are becoming more involved in the management of intellectual properties – both the facility's rights and the sponsors/advertisers' rights. Intellectual properties are creative intangible assets that have commercial value. There are three major categories of intellectual properties – patents, copyrights, and marks. A patent is any new and/or useful invention or improvement on a process, machine, or manufacturing method. While sport facilities rarely deal with this intellectual property, there are times when the personnel may be able to create a patented invention or improvement. At that point, the ownership or personnel should secure the services of a patent lawyer.

A copyright gives the owner of an artistic creation the exclusive right to copy, reproduce, distribute, publish, perform, or display the work. For copyright protection to be legal: (1) the work usually needs to be original, and (2) it must be in a tangible form that can be reproduced. For sport facility managers and owners, any document, manual, or form may have the right to be copyrighted if it meets the above criteria. Understanding copyrights is also important as related to the operations or events in a facility. The use of music, public performances, and broadcasts are protected under copyright law. Any of these types of events that take place in your sport facility, should they be scheduled for rebroadcast, may be subject to copyright approval by the ownership for a fee.

The final area of intellectual property law that sport facilities will engage in are marks – specifically trademarks. A trademark is a word, phrase, symbol or design, or a combination of words, phrases, symbols or designs, that identifies and distinguishes the source of the goods of one party from those of others. Sport facilities have their own trademarks, and also need to manage the trademarks of those organizations associated with the sport facility. The purposes of a trademark include:

- Articulating the source and the standard of quality for the product or service offered by the sport facility, hence protecting the public from confusion and deception.
- Distinguishing the products and services of the sport facility from their competition – often through the licensing process.
- Serving as a major element of the advertising campaign for the sport facility.

One of the major challenges to intellectual property right protection for sport facilities is twofold. First, who is the true owner of the intellectual property – an event or the facility? This question should be answered in the contracting process. The second and bigger question today is the protecting of intellectual properties from ambush marketing efforts.

## Ambush marketing

Ambush marketing is the attempt by a third party to create a direct or an indirect association with a sport facility, the event it is hosting, or its participants without their approval, hence denying official sponsors', suppliers' and partners' parts of the commercial value derived from the 'official' designation. This association is without the permission of the sport endeavor or its official partner(s), and the desire is to deceive the sport consumer into believing that there is an official association. Entities engage in ambush marketing because of their desire to be associated with a sport facility or the event being housed there. Reasons include not being able to pay the sponsorship fees, or they are prevented from entering into an association with sport event due to a contract of exclusivity or long-term association with a competitor.

# Global anti-ambush marketing laws

For many municipalities around the globe, it has come to pass that governmental intervention is necessary to ensure sponsor protection during hallmark events. As a sport facility manager, you will need to be aware of these various legislations and work with local authorities and your sponsors to ensure that ambush marketing is limited. We take a look at some of the laws around the globe:

## United States

As print, there is no federal legislation, but municipalities hosting hallmark events have taken steps to ensure that ambush marketing will not take place in their city when the country and potentially the world is watching. One example was in 2006 in Detroit, Michigan, where an anti-ambush marketing law that created a no-ad zone around stadiums during the Super Bowl and the World Series. Similar laws were enacted for Super Bowls in Glendale, Arizona and Tampa, Florida.

## Australia

Australia has been at the forefront of controlling ambush marketing. With the 2000 Summer Olympics coming to Sydney, the Australian government passed the Sydney 2000 Games (Indicia and Images) Protection Act 1996, and the New South Wales government passed the Olympic Arrangements Act 2000. A significant part of both laws was "Games specific legislation enacted to prevent ambush marketing and provide for 'clean' Games venues to equip New South Wales and Australia for future sporting and large marketing programs." Since these Olympics, the Australian government has enacted similar laws for hallmark sport events, the most recent being the Melbourne 2006 Commonwealth Games Protection Act 2005.

## South Africa

The South African Parliament has passed wide-ranging ambush marketing legislation to create boundaries for the sports marketing industry. The new restrictions tackle 'intrusion' marketing where a company seeks subtle exposure of its brand through the publicity generated by the event. The legislation, which amends the Merchandise Marks Act 1941, enables South African Government to designate certain events, such as the cricket World Cup and the FIFA World Cup, as being subject to new restrictions. Once an event is so designated, it will be a criminal offense to conduct ambush marketing in connection with the event and perpetrators could face jail. The laws prohibit use of any brand in relation to a designated event in such a manner which is calculated to achieve publicity for that trademark and thereby derive promotional benefit from the event without prior authority of the organizer.

*Continued*

## Global anti-ambush marketing laws—cont'd

### New Zealand

New Zealand has passed legislation to provide greater protection to sponsors of important events from ambush marketing: the Major Events Management Act 2007. The purpose of the anti-ambush marketing part of the law is to prevent unauthorized commercial exploitation at the expense of either a major event organizer or a major event sponsor. Specifically, the law (1) prohibits representations that suggest persons, brands, goods, or services have an association with a major event when they do not; (2) prohibits advertising from intruding on a major event activity and the attention of the associated audience; and (3) prohibits the use of certain emblems and words relating to Olympic Games and Commonwealth Games (and other designated events) without appropriate authorization.

### China

After being selected as the host of the 2008 Summer Olympic Games, the Chinese government passes the Protection of Olympic Symbols Relations 2002. This law not only protects Olympic symbols and names, but also includes an anti-ambush marketing clause. Ambush marketing is vaguely defined as activities that might be deemed by others as an existing sponsorship or other supportive relationships.

*Source*: excerpts from Schwarz, E. C. (2009). The evolution of global anti-ambush marketing laws. Paper presented at the 7th annual conference of the Sport Marketing Association, Cleveland, Ohio.

### Suggested discussion topics

1. Research the following:
   a. The London Olympic Games and Paralympic Games Acts 2006 – and explain the provisions to reduce ambush advertising at the 2012 Summer Olympics.
   b. The Olympic and Paralympic Marks Act of 2007 in Canada – and explain how the law addresses Olympic mark protection and ambush marketing challenges, as promised by the Canadian government when they bid for the 2010 Vancouver–Whistler Winter Games.
2. Brazil will be hosting the FIFA World Cup in 2014 and the Summer Olympic Games in 2016. What preventative measures are the Brazilian National Institute of Industrial Property and the Brazilian government seeking to implement to combat ambush marketing?

# How much legal expertise is enough?

On a final note for this chapter, the question is raised 'how much legal expertise is enough for a sport facility manager or owner?' The reality is that with all the other responsibilities in management and operations of the sport facility, also dealing with keeping up-to-date on all the federal/parliamentary, state/regional, and local/municipality law changes and enactments is nearly impossible. In fact, it would be irrational for facility managers and owners to believe that they can possess legal expertise in all of these areas as described in this chapter – as this is only a snapshot of the total breadth and depth of the law. Therefore, we cannot stress enough the importance of having access to legal expertise, and if possible, have legal council on retainer to stay on top of the legal concerns that affect sport facilities.

# Chapter review

The law has a significant relationship to almost entirely all aspects of sport facility operations management. Laws are a body of rules that govern individual or collective actions and conduct as defined by an authorized governing body and having binding legal force. The challenge is that laws are constantly evolving through modifications and change, and that evolution has a direct effect on the daily conduct of the management and operation of a sport facility. The four major areas of law that sport facility managers and owners deal with include constitutional law, statutory law, common law, and administrative law. While it would be impossible for a sport facility manager or owner to know every law that will have a direct effect on the management and operation of the sport facility, they do have a duty of care to their users and associated constituents to act in a legal manner.

Sport facility managers and owners must have a basic understanding of the legal principles and standards that will directly affect them. Negligence law involves unintentional torts related to a failure to act in a manner equal to how a reasonable person would act under the same circumstances. Criminal law is an intentional tort (i.e.) a civil wrong based on an intentional act that becomes a detriment to the general health, safety, and welfare of the general public. In sport facilities, the civil wrongs most often seen are assault, battery, defamation, and invasion of privacy. Contract law is a major part of facility management, especially as related to employment contracts, event contracts, and sponsorship contracts. Event contracts are usually more detailed because there are a number of specialized elements that need to be included such as pre-event set-up and post-event breakdown; specialized lease agreements for facilities, equipment, and rentals; and other ancillary benefits and options, including marketing and sponsorship efforts, concessions and merchandising offerings, and personnel inclusions. Sponsorship contracts could be for naming rights on the entire complex, or for a specific part of the facility (a court, field, or room). In addition to advertising and promotion specifications, the contracts may also include statements of exclusivity or non-exclusivity, options to renew, rights of first refusal for renewal, and any intellectual property rights concerns. In addition, marketing-based legislative issues related to intellectual properties (especially copyright and trademarks) and ambush marketing are significant legal issues that should be understood and addressed.

One of the biggest issues is determining how much legal expertise should sport facility managers or owners have. In general, they cannot possess legal expertise in all of these areas as described in this chapter, and it is crucial to have access to legal expertise to stay ahead of the changes in laws affecting sport facilities.

# Section Three

## Ancillary Issues in Management and Operations

# 10 Facility marketing management

## Chapter outline

## Chapter objectives

This chapter will cover the basic theories and principles of global sport marketing and communications related to sport facilities. The goal is for the reader to develop knowledge and skill in the marketing process as it relates to understanding the sport consumer, logistics, promotions and public relations activities in sport facilities that focus on: (1) studying and understanding the consumer in terms of marketing a sport facility, (2) developing marketing strategies for the sport facility, and (3) clarifying a sport facility's needs and goals – through the marketing mix, market research and information systems, and consumer behavior. In addition, the implementation of sport marketing plans will be discussed – both through logistical functions including product management, sales management, supply chain management; and promotional efforts including advertising, sponsorship, and other communication management efforts.

## Introduction to sport facility marketing management

One of the biggest misconceptions in sport facility management is that the facility manager does not need to be involved with marketing – that their sole job is related to the operations and management of the actual facility. On the contrary, facility managers need to have a solid foundation in marketing and should be involved in all aspects of marketing that relate to the sport facility. The knowledge of the sport facility manager with relation to operations and management of the facility actually can serve as a significant asset in the development of marketing plans, helping with the understanding of the consumers who use the facility, efficient logistical administration of marketing efforts, and effective application of promotional activities through facility advertising, sponsorships, and atmospherics.

The purpose of this chapter is to provide an overview of how the association of sport marketing and sport facilities can interact to best provide products and services that satisfy the needs, wants and desires of the consumer; aid in the planning, organizing, directing, controlling, budgeting, leading, and evaluating a facility whose primary product and service is related to sport, recreation, leisure, and entertainment; and how the sport facility managers' understanding of the application of marketing can help with the transfer of goods and services from the producer (the sport facility, the events in the facility, and the organizations utilizing the facility) to the consumer (spectators and participants).

## The sport marketing mix and sport facilities

The focal point of these marketing functions is in four specific areas known as the 4 C's of marketing analysis: the consumer, the company itself, the competition, and the climate. The consumer is an individual or organization who purchases or obtains goods and services for direct use or ownership. In the case of the sport facility, it is most often the purchase of a ticket to gain access to a facility for the purpose of experiencing an event. Sport marketers reach sport consumers through a series of processes – (1) segmentation is the concept of dividing a large, diverse group with multiple attributes into smaller groups with distinctive characteristics, (2) targeting seeks to find the best way to get a product's image into the minds of consumers, and hence entice the consumer to purchase the product accomplished by focusing on the P's of sport marketing (product, price, place, promotion, and publicity), (3) positioning focuses on how a company seeks to influence the perceptions of potential and current customers about the image of the company and its products and services, and (4) delivery is the concept of producing or achieving what is desired or expected by the consumer. With regard to the company and competition, the framework is centered on the SWOT analysis. The managerial function of the company itself is most concerned with internal strengths and weaknesses. The leadership of the company tends to focus on the external opportunities and external threats posed by competition and the environment. The climate involves forecasting the factors that will have a direct effect on the internal and external functioning of the sport facility, including changes in societal values and beliefs, the economy, legal and political issues, the media, and changes in technology.

The sport facility managers, because of their experience within the climate, their understanding of the diverse consumers who come to the facility for various events, their knowledge of how similar facilities operate, and their direct involvement with the internal functions of the sport facility, make themselves a crucial part of the marketing management team for the sport facility. However, there are significant challenges for the facility manager, because while the sport facility itself is a tangible building, the sport product is generally intangible, subjective, and variable. This makes the sport marketing efforts for a sport facility unique for numerous reasons, but most importantly because the primary sport product, and hence the market, is traditionally demand based, whereas most generic products are marketed based on need. The sport product takes many forms including a consumer good, a consumer service, a commercial good, or a commercial service; hence it has a wide and varied appeal. The sport facility manager should have an equally wide and varied understanding of the multiple types and aspects of sport products and services that may take place in their sport facility, and how best to deliver what is promised to the consumers.

The sport facility manager must also recognize that since the sport product is normally publicly consumed, and consumer satisfaction is directly affected by the environment – which is most often provided by the facility. As a result of the strong emotional connections elicited by the involvement of the sport product, and the fact that since the sport product is a perishable commodity (when the game or event is over, it is the memory of the experience that remains), the sport facility manager must do everything possible to ensure that from the facility standpoint – the customer is satisfied. This is most often accomplished by working with all sub-departments associated to the facility to ensure that the product extensions within the sport facility are adequate – including such things as quality concession stands, functional and clean lavatories, simple ingress/egress, good flow within the facility (including directions within the facility), top quality security, and overall cleanliness of the sport facility. Anything a sport facility manager can do to enhance the customer experience aids in marketing efforts.

## Understanding the sport consumer in sport facilities

### Marketing information systems

In order for the sport facility manager to understand these consumers, they must be able to effectively and efficiently incorporate a marketing information system into their marketing efforts. The purpose of a marketing information system is to collect the various data available in one place for use and to make sport marketing decisions through an intricate structure involving the interaction of people, infrastructure, and techniques to gather, sort, analyze, evaluate, and distribute relevant, well-timed, accurate information for use by sport facility directors, so that they can develop, implement, and manage marketing plans. The marketing information system is made up of four elements – the marketing research system, the internal reports system, the marketing intelligence system, and the marketing decision support system.

### Marketing research

The marketing research system is the process of designing, gathering, analyzing, and reporting information that is utilized to solve a specified sport marketing issue or problem. The sport facility manager must engage in a process to determine where there is a lack of information available about a need – ranging from the available target market to a need within the facility. As a result of a problem being defined, the sport facility manager comes up with a list of potential solutions articulated in terms of goals and objectives, and then engages in the research process. This process includes collecting primary and secondary data through various methods (surveys, focus groups, case study analysis, market tracking studies, industry standard reports, etc.); tabulate and evaluate the data collected; and utilize the information to develop programs to meet the needs of the consumer; or modify policies and procedures as necessary.

## Internal reports system

The internal reports system serves as a framework for the marketing information system by allowing the sport facility director the ability to examine the internal operations of the sport organization to enhance the marketing efforts of the facility and the associated events. Utilizing the information collected from various departments through inputs from the order-to-payment cycle; the point-of-sale system; and data mining, the sport facility manager is better able to understand the sport organization they are working with, and hence its relationship to prospective and current customers.

## Marketing intelligence system

The marketing intelligence system is a crucial element of the marketing information system, because it opens the door to understand the external environment that affects the sport facility and the organizations it serves. By using the primary and secondary intelligence collected through the various methods of scanning, and evaluating that data through the scanning dissemination process, the sport facility manager can gain a better understanding of the opportunities, threats and trends that can affect the sport facility. In addition, this intelligence is utilized to enhance the internal reports of the sport facility, and can serve as a framework for future sport marketing research.

## Marketing decision support system

The marketing decision support system (DSS) assists sport facility managers and other decision makers both within the sport facility and the organizations it serves by taking advantage of information that is available from the various sources and using that information to make strategic decisions, control decisions, operational decisions, and marketing decisions. This system looks at both the decision process and decision outcomes, with the goal of making changes in selected sport marketing that lead to higher profits, a stronger and more positive image for the sport facility, and to increase sport consumer satisfaction. Therefore, the results from the decision support system are utilized to make strategic, control, operational, and marketing decisions that interact with all parts of the sport facility and the associated organizations.

## Consumer behavior

While it is important to have knowledge about the marketing information system, this is only the functional part of understanding the sport consumer. The sport facility manager, to effectively engage in marketing management, must also comprehend and apply the principles of consumer behavior. Consumer behavior is the conduct that consumers display in seeking out, ordering, buying, using, and assessing products and services that the consumers expect will satisfy their needs and wants.

The sport facility manager must understand the internal and external factors that affect sport consumers. The internal factors include the personality of the sport consumer, the learning process of sport consumers, the process of motivating sport consumers, the attitudes of the sport consumer, and the perceptions developed by sport consumers about a sport product. External factors resulting from environmental influences include culture, subculture, international and global interaction, social setting, and social class.

In order to effectively understand the consumer behavior, sport facility managers must understand the marketing concept, which is a consumer-oriented philosophy that suggests that satisfaction of consumer needs provide the focus for product development and marketing strategy to enable the firm to meet its own organizational goals. In terms of sport facility management, the marketing concept focuses on the socialization, involvement, and commitment of spectators and participants through the sport product itself, the production of sport (through the experience of the 'event'), and the sale of sport (including the product extensions).

The sport facility manager will be an active member of the problem solving and decision making processes to ensure that the needs and wants of the consumer are being met. In problem solving, the sport facility manager will engage in brainstorming, formulating various solutions, analyzing all solutions to determine a course of action, implementing the course of action, and evaluating the success of the course of action chosen to ensure that optimal success is attained from a facility operations standpoint. The decision making process that works hand-in-hand with problem solving focuses on the economic, passive, cognitive, and emotional needs of customers before they enter the facility, while they are in the facility, and after they have left the facility. Ultimately, sport facility managers look at three key determinants of success as related to marketing management: (1) Did the marketing program influence sport consumers to come to the facility? (2) Did the advertisements and other collateral materials stimulate sport consumer purchases to come to the facility? and (3) Was the spread of information about the sport facility via word of mouth in an effective, controlled, and positive manner?

The over-riding goal is to market the facility utilizing the various processes in consumer behavior to influence the sport consumer coming into the sport facility for an event. Once in the facility, the goal is to have the sport consumer believe that the sport facility is delivering a sport product and experience that meets and satisfies their needs, which in turn results in the sport consumer purchasing another sport product in the future, and hence using the sport facility.

---

## So who is the sport consumer?

There has been much discussion as to the true identity of the consumer for a sport facility. Traditionally, they were grouped into two categories – participants (individuals who are involved or plays a part in a spectacle – such as a sport event or concert), and spectators (individuals who are present and observes a spectacle such as a sport event or concert). Participants are fairly easy to identify – the players, the coaches, the trainers, and the management. Sport facility managers must understand each of these groups, and market their facility to these constituents every day, ranging from the quality of the field/court of play to the amenities of the offices and locker rooms. The participants are the direct internal clients of the sport facility, and it is the goal of the sport facility manager to meet the needs and wants of these clients in order to assure continued use of the facility by those clients.

Spectators are a bit more complex to identify. However, a study conducted by A.T. Kearney (an innovative, corporate-focused management consulting firm that provides management advice concerning issues on CEO agenda) classified the sport consumer into different traditional (sport fanatics; club/team loyalists) and new (social viewers, opportunistic viewers, starstruck spectators, and sport indifferent consumers) segments. More details of this can be found in the online supplements of the text.

---

## Sport marketing logistics in sport facilities

After the sport facility manager understands the intricacies of the sport consumer, they then need to understand the major logistical functions in sport marketing that affect how they position their sport facility, and deliver the sport product through the sport facility. The major logistical functions a sport facility manager must understand in terms of sport marketing are product and service management, and sales management.

### Product and service management

Sport product and service management usually starts as a function of the sport marketing planning process. This process involves the development of the sport organization's products and services marketing strategies, including the tactics and programs to be implemented during the lifespan of the plan. It starts by defining the competitive set, which is the process of determining the direct competitors to a sport organization in the specific product or service area. Then the sport organization engages in category attractiveness analysis, in which aggregate marketing factors, segment factors, and environmental factors are considered. This is followed up with competitor and consumer analyses.

Sport facility managers have products and services they have total control over (internal), and products and services they have limited control over (external). Internal products include the facility itself – the playing surface and related equipment, seating, scoreboard/message boards, bathrooms, concession areas, and the general infrastructure. Internal services include maintenance, housekeeping, security, customer service, and first aid. External products include all aspects of the event taking place in the facility. External services are the added benefits provided by the event and other external entities to enhance the experience of the customer.

Marketing of the internal products and services is an important job that the facility manager must undertake. Just as with any other product or service, increasing awareness and image is crucial to not only attracting events to the facility, but also attracting customers to attend the events in the facility. Hence, the sport facility manager must be acutely aware of the sport product and service life cycle, and how each stage is directly affected by the realities of competition, saturation, and change. The internal development stage begins with the idea of a new product or service (in the case of a new facility) or a new twist on an existing product or service (in the case of a modified facility). Introduction to market is the time when the sport organization puts its plan into action and starts capturing market share by introducing products and services to the market. In this stage, the benefits of holding events in the facility to event coordinators, and building brand awareness and equity within the community, is vital. The growth stage is when the facility that offers the best product and/or service (both in the types of events and the experience within the facility) rises to the top and separates itself from the competition. Maturity refers to the time at which the sport facility has maximized profits and is seeking to maintain a stable place in the market through regular events and a standard schedule. The goal is to maintain a regular place in the market as long as possible. However, as with any product, there will come a time when the saturation point is reached. This is when the sport facility must come to the realization that it needs to reevaluate the sport product or service life cycle, because they are no longer increasing their market share. Often, this means that events and people are not coming to the venue, because it is viewed as deteriorating or moving towards obsolescence. The decline stage is the last stage before obsolescence, and either the sport facility should have introduced new services or a next generation of the product (such as a renovation or refurbishment), or the facility needs to exit the market (usually through demolition and replacement).

Marketing of the external products and services works in a similar manner. The sport facility manager keeps their eye out for new products or services that can be presented through the sport facility, such as a new event in the marketplace that is of interest to the general public. At the same time, both regular events involving local teams and annual events need to be on the radar of the sport facility manager, and plans need to be made to attract them to the facility. When the event is introduced to the market, the goal is to attract these new events to the facility – hence capturing market share. The growth stage is when the reputation of the facility grows and the best events want to appear in the facility. As that calendar of events grows, there will be a time of maturity, where the image and awareness of the facility is at its highest, and the job of the facility manager is to balance the schedule and not extend beyond the capability of the facility. A sport facility manager also needs to realize at this time of maturity that as events grow in scope (and hence their needs expand), and more modern facilities open, it is possible that events may move on to other venues. The goal, as with the internal plan, is to maintain a regular place in the market as long as possible through positioning and differentiation.

## Sales management

Sales are the backbone of any sport organization, and this is equally true of sport facilities. While the facility manager may not necessarily have direct involvement in the sales process, they need to have an acute awareness of the entire process, and be prepared to offer advice, consultation, and opinions about sales efforts related to facility inventories. In addition, the facility manager, through their staff, build and nurture personal relationships with customers – since many of the facility staff become the face of the facility, because of their direct contact with the guests.

Facility managers are involved with the sales process of numerous facility inventories including leasing/rental of the facility for events; ticketing and box office management; premium access (suites, club seating, public seating licenses/ debentures); product branding through pouring rights, and various promotional sales efforts including advertising (signage and promotions) and sponsorships (naming rights and endorsements).

Facility managers are often in charge of selling their facility to potential clients for a variety of events, including sports, concerts, corporate rentals, hospitality events, graduation, fundraisers, and a number of other types of events. The facility manager is often involved in the negotiation of these rental contracts – covering everything from costs of the spaces to be used to various costs including set-up/break-down, security, housekeeping, electrical/technology, special equipment usage, permits, fire/police clearance, storage, and insurance.

Another major area facility managers must oversee is ticketing and box office management. From a ticketing standpoint, the facility manager needs to coordinate with teams and events to understand the various ticketing structures, inform ticket taking staff of those structures, employing enough staff to service the guests, and ensure that ushers and security understand the level of access that tickets (and in many cases credentials) allow. As far as the box office, many do not realize that the facility owns the box office – not teams or events. There are times when some of the box office operations are outsourced (example – via team/event ticketing or outside vendors such as Ticketmaster and RazorGator), but in all ticketing for events at some point must go through the box office. Usually there is a box office staff who reports to and works with the facility manager to determine ticketing based on space available, facility configuration for a specific event, and changes that may occur after the event has been set up. The box office is also responsible for creating a manifest, which is a listing of every seat available in a facility that is used to coordinate with teams, customers, promoters/booking agents, and outsourcing vendors to track pricing and availability of seating in the venue. This master list serves as the main source of information for every event. In addition to manifesting and ticketing, the facility manager – through the box office – is also responsible for coordinating relationships with the tenants of the facility, on-sales for new events coming to the facility (both marketing of the on-site and the management of the on-sale day), security of the box office (since a lot of money does go through the box office daily), and event day ingress/egress.

Premium access is a financially lucrative part of running a sport facility, and facility managers need to pay special attention to ensure that users of these inventories are receiving value for the money they have paid. There are four main types of premium access seating – premium seating, club seating, luxury boxes/suites, and personal (or sometimes permanent) seat licenses (PSLs). Premium seating is the best seats in the facility – front row at the basketball game, behind the plate or dugout at a baseball game, or midfield at a soccer or rugby game. Club seating is a specialized seating in the facility with special access and amenities that usually includes food and beverage with the price of admission. Luxury boxes/suite are private rooms with seating for those who have access to the box/suite, a lounge area, private bathroom, and food/beverage service either catered or available through wait staff. PSLs, which are also known as debentures, are where customers pay a one-time fee to gain ownership of a specific seat, and then must pay a yearly season ticket fee to maintain the license.

The food and beverage industry is an integral part of the sport facility. While the operations may be kept in-house or outsourced to another company, product branding through pouring rights is one area in which the facility manager must be closely involved. As a result of exclusive agreements where beverage companies such as Coca Cola and Pepsi, or alcohol companies such as Anheuser Busch, Miller, or Coors have the pouring rights in a facility, the facility manager is often the individual who is involved with these negotiations. Usually their involvement involves leveraging the contract to include dedicated funds for facility upgrades and improvements, and specific guidelines on how the branding of the facility by the vendor can be implemented.

Sport facility managers are also involved with numerous promotional sales efforts, including advertising and sponsorship sales. The final section of this chapter will cover the promotional aspects of the sport, and how the facility manager involvement in promotional mix elements includes and goes beyond just the sale of advertising and sponsorship.

## Promotional aspects of sport marketing for sport facilities

Promotions are a very involved communications process that aids in providing information about the sport facility to consumers through the promotional mix. The elements of the sport promotional mix that sport facility managers work with include advertising, sponsorship, public relations, and atmospherics. To coordinate the interaction between the elements of the sport promotional mix, a strategy must be developed that focuses on building brand loyalty and product credibility, developing image, and positioning the brand. The strategic process involves promotional integration, which is the actual creation and delivery of the promotional message that involves defining how the message is to reach the consumer, ensuring that the promotional message will be received and understood, and that the promotional message will lead to the purchase of a product or service – in the case of a sport facility, attending an event at the facility. The ultimate goal is to build brand awareness for the facility through a series of integrations (image, functional, coordinated, consumer-based, stakeholder-based, and relationship management) that will lead to the overall strategic promotional implementation.

There are a number of generalizations that can be made about promotions. Promotions temporarily increase sales substantially; promotion in one product category affect sales of brands in complementary and competitive categories; and promotions can result in increased traffic to the sport facility. Most of the generalizations are true, however it is important to understand how to utilize these elements in order to ensure that the results are long-lasting, and lead to maintaining current and attracting new customers to the sport facility.

## Advertising

Advertising is the process of attracting public attention to a sport product or sport business through paid announcements in the print, broadcast, or electronic media. As a primary element of the sport promotions mix, it is the communication process utilized most often in sport marketing for sport facilities. Through advertisements, advertising campaigns, and integrated brand promotion, advertising helps establish and maintain relationships with the sport consumer by providing a conduit for listening and reacting to the sport consumer through their attendance at an event hosted by a sport facility.

Advertising in sport facilities is an integral tool of marketing as related to brand development and management, segmentation, differentiation, and positioning. As a result, advertising efforts need to be in congruence with the sport facility's brand strategy and the branding process. The brand strategy has a direct impact on the sport facility's value in terms of market capitalization and corporate value. The branding process provides the sport consumer with a clear understanding of the attributes and values of the sport facility. Sport facility advertising efforts will be unique to each facility and on the events and services being offered, however the ultimate goal is to utilize the advertising efforts to enhance sport facility loyalty through brand association, and build image through the association with the brands being advertised.

The sport facility manager is involved with the marketing, sales, and implementation of advertising in a sport facility. The goal of sport facility advertising is to maximize the visibility of the brand's image and build brand association and loyalty with customers to the sport facility – while enhancing the image and awareness of the sport facility. Sport facility managers are involved in developing the partnerships since they are the individuals who will ultimately be involved in implementing and managing the advertisement efforts within the sport facility. The majority of this implementation usually involves signage in the facility. The most common types of signage include banners, infrastructure (embedded onto the facility framework), field/court surfaces, and computerized scoreboards. However, in recent years, sport facility managers have become very creative with the inventories available for advertising signage. These include step signage, wall wraps, turnstiles, garbage cans, bathrooms, and in-game equipments (such as silhouetted advertisements on nets above the glass in ice hockey arenas or field goal nets behind football uprights).

## Sponsorship

Sport sponsorship involves acquiring the rights to be affiliated with a sport product or business in order to obtain benefits from that association. Sport sponsorships play a significant role in the sport promotional mix, and take place at multiple levels of the sport business landscape. Especially in the United States, the most lucrative sponsorship agreements are naming rights with sport facilities. As such, sport facility managers are involved with the management of these sponsorships to ensure that these terms of the sponsorship are being upheld in terms of exclusivity, signage within the facility, implementation of promotional activities, and accuracy in the delivery of the corporate image and likeness.

Sport sponsorship agreements between corporations and sport facilities are documented within a sponsorship proposal. These packages are designed to articulate the benefits derived from the agreement for all parties involved. The reason for entering into a sport sponsorship agreement varies from organization to organization. Corporations have numerous goals as a result of sport sponsorship, including increasing public awareness, enhancing their company image, building business and trade relationships with other sponsoring organizations, changing or improving public perception of their company, increasing community involvement in the target area, and enhancing personnel relations by offering opportunities for employees to attend sponsored events, including attendance at hospitality areas. The goals of sport facility as a result of sponsorship include taking in additional revenue from the agreement, and increasing target market awareness, image, sales, and market share.

Sport facility sponsorships are naming rights agreements for stadiums, arenas, and other sport facilities. Since 2000, this is the fastest growing area of sport sponsorship, as many sport facilities around the world have sold their naming rights to sport corporations. These deals are usually long-term and significant in value. Also, the value of the sponsorship will vary with the size of the market, the level of competition playing, and the assortment of events scheduled by the facility. Below are some examples of major sport facility naming rights deals that are currently in place around the world. You will note that the deals in the United States are significantly longer in term and have a higher cost per year than other parts of the world.

| Location | Name of facility | Location | Sponsor | Terms (in millions) |
| --- | --- | --- | --- | --- |
| United States | Citi Field | New York | Citi Bank | $400 M for 20 years. |
| | University of Phoenix Stadium | Glendale, AZ | University of Phoenix | $154.5 M for 20 years. |
| | Reliant Stadium | Houston, TX | Reliant Energy | $310 M for 31 years. |
| | FedEx Field | Washington, DC | Federal Express | $205 M for 27 years. |
| | American Airlines Center | Dallas, TX | American Airlines | $195 M for 30 years. |
| | Philips Arena | Atlanta, GA | Royal Philips Electronics | $182 M for 20 years. |
| Canada | Bell Centre | Montreal, QC | Bell Canada | $64 M for 20 years. |
| | Air Canada Centre | Toronto, ON | Air Canada | $40 M for 20 years. |
| | Scotiabank Place | Ottawa, ON | Scotiabank | $20 M for 15 years. |
| | Pengrowth Saddledome | Calgary, AB | Pengrowth Energy | $20 M for 20 years. |
| | Ricoh Coliseum | Toronto, ON | Ricoh Electronics | $10 M for 20 years. |
| Europe | Emirates Stadium | England | Emirates Airlines | £100 M* for 15 years. |
| | Allianz Arena | Germany | Allianz Insurance | £60 M for 15 years. |
| | O₂, Dublin | Ireland | O₂ Telecom | €25 M for 10 years. |
| | Aviva Stadium | Ireland | Hibernian Aviva | €50 M for 10 years. |
| Asia | Nissan Stadium | Japan | Nissan Automobile | ¥470 M for 5 years. |
| Africa | Coca Cola Stadium | South Africa | Coca Cola | R45 M for 4.5 years. |
| Australia | ANZ Stadium | Sydney, NSW | ANZ Bank | AU$31 M for 7 years. |
| | Suncorp Stadium | Brisbane, QLD | Suncorp Bank | AU$6.6 M for 5 years. |
| | Etihad Stadium | Melbourne, VIC | Etihad Airways | AU$5 M for 5 years. |

* Includes 8-year shirt deal.

## Enhancement of other promotional mix elements

Sport facility managers are also involved in enhancing other aspects of the promotional mix – especially public relations and atmospherics. Public relations is the collection of activities, communications, and media coverage that convey what the sport organization is and what they have to offer, all in the effort to enhance their image and prestige. Through public relations, the sport facility director focuses on getting information out to the public through various methods to enhance the image and awareness of the facility and the events to be hosted. In order to get the best value, facility managers focus on the use of unpaid, non-personal promotion of the facility through a third party (usually the media) that publishes in print media or presents information through radio, television, or the Internet. The goal of any good publicity is that it is viewed as coming from an unbiased, neutral source. A sport facility manager understands that utilizing public relations is critical to success, as it is the management function that helps to evaluate public attitudes, articulate policies and procedures of an organization that may be of public interest, and execute programs of action to acquire public understanding and approval.

The most important relationship is with the media. Media relations are the activities that involve working directly with individuals responsible for the production of mass media including news, features, public service announcements, and sponsored programmes. Effective media relations maximize coverage and placement of messages and information in the mass media without paying for it directly through advertising. Most media relations activities are designed to get free media coverage for programs and issues. As such, the sport facility manager engages in a number of efforts to give the media more access than the general customer. This includes a press box/press row exclusively for the media; credentials for sideline/on field access/locker room, and behind-the-scenes access; areas for holding exclusive and group press conferences/interviews; and access to communications (phones/faxes/Internet technology) to file stories efficiently. Since the media will also be at the events in the facility for longer than the general public, the facility manager works with catering to ensure that food and beverage services are provided either in the press box or in a press-only dining area. The goal of providing a significant amount of access and service to the media is for the purpose of getting free media coverage that shows the sport facility in a positive light among the significant competition that is vying for limited amount of air time or print space.

Another aspect of promotions that is under the major control of the sport facility director is atmospherics. Atmospherics utilizes the design of visual communications in an environment to entice the sport consumer's perceptual and emotional responses to purchase the sport product or service. As a result of the operational function, the sport facility manager is able to control the environment based on the needs and wants of the consumer. Examples include:

- *Temperature*: control the heating, ventilation, and air conditioning (HVAC) systems, or in the case of a retractable roof facility – opening and closing the roof.
- *Lighting*: control the type of bulbs, the angle of lighting, and the control of natural lighting.

- *Sound*: ensure the speakers and public address systems are maintained to allow for maximum clarity.
- *Color*: since the facility manager is in charge of the in-house maintenance staff, the facility areas can be painted in colors that create an aesthetically-pleasing appearance.
- *Traffic flow*: by alleviating the clutter throughout the facility – especially in concourses and entryways – the movement/ingress/egress of guests will be more efficient.

## Chapter review

Facility managers need to have a solid foundation in marketing and should be involved in all aspects of marketing that relate to the sport facility. The association of sport marketing and sport facilities interact to best provide products and services that satisfy the needs, wants and desires of the consumer; and aid in the planning, organizing, directing, controlling, budgeting, leading, and evaluation of a facility whose primary product and service is related to sport, recreation, leisure, and entertainment.

The focal point of these marketing functions is in four specific areas known as the 4 C's of marketing analysis: the consumer, the company itself, the competition, and the climate. Sport marketers reach sport consumers through segmenting the population, targeting specific groups, positioning the sport facility to influence potential customers to attend an event at the facility, and then deliver on what is promised. With regard to the company and competition, the framework is centered on the SWOT analysis – internal strengths and weakness of the company, and external opportunities and threats posed by competition and the environment. The climate involves forecasting the factors that will have a direct effect on the internal and external functioning of the sport facility.

While sport consumers are often viewed simply as spectators and participants, the reality is that they can be broken down in numerous categories. There are multiple levels of spectators, including sport fanatics, club/team loyalists, social viewers, opportunistic viewers, starstruck spectators, and sport indifferent consumers. In order to understand these various consumers, sport facility managers must be able to effectively and efficiently incorporate a marketing information system into their marketing efforts. The purpose of a marketing information system is to collect the various data available in one place for use and make sport marketing decisions through an intricate structure involving the interaction of people, infrastructure and techniques to gather, sort, analyze, evaluate and distribute relevant, well-timed, accurate information for use by sport facility directors, so that they can develop, implement, and manage marketing plans. The marketing information system is made up of four elements – the marketing research system, the internal reports system, the marketing intelligence system, and the marketing decision support system. In addition, the sport facility manager must also comprehend and apply the principles of consumer behavior – the conduct that consumers display in seeking out, ordering, buying, using, and assessing products and services that the consumers expects will satisfy their needs and wants. The various factors of consumer behavior that a sport facility manager must understand include internal factors (personality, learning processes, motivation, attitude, and perceptions) and external factors (culture, subculture, international/global interaction, social class, and social setting).

The sport facility manager must also understand the major logistical functions in sport marketing that affect how they position their sport facility, and deliver the sport product through the sport facility. The major logistical functions a sport facility manager must understand in terms of sport marketing are product and service management, and sales management. Product and service management includes the products and services they have total control of (internal), and products and services they have limited control over (external). Internal products include the facility itself – the playing surface and related equipment, seating, scoreboard/message boards, bathrooms, concession areas, and the general infrastructure. Internal services include maintenance, house-keeping, security, customer service, and first aid. External products include all aspects of the event taking place in the facility. External services are the added benefits provided by the event and other external entities to enhance the experience of the customer. The sales management function is the backbone of sport facilities, because without customers – the facility would have no purpose for existence. Facility managers are involved with the sales process on numerous facility inventories including leasing/rental of the facility for events; ticketing and box office management; premium access (suites, club seating, public seating licenses/debentures); product branding through pouring rights, and various promotional sales efforts including advertising (signage and promotions) and sponsorships (naming rights and endorsements).

Hand-in-hand with logistics are the promotional aspects involved with marketing sport facilities. Promotions are a very involved communications process that aids in providing information about the sport facility to consumers through the promotional mix. The elements of the sport promotional mix that sport facility managers work with include advertising, sponsorship, public relations, and atmospherics. Advertising in sport facilities is an integral tool of marketing as related to brand development and management, segmentation, differentiation, and positioning. As a result, advertising efforts needs to be in congruence with the sport facility's brand strategy and the branding process. Sport facility managers are involved with the management of sponsorships to ensure that the terms of the sponsorship are being upheld in terms of exclusivity, signage within the facility, implementation of promotional activities, and accuracy in the delivery of the corporate image and likeness. Through public relations, the sport facility director focuses on getting information out to the public through various methods to enhance the image and awareness of the facility and the events to be hosted. The most important relationship is with the media, and therefore the sport facility manager engages in a number of efforts to give the media more access than that of the general customer – including press box/press row exclusively for the media; credentials for sideline/on-field access/ locker room, and behind-the-scenes access; areas for holding exclusive and group press conferences/interviews; and access to communications (phones/faxes/ Internet technology) to file stories efficiently. As far as atmospherics, the facility manager is able to control the environment based on the needs and wants of the consumer – including temperature, lighting, sound, color, and traffic flow.

# 11 Event planning in facility management

## Chapter outline

## Chapter objectives

Without events, there would be no purpose for a sport facility. Events can range from free open recreation time to a full-scale hallmark event such as the Olympics or World Cup. The purpose of this chapter is to explore the relationship between facility operations and management and event planning. This chapter is not intended to provide an in-depth analysis or explanation of event management; it is intended to articulate the role facility management plays in supporting event management. This first important factor to understanding is the entire sport facility event planning process, as well as the various event relationships that a facility manager may engage with. This will lead to examining the sport facility's role in pre-event, during event, and post-event operations including the activation of a facility event marketing plan, event implementation, level of involvement in managing events, preparation for the unexpected, and evaluation after the event has taken place.

## Sport facility event planning process

The sport facility event planning process involves the development of the event from conceptualization through activation to implementation and eventual evaluation by event managers. However, a part of the process that is often not described is that sport facility management and ownership go through a similar process in preparation for events coming to the sport facility. Hence the sport facility event planning process mirrors the sport event planning process, but with some intricate differences. This first section of this chapter will discuss the planning process from setting objectives and developing conceptualizations to contract signing and moving forward towards implementation of the event.

The first step in the event planning process is setting objectives. All sport facility managers and owners need to make some decision as to what type of events they want their facility to host. Often, these decisions go back to the philosophy, mission, and vision of the sport facility. For instance, if this is a community-based recreation facility, the types of events to be hosted there would need to be focused on community building and the needs of that local municipality. In contrast, a large, commercial-focused stadium or arena is seeking to maximize revenues through high attendance rates at high-profile events. However, there will always be questions at this stage, especially for commercially focused facilities, but not immune to community-based facilities, about events that may be beneficial socially or financially, but are contrary to the mission of the sport facility. These may include events that may be politically (ranging from a local politician's speaking engagement to a political convention), culturally (religious ceremonies), or socially (events such as an arts and crafts show) motivated, and may raise questions in the community. In addition, certain sporting events, depending on the jurisdiction, may not be considered appropriate, the most common sport that occurs today is mixed martial arts (MMA). In general, when setting objectives for determining what events will be held in a sport facility, there will be a general list of accepted events, but there also needs flexibility to consider other options that may be financially and socially viable. Some of the questions that should be answered to set these objectives include:

- What does the sport facility management ownership want to achieve by hosting the event?
- Who are your target audiences and participants?
- Is there an understanding of the history of the potential event?
- Does the event have a track record of success or failure?
- Does the sport facility have access to partnerships that can aid in the success of the event?
- Is there support from key stakeholders and partners for hosting the event in the sport facility?

After objectives are understood, the sport facility needs to develop concepts of how they view these potential events in their facility. In conjunction with all pertinent personnel from the facility, the ownership and management will lay out what the general framework of these various events would look like. This includes the functions of ingress/egress, seating, timing, scale, facilities and equipment needed, marketing plans, set-up, during event responsibilities, breakdown, and evaluation processes. As a part of this process, the sport facility will develop a series of strategies for success of the event. These strategies should be: (1) realistic; (2) results in having a positive influence on the sport facility, the event, and the community; (3) should be able to be accomplished within the available infrastructure; (4) and be able to be realized within the available budget. In conjunction with effectively creating these strategies, three main questions need to be answered:

- What is the importance of the event to the sport facility and the community?
- What are the benefits of hosting the event to the sport facility and the community?
- Who are the parties within the sport facility (and potentially the community) that should have input into creating the strategies?

Once these functions are analyzed, the sport facility ownership and management must determine whether it is feasible to host each type of event being analyzed. Feasibility is determined by first conducting a situation analysis (SWOT) to see what strengths the sport facility brings to the table for this type of event, where are the weaknesses that can prevent success, and what opportunities and threats does this event bring to the sport facility. In addition, a competitor analysis will be conducted for two reasons: (1) if there is a bid process for a larger event, to try to gain information that will aid in the success of securing the bid; and more importantly (2) to see if those competitors have run similar events, and try to acquire information that will help in managing that type of event.

Once all of this research and analysis is completed, the information is evaluated and a determination needs to be made whether to proceed with this type of event being hosted in the sport facility. If the evaluation is no, then either reconceptualization of the event needs to take place to determine whether through modification the event would be appropriate for the facility, or the event is deemed not appropriate, and negotiation for those types of events will not be conducted. If it is determined that the event would be a good fit for the sport facility, it is time to seek out those events (just as events are seeking out facilities) and get the parties together to negotiate contracts.

Prior to negotiating contracts, the sport facility managers and owners will develop a pro forma budget to anticipate what the general costs of hosting an event will be for the sport facility. This budget will become more detailed once contracts are negotiated and signed, but this advanced budget creates a general financial framework place for the specific type of events and a starting place for negotiations. If similar events have been held at the sport facility in the past, those final budgets can be used to support the developing budget for the new event. It is also important that the developers of the budget keep in mind political, economic, and infrastructural issues that may skew or change costs. In general, when creating the budget, the following questions should be considered:

- Do you have information from previous event budgets that can help create the current event budget?
- Have all pertinent costs been included in the budget?
- Have all internal and external factors related to the sport facility been taken into account in the budget?
- Have errors and omissions been built into the budget for unforeseen expenses, unexpected costs, or miscalculation of budget number that causes going over budget?

- Who from the sport facility is ultimately in charge of managing the budget and control cash flow?
- Who will be the secondary level of budget management in charge of auditing and monitoring the budget?

When the parties responsible for negotiating on behalf of the sport facility and the event get together, there are two end goals: (1) signing a contract agreeing to the use of the facility to host the event; and (2) discussion about the implementation of pre-event processes. Usually representing the sport facility is the facility manager and their designee (depending on the scope of the facility and/or the event), as they are usually the person responsible for scheduling and booking the facility, and have been actively involved in marketing the facility to event managers and promoters. From the event side, usually a promoter will negotiate on behalf of an event, however again depending on the scope of the event, the actual event manager or owner may be involved. The biggest challenge in this process is that the event (ranging from team owners to concert promoters to hallmark event managers) is only concerned about the event itself and maximizing profits through the event, whereas the facility is mostly concerned about how the event is presented and produced, as the appearance is a reflection on the sport facility in the community. These clashing philosophies often lead to some contentious discussions, and hence it is strongly recommended that all discussions and agreements are documented and clearly stated in all contracts. This includes the implementation of pre-event planning, such as determining:

- Who is responsible for marketing specific aspect of the event?
- What event staff is going to be provided through the sport facility, and what staff will the event be providing?
- How long before the event can ingress for set-up begin?
- How long before the event must set-up be completed so proper authorizations (as needed) can be given by the facility manager, police department, fire marshal, etc.
- What time will doors open?
- Who is responsible for what from the time doors open through the event and until doors close?
- How long does the event have to break down and egress from the facility?
- How will any financial issues be settled at the end of the event?

The list above is only an example of the numerous questions that should be answered during the pre-event planning process. This time of negotiating contracts and responsibilities not only serves to set parameters for the event's use of the facility, it provides an opportunity for the sport facility manager (and in some cases the ownership) to understand the relationships that are being forged. The most significant of these relationships is between the facility manager (and the appropriate staff) and the event manager (and their designated staff) as discussed above. However, depending on the scope of the event, there may be additional relationships forged as a result.

One such relationship is with the media. The scope of the event will gauge the interest from the media – the relationship with media for local, small events will be limited, whereas for larger events media involvement will grow. For instance, a local secondary school football tournament as a municipal facility will certainly have less media coverage than a professional football match at the new Cowboys Stadium or the new London Olympic Stadium, and obviously that media coverage will pale in comparison to the media coverage when the Cowboys Stadium expects to have 80,000 fans for the 2010 NBA All-Star Game, or when the London Olympic Stadium hosts the Opening Ceremonies of the 2012 Summer Olympics.

## Conflict between facility sponsorship and sponsored hallmark events

Another relationship is with potential sponsors. Depending on the scope of the event, this relationship could be minimal or on a grand scale. The biggest issue regarding this relationship is ensuring that facility sponsors do not clash with event sponsors. When this happens, significant problems can occur.

A significant example of this can be found in two separate incidents at the Pepsi Center in Denver, Colorado. In 1999, the Colorado Avalanche of the National Hockey League (NHL) submitted a bid for the 2001 All-Star Weekend in the arena they played in at that time – McNichols Arena. During this same time in Denver, a new arena was being built to house the Denver Nuggets of the National Basketball Association (NBA) and the Colorado Avalanche (NHL). Naming rights were sold later that year (1999) to PepsiCo for $3.4 million US per year for 20 years. The major dilemma came because Coca Cola is the official non-alcoholic drink sponsor of the NHL. So the NHL All-Star Game, with the NHL's sponsor Coca Cola in tow, would be held at the Pepsi Center.

At the same time, The Denver Nuggets of the NBA were keeping a close eye on this situation. They were looking for ways to host the 2003 NBA All-Star Game at the Pepsi Center, but the NBA contract with Coca Cola is even stronger than that of with the NHL. The contract between the NBA and the Sprite brand-name is a 100-year global marketing alliance estimated to be worth well in excess of $1 billion US.

How could the clashing naming rights of the facility and the sponsorship of the hallmark event be solved so Denver could reap the rewards of hosting these two All-Star events? Go to the online supplements for the text to read the scenario, understand the similarities and differences between how this conflict was solved for each event, and additional discussion topics to consider.

## Activating the facility event marketing plan

Just as an event would engage in marketing, a sport facility also will engage in marketing of events they host. Some of these marketing efforts will be in partnership with events, while others will be independent of each other. Ultimately, it is important to remember that marketing efforts will be developed based on the philosophy of the organization. Therefore, the majority of partnered marketing efforts will focus on the event's desire to maximize attendance and profits, and the independent facility marketing will focus on the presentation and production of event desired by the community, and the appearance of the facility as a significantly positive reflection of that community.

The facility event marketing plan is a comprehensive framework for identifying and achieving a sport facility's marketing goals and objectives through the event. A marketing plan is developed by the sport facility managers and personnel for each individual event, and includes the following steps:

- Identify the purpose of the plan in terms of the event, including developing mission and vision statements; creating goals and objectives; and ensuring involvement and communication with all pertinent sport facility personnel.
- Analyze the event in terms of tangible goods, intangible support services, and the event itself.
- Conduct a SWOT analysis to forecast the market climate/environment in terms of the event.
- Position the sport facility in terms of the event to your primary and secondary markets.
- Segment and target the market based on pertinent market research concepts related to the event – i.e. demographics, psychographics, and geographics.
- Package the event so it becomes attractive to the consumer. This may include special packages with hospitality opportunities or advanced on-sales of tickets.
- Work with the event management and the box office to price the event appropriately.
- Promote the facility first, and the event as an add-on, through advertising, the media, community relations, word-of-mouth, promotional efforts, public relations, and sponsorship partnerships.
- Set up a plan for effective distribution of tickets or other admissions efforts for the event. This includes coordination with the facility box office, and working with the box office to meet the needs of secondary and tertiary box offices such as teams, events themselves, and online ticket agencies (Ticketmaster, Ticketek, StubHub, RazorGator).
- Once marketing efforts have started, and throughout the process of marketing the facility and the event, conduct constant evaluation and collect feedback to maximize marketing efforts.

There are two main issues to remember here. It is important to make sure that although some marketing efforts by sport facilities and sport events may be conducted independent of each other, both parties must be aware of what the other is doing to avoid conflicting information being publicized. Second, if there is conflicting information being publicized, the two parties must get together and ensure that the problem is rectified immediately. Ultimately, both parties want a full facility for the event, and confusion among customers will only lead to problems, and in most cases the facility personnel will be the individuals to deal with the problem as they are the local entity the customer will expect to get answers from, and the facility wants to ensure that their image is not tarnished in the mind of the community.

# Event implementation and activation from the facility viewpoint

Event implementation planning from the sport facility viewpoint starts the day a contract is signed with an event. From that point, the facility management will determine the scope of the work necessary to have the event staged in the facility; tasks that need to be completed will be analyzed and itemized; schedules and timelines will be established; and personnel given responsibilities to complete. The scope of the work to be completed will vary based on the size of the event, the contract stipulations, and the amount of work that can be conducted prior to the day of the event.

The busiest time for sport facility is the 24-hour period that encompasses the ingress, set-up, implementation, activation, breakdown, and egress of the event. This usually includes 12–16 hours or so before the doors open, the entire duration of the event, and usually the four hours after the doors close. During this time, the level of involvement of facility personnel with the event significantly increases. There are also special relationships that need to be addressed, including those with unions and outsourced vendors. In addition, throughout this process, there is a constant need to prepare for unexpected situations that may cause chaos during the event.

## Level of involvement of facility personnel in managing events

Again, the level of involvement in the activation will be strictly stipulated in the contract between the sport facility and the event. The sport facility manager will often have a checklist of responsibilities that need to be accomplished prior to opening the doors. These checklists usually encompass three parts: (1) work breakdown structures, which are itemized by task, personnel, and operational area; (2) an inventory of assignments sequenced in a priority listing to ensure which tasks are accomplished first, and how long it should take to complete the tasks; and (3) an event life cycle, or schedule/timeline of events scripted to the minute. Probably the biggest challenge for the sport facility manager is when there are two events that are back-to-back, and an even greater challenge when there are multiple events in a single day. This means that while one event is breaking down, another is trying to set up. Keeping this phase of event activation organized is crucial to success.

## Working with unions

However, in many facilities, these processes of set-up and breakdown are not totally controlled by the management of the sport facility. Many sport facility managers and event promoters have the additional challenge of coordinating operations within a unionized facility. As such, many of the functions that need to be accomplished as related to daily operations, event set-up, event activation and implementation, and event breakdown are controlled by the union guidelines. This may include number of hours a person can work and require breaks, minimum number of union employees for certain tasks, weigh limitations on lifting and moving, specialists required for certain tasks (examples include forklift drivers, electricians, plumbing, construction, and sound/lighting), and overtime stipulations.

## Working with outsourced service vendors and facility services

In addition, as most events come in from the outside, the management of the sport facility also has a responsibility to act as a liaison between the events and ancillary services. These ancillary services may be managed in-house to the sport facility, or may be outsourced to vendors. One of the biggest challenges for a sport facility manager is maintaining the quality expected of the sport facility, and dealing with the multitude of expectations of an event. Coordination of event needs has to be communicated to various constituencies including concessionaires (especially food service and catering), parking, security, and housekeeping/custodial. In some cases, the sport facility will provide these services for a fee within the event contract. The bigger challenge is when the event has its own ancillary services (such as their own concessionaires and security personnel). The need to communicate and coordinate with the sport facility services to ensure that everyone is on the same page and understands the parameters of his/her responsibilities is vital to the success of both the event and the proper management of the sport facility.

## Preparing for the unexpected

As with any event within a sport facility, problems are bound to occur. The sport facility manager's reaction to these unexpected issues is crucial to the event success, and to keeping the reputation of the sport facility at its highest level. There will be some issues that are beyond the control of the facility manager such as acts of God and Power outages. Others are fully within the grasp of the facility manager and their personnel to deal with. The best piece of advice to provide here is twofold. First, always remember Murphy's Law, which states that 'anything that can go wrong will go wrong with little advanced notice'. Facility managers and personnel who can, on a moment's notice, dissect a problem and solve it without customers knowing that anything happened are high-quality sport facility personnel. The second item to always remember is the 6 Ps of facility and event management: 'prior proper planning prevents poor performance', which is also stated as 'if you fail to plan, then you plan to fail'. Therefore, if you engage in quality and complete planning as far in advance as possible, the likelihood of a problem or poor performance is reduced exponentially.

## Evaluation of events by the facility ownership and management

Once you have supported an event and the event has left the building, it is time to sit back and reflect on the successes and failures of the event. This is usually accomplished through an outcomes assessment process. When the facility event management plan was put together, there should have been goals and objectives created. Those goals and objectives need to be measurable in order to effectively measure them. This will include measurements of the event as a whole, specific task analyses, and performance evaluations of both the facility personnel and of the outside event. These evaluations will result in one of four decisions: (1) have the type of event at the sport facility again in the future with no modifications (which 99.9% of the time does not happen); (2) have the type of event at the sport facility again with enhancements or modifications; (3) have that type of event again, but significant changes need to occur before the event is repeated; or (4) no longer hosting that type of event in the future.

## Chapter review

No matter the size or type, facilities need events – and events need facilities. Sport facilities engage in their own independent sport event planning process as a part of its operations and management. The sport event planning process from the standpoint of the sport facility involves the development of the event from conceptualization through activation to implementation and eventual evaluation as related to the infrastructure and support services offered. This planning process involves setting objectives; developing a conceptualization of how the event will be implemented; creating realistic strategies that can be accomplished within the infrastructure, at a cost that is affordable, and brings a positive image to all constituencies; and finalizing feasibility studies and SWOT analyses. Once accomplished and a decision is made to move forward with an event, the sport facility manager and ownership will enter into negotiations to host an event. This may be accomplished through a series of bid processes or through direct contact with an event promoter. As a part of negotiating contracts, a pro forma budget would be created in advance to anticipate what the general costs of hosting an event will be for the sport facility. Once all terms are agreed upon, contracts are signed and pre-event preparation begins immediately.

A major responsibility of the sport facility manager at this point is ensuring that the event is presented and produced in a professional manner, as the appearance is a reflection of the sport facility in the community, and that the facility is not damaged. This is a challenge at times because event promoters are often only concerned about the event itself and maximizing profits. In addition, as a result of the event, the sport facility manager must often also forge additional relationships with the media and sponsors to ensure that there are no conflicts.

Some of the responsibilities of the sport facility manager at this point include activating the facility's event marketing plan, implementing and activating the event plan (set-up, pre-event, during the event, post-event, and breakdown), determining the level of involvement of facility personnel, coordinating tasks with unions and facility services (both in-house and outsourced), and preparing for any unexpected problems that may occur. Once the event has left the facility, an evaluation process must take place to determine whether to have the event at the sport facility again in the future with no modifications; have the event at the sport facility again with enhancements or modifications; have the event again, but with significant changes; or choose to no longer host the event in the future.

# 12 Risk assessment in facility management

## Chapter outline

## Chapter objectives

Sport facility managers must plan for all types of emergencies that may disrupt normal operations. In order to manage and mitigate potential incidents such as terrorism, hooliganism, and crowd control issues, facility managers need to possess a sound knowledge of risk management practices. Most critical is the process of risk assessment to identify potential facility threats, vulnerabilities, and security countermeasures. Identifying risks helps management prioritize safety and security measures, choose appropriate financing methods, and implement effective risk management plans and policies. This chapter will cover risk management concepts, including risk assessment, risk control strategies, and risk planning options.

## Risk management

Risk is the possibility of loss from a hazard such as personal injury, property damage, or economic loss. Risk cannot be eliminated from the environment, but with careful planning it can be managed. Risk is best understood as the product of the consequence (severity) of an event and the probability (frequency) of the event occurring, also represented as:

Risk $=$ probability $\times$ consequence severity

Risk increases as the consequences and probability of occurrence increase (see Figure 12.1). When risk probability is low and consequence severity is low, the risk level is depicted in Figure 12.1 as RP1, CS1. As the level of risk probability and level of consequence severity increase, the risk level increases to RP2, CS2.

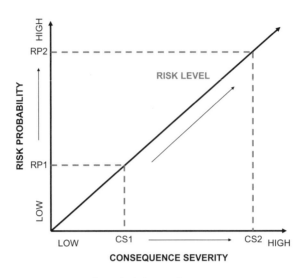

**Figure 12.1** Risk probability and consequence severity.

The three main types of risk are mission (function) risks, asset risks, and security risks. Mission risks prevent an organization from accomplishing its mission. Asset risks may harm an organization's physical assets, and security risks have the potential to harm actual data and people.

Quality risk management practices are imperative to reduce legal exposure, prevent financial and human loss, protect facility assets, ensure business continuity, and minimize damage to the sport organization's reputation. First and foremost, a facility owner or operator must act in a prudent manner. He or she has a duty of care to provide a reasonably safe environment for patrons. In the event of an incident, organizational plans and policies will be reviewed to assess the standard of care provided. Sport managers understand the value of risk management practices but sometimes fail to do the necessary planning. Sport managers should be proactive and implement plans and policies to reduce risk and prevent financial losses. Sport facility managers must develop an effective risk management program to reduce risks and mitigate consequences of incidents.

## Risk assessment

The U.S. Department of Homeland Security identified major sport stadiums and arenas as key assets. Key assets are individual targets whose destruction could create local disaster or damage to the nation's morale or confidence. Sport facility managers face a significant challenge in determining potential threats and must prepare for a wide range of possible incidents. In order to identify potential threats, sport facility managers should conduct a risk assessment of their facility. Risk assessment is the process of evaluating security-related risks from threats to an organization, its assets, or personnel. The assessment process gathers critical information to aid the facility manager in the decision-making process.

### Sport venue risk assessment model

The National Center for Spectator Sports Safety and Security (NCS4) developed a sport venue risk assessment model based on U.S. Department of Homeland Security risk assessment principles (see Figure 12.2).

### Step 1.0: identify the sport event security action team (SESAT)

Step 1.0 involves identifying the sport event security action team (SESAT) or 'Working Group'. These individuals are key players in the security operations and planning at facility sport events. The team is responsible for providing information about the sport facility and surrounding area. SESAT members may include sport facility manager, local police chief, local emergency management director, emergency medical services, fire/HAZMAT, public health, and public relations. A combination of representatives from all agencies ensures multi-discipline cooperation and the ability to gather knowledge and information from different perspectives.

### Step 2.0: characterization of assets

Step 2.0 allows managers to characterize assets. An asset is a person, place, or thing and can be assigned a monetary value. Assets to be assessed include both

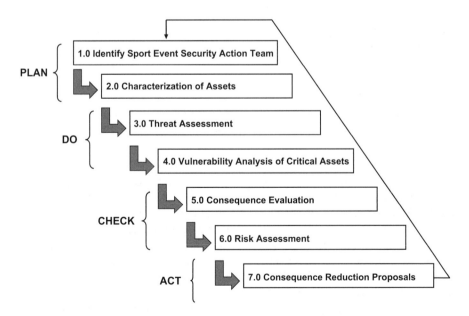

**Figure 12.2** Sport event security assessment model (SESAM).
*Source:* The National Center for Spectator Sports Safety and Security.

facility assets and surrounding area (community) assets. Assets to be protected may include people (i.e. athletes), physical assets (i.e. stadium), information (i.e. electronic data), and processes (i.e. supply chains and procedures). The following outline provides examples of assets under each category:

| Human assets | Physical assets | Information and processes |
| --- | --- | --- |
| Athletes | Facility buildings | Electronic data |
| Spectators | Stadium and contents | Non-electronic data |
| Staff | Command post | Supply chains |
| Contractors | Police department | |
| Visitors | Fire department | |
| Community residents | Hospitals | |
| | Public works | |

### Step 3.0: threat assessment

Step 3.0 identifies potential threats. A threat is a product of intention and capability of an adversary to take action which would be detrimental to an asset. Most relevant threats to the sport industry can be categorized as: terrorism, hooliganism, crowd disorder, vandalism, personal assault, theft, fraud, logistical failure, and inclement weather. Facility mangers must decide what their main threats are at an early stage and determine how vulnerable the organization is to an incident. Terrorism is one of the most common cited risks associated with the security of sport venues. Sporting events are at high risk due to the common elements of large crowds, national/international participants, national/international audience, and the known date, time, and location of events.

There are numerous sport facility threats that need to be assessed, including terrorism, hooliganism, crowd disorder, vandalism, personal assault, theft, fraud, logistical failure, and inclement weather.

### Terrorism

The U.S. Federal Bureau of Investigation (FBI) defines terrorism as the unlawful use of force or violence against persons or property to intimidate or coerce a government, the civilian population or any segment thereof, in furtherance of political or social objectives. A sport stadium or arena is considered a high value terrorist target because of the potentially high casualty rate. There are two primary categories of terrorism: domestic terrorism and international terrorism. Domestic terrorism is the unlawful use, or threatened use, of force or violence by a group or individual based and operating entirely within the home country. International terrorism is the unlawful use of force or violence against persons or property committed by a group or individual who has some connection to a foreign power or whose activities transcend national boundaries (FBI).

## Hooliganism

Hooliganism involves disorderly fans and criminal activity that occurs before and after events. Incidents may be organized (pre-planned) or spontaneous. Spontaneous hooliganism is a low-level disorder in or around stadiums and is not so violent. Organized hooliganism is the more serious form of hooliganism where violence is the norm and people get injured or killed. The primary purpose is to fight with rival supporters, police officials, and cause disruption at the event and destroy property. Hooliganism has been known as the 'English Disease' because of its origin in Britain, but it is prevalent elsewhere in Europe too.

## Crowd disorder

Crowd disorder may involve demonstrations or protests inside and outside the venue, or spectator intrusions onto the playing field. Fan celebrations are sometimes over exuberant resulting in 'rushing the field'. Crowd congestion has been the cause of many horrific incidents in the sporting world. This problem has primarily been the result of the number of fans exceeding venue capacity. Other reasons may include excess alcohol consumption, inadequate access control, or inadequate design of facility structure.

## Vandalism

Webster's dictionary defines vandalism as the willful or malicious destruction or defacement of public or private property. Individuals or groups may cause damage to the stadium or arena building or equipment installed at the venue. Acts of vandalism normally occur during non-event days when security is lenient and can range from graffiti to arson.

## Personal assault

Sport facility managers must plan for all types of assault, including player and fan violence. Assault cases on and off the playing field have become a major problem in recent years, especially at youth sport events. In many previous cases, parents have assaulted one another or an officiating referee.

## Theft

Sport organizations and associations need to plan for financial loss caused by the illegal disappearance of money or inventory. Management, employees, and visitors are all susceptible to theft and/or embezzlement. Many organizations experience 'shrinkage' of inventory that may be attributed to an outsider or a staff member. This reinforces the need for employee background checks or similar policies to prevent hiring dishonest staff.

## Fraud

Ticket scalping and fraudulent tickets are a problem in the sport industry. Entities selling tickets are sometimes selling above face value which is illegal in some parts of the world. Furthermore, fraudulent tickets infiltrating the ticket market have caused serious problems in the past, especially the sale of these tickets through online Internet sites. An example of this problem transpired at the 2007 Liverpool–Milan Union of European Football Associations (UEFA) Champions League Final in Athens, Greece. Many fans with valid tickets were locked out of the Athens Olympic stadium for the final match because fans with counterfeit tickets purchased on the black market had successfully gained entry to the venue.

## Logistical failure

Sport facility event operations may be disrupted due to logistical failure (i.e. loss of power and/or resources). Plans need to be developed to address unplanned events and ensure continuity of operations through back-up systems or event relocation agreements. Mutual aid agreements with a neighboring facility may provide relief in case the unexpected happens and the facility is unable to host an event.

## Inclement weather

Natural disasters or inclement weather can cause chaos to sporting organizations and their events. In fall 2005, Hurricane Katrina, known as the worst natural disaster in U.S history, caused massive devastation to the U.S. Gulf South region and New Orleans area. Many professional and collegiate sport programs in the affected areas suffered major destruction and financial loss. Some programs were eliminated or relocated to another part of the U.S. The New Orleans Saints Football team relocated to Baton Rouge, Louisiana for the 2005 season. The team returned to their home venue in September 2006. It cost an estimated $180 million to renovate the Superdome facility. The sudden onset of storms, tornadoes, or lightening can pose real problems for facility operators resulting in mass evacuations of stadiums and arenas.

Table 12.1 provides examples of sport event incidents from around the world. Besides major threats to sport facilities previously discussed, the facility manager must also identify specific risks associated with the venue and its activities. These may include employee accidents, breach of contract, negligence, product defects, discrimination, environmental hazards (i.e. slippery surfaces), infrastructure hazards (i.e. design defects), programmatic hazards (i.e. supervision and training), emergency care hazards (i.e. appropriate treatment), and transportation hazards (i.e. properly maintained vehicles).

### Step 4.0: vulnerability assessment

Step 4.0 assesses current vulnerabilities. Vulnerability is defined as an exploitable security weakness or deficiency at a facility. Vulnerabilities expose the facility to a threat and eventual loss. A vulnerability assessment identifies weaknesses in physical structures, personnel systems, and processes that may be exploited and is a key component of the risk assessment process. Common vulnerabilities at major sport venues include the lack of emergency preparedness, perimeter control, physical protection systems, access control, credentialing, training, and communication capabilities.

**Table 12.1** Global sport event incidents

1972: At the Munich Olympic Games a group known as Black September took several Israeli athletes hostage.

1984: Violence erupted outside the Tiger Stadium after the Detroit Tigers defeated the San Diego Padres in the World Series.

1985: European Cup soccer match between English and Italian teams at Heysel Stadium, Brussels, Belgium, where 41 persons died when a crowd barrier collapsed under the weight of people trying to escape from the rioting between rival fans.

1988: Nepalese Hailstorm – a violent hailstorm resulted in 93 fatalities and over 100 casualties during a soccer match at the national stadium in Nepal. Hundreds of spectators attempted to exit the open stands when the storm broke, although, the gates were locked and many fans were trampled to death.

1989: San Francisco earthquake during Game 3 of the Major League Baseball (MLB) World Series between San Francisco Giants and Oakland As at Candlestick Park. Stadium remained intact and no fan received serious injuries.

1989: Hillsborough Stadium Disaster resulted in the deaths of 96 people. An influx of thousands of fans through a narrow tunnel into a crowded standing area caused a hug crush at the front of the terrace. People were being pressed up against the fencing by the weight of the crowd and officials were slow to detect the crush and relieve the pressure.

1993: Monica Seles Stabbing – during the second set of a quarterfinal match in Hamburg, Seles was stabbed between the shoulder blades with a 25-cm knife by a fan. Seles was unable to return to playing tennis for 28 months because of the psychological harm.

1993: Twelve thousand fans rushed to the field in Madison at college football game between Michigan and Wisconsin at Camp Randall Stadium. Fans were hurt when chain link and rail fences collapsed under a wave of jubilant Wisconsin fans, who pushed towards the field after the game.

1996: At the Atlanta Olympic Games two people died and 110 injured from a pipe bomb blast at Centennial Olympic Park during an open-air concert.

1996: One hundred died in a crowd crush at a tunnel leading to soccer stadium seating in Guatemala City at a World Cup qualifying match. Too many tickets had been sold.

2000: Thirteen people were trampled to death in a riot at a 2002 FIFA World Cup Qualifying match in Zimbabwe between South Africa and Zimbabwe.

2002: An FBI alert warned that Al-Qaeda's Manual of Afghan Jihad proposed U.S. football stadiums as a possible terrorist target. People with links to terrorist groups were downloading stadium images.

2002: A father and son attacked Major League Baseball (MLB) Kansas City Royals first base coach Tom Gamboa at Comiskey Park.

*Continued*

**Table 12.1** Global sport event incidents—Cont'd

2004: Mayhem broke out at a National Basketball Association (NBA) Indiana-Pacers game in which fans and players exchanged punches in the stands.

2004: A street reveler was killed at a Boston Red Sox celebration when she was hit in the eye by a projectile filled with pepper spray.

2005: UEFA Champions League quarterfinal match between AC Milan and Inter Milan was abandoned after Inter fans threw missiles and flares onto the pitch. One of the flares hit the AC Milan goalkeeper.

2005: Hurricane Katrina caused the displacement of many professional and collegiate sport programs in New Orleans and the Gulf Coast region of the United States.

2005: An Oklahoma University student killed himself by prematurely detonating a bomb strapped to his body outside an 84,000-seater stadium.

2006: The National Football League (NFL) received a radiological dirty bomb threat that indicated several stadiums were subject to attack.

2006: A major on-field altercation between Florida International and Miami University collegiate football players led to the suspension of 31 players. It took two dozen police officers to control the situation.

2006: Ten players were ejected following the NBA New York Knicks–Denver Nuggets brawl.

2007: A police officer was killed in Sicily, Italy, when fans rioted at a Serie A soccer match between Catania and Palermo, leading to the suspension of all league matches and a safety assessment on all stadiums.

2007: UEFA Champions League lockout – many fans with valid tickets were locked out of the Athens Olympic stadium for the final match between Milan and Liverpool. It is alleged that fans with counterfeit tickets purchased on the black market had successfully gained entry to the venue.

2008: At the Summer Olympics in China, Cuban Taekwondo champion Angel Matos kicked a Swedish referee in the head, pushed a judge, and spat on the floor after being disqualified in the Bronze Medal match due to his Kye-shi time-out elapsed.

## Step 5.0: consequence evaluation

Step 5.0 evaluates potential consequences of an incident. This includes analyzing the potential number of people requiring hospitalization, potential loss of life and infrastructure, economic impact, and level of social trauma. There will be consequences to all types of incidents, for example, a slip and fall accident may result in one personal injury and a single lawsuit. Alternatively, a major crowd crushing incident could cause hundreds of casualties, huge financial loss, and a social stigma to the sport team, league, or governing body. Consequence is also referred to as the 'criticality' impact of loss which differs at each facility, the greater the potential for loss or damage to human and physical assets, the higher the impact of loss. Consequence evaluation can be classified as essential (catastrophic loss), critical (serious loss), important (moderate loss), or not important (minor loss). Consequence classifications are discussed later in this chapter.

## Step 6.0: risk assessment

Step 6.0 involves determining the *overall* risk level for the facility. After analyzing the threat, vulnerability, and consequence levels of each potential incident, a total risk level for the facility is determined. The level of risk may be categorized as high, moderate, or low. The facility manager must decide whether the determined risk level is acceptable or not and make necessary adjustments to safety and security policies and procedures.

## Step 7.0: consequence reduction proposals

Step 7.0 is the final stage in the process which offers the opportunity to provide consequence reduction proposals (countermeasure improvements). They are provided to management to enhance decision-making abilities. Possible security measures to reduce risk may include physical security, good personnel practices, and information security. Facility managers should conduct regular reviews of security measures and exercise plans to ensure that they remain accurate and workable. Furthermore, all staff should understand the importance of security and assume responsibility to raise concerns and report observations. Other consequence reduction thoughts include policy review, evacuation routes, traffic rerouting, vendor/usher/volunteer training, stadium lockdown, lighting upgrades, parking restrictions, and emergency lights and signs.

The sport venue risk assessment model is a cyclical model. Assessments must be continuously completed on facilities to ensure adequate plans and security measures are in place and updated over a period of time. A sport facility's threat and vulnerability level may change depending upon circumstances in the country or local community. Evaluations of potential threats and existing vulnerabilities are used to determine what dangers to prepare for, how to address them, and how to prioritize preparedness efforts. Determining which threats are the most dangerous allows managers to decide where they should invest their time and effort in preparedness methods.

# Case study: Sportsplex threat assessment

The XYZ Sportsplex is a multipurpose outdoor facility, hosting soccer, rugby, and athletic events. The facility management team has decided to conduct a threat assessment in order to identify potential risks and gaps in their security operational system.

The XYZ facility management team appointed a sport event security action team (SESAT), representative of police, fire, emergency medical services, public relations, and public health officials. A pre-planning meeting occurred to inform agencies of the situation and their role in the assessment process. Facility and surrounding assets were characterized, and potential facility threats were discussed.

Stadium location and features:

- Built in 1994
- 60,000 club seats plus 1000 box seats
- Located in a major metropolitan city
- Access to major public transportation systems
- Residential and business area surrounding facility
- 16 main entrances with turnstiles
- Parking immediately adjacent to facility
- Press box with CCTV capabilities
- Command Post in Press box area
- Concession deliveries scheduled once a week
- Event security is outsourced to local security provider
- Local police, fire, and emergency medical services available on event day.

Assets:

- Stadium infrastructure
- Human asset (i.e. spectators, athletes, officials)
- Equipment storage area
- Residential and business assets
- Public transportation infrastructure
- Local response agencies.

Threats:

- Active political activists in city area
- Biological agent release in facility
- Active shooter incident
- Suicide bomber
- Fan/player violence
- Tornado warning
- Vehicle Borne Improvised Explosive Device (VBIED).

*Continued*

## Case study: Sportsplex threat assessment—cont'd

The sport event security action team discussed the following issues:

1. The facility was built in 1994 with little focus on security features.
2. The multipurpose facility hosts soccer, rugby, and athletic events.
3. Fan demographics are different as per the sport.
4. Previous incidents of fan violence.
5. Screening of spectators entering facility.
6. Alcohol consumption.
7. Evacuation procedures (full, partial, or shelter-in-place) have not been established.
8. Concern over training requirements for security staff and volunteers.
9. Facility break-ins have occurred in the past year resulting in theft of property.
10. Restricted areas of facility are unsecured during event time.
11. There is inadequate facility lighting at entry gates and in parking areas.
12. Credentialing of athletes, officials, and security staff.
13. Control and monitoring of concession deliveries.
14. Facility equipment and maintenance storage is unsecured and stores chemicals that may be used for terrorist purposes.
15. If an incident were to occur, the possible hospital surge of casualties would overwhelm current emergency medical resources in the city.

After further discussion, the team decided to implement the following countermeasures improvements:

1. Conduct a structural assessment of the facility and reevaluate/redesign security features within the facility.
2. Evaluate threats and risks for each event as they may differ.
3. Utilize security technologies, i.e. text messaging system, to identify troublemakers.
4. Develop emergency response and evacuation plans.
5. Practice evacuation drills to test operations.
6. Require all staff to complete security training, i.e. terrorism awareness training.
7. Ensure proper and consistent screening procedures.
8. Schedule concession deliveries when security officials are present.
9. Ensure all restricted areas (e.g. press room, storage space) are secured at all times.
10. Establish mutual aid agreements with response agencies and ensure alternative playing sites for continuity of operations.

### Suggested discussion topics

1. Discuss the risk assessment process. Are there any other potential threats or vulnerabilities to the XYZ Sportsplex? What additional countermeasure improvements would you recommend?
2. Review the 1996 Atlanta Centennial Olympic Park bombing incident. Discuss the event operations and response strategies.

# Risk evaluation, control, and response

## Risk probability, consequence severity, and financial loss

Risk probability refers to how frequent a risk may occur. How frequent a risk may occur is dependent on the current vulnerability levels. If existing countermeasures are effectively protecting the facility from all threats, the vulnerability will be low and in essence the risk probability will be low. However, the reverse is also true. If current facility vulnerabilities are not protected the facility is exposed to a high potential for loss. Sport organizations can classify the probability (frequency) of risks into four categories – extremely high, high, medium, and low.

The consequence severity of a threat and eventual loss must also be evaluated. The manager must consider both the severity and financial impact on the sport program. Each threat must be evaluated individually and the impact it will have on the facility or organization to perform its mission. Consequence severity (impact of loss) can be classified into four categories – essential, critical, important, and not important. Subsequently, the resulting financial loss is equated as catastrophic, serious, moderate, or minor:

- Essential: a successful threat would cause complete loss of facility operations, resulting in a *catastrophic* loss.
- Critical: a successful threat would cause severe impairment to facility operations, resulting in a *serious* loss.
- Important: a successful threat would cause noticeable impact on facility operations, resulting in a *moderate* loss.
- Not Important: a successful threat would not cause a noticeable impact on facility operations, resulting in a *minor* loss.

A catastrophic loss is one that requires major tax or fee increases; or in private industry it may result in bankruptcy. Critical loss would require major service cutbacks, facility closings, and/or program cancellations. Moderate loss indicates temporary service reductions or minor fee increases. Minor losses can be absorbed by the organization with current operating revenues and no program reductions. In order to aid sport facility managers in risk management decisions, consequence and probability data is presented in a risk logic matrix (see Figure 12.3).

## Risk control and response strategies

Evaluating risk and potential loss assists the facility manager's decision-making process to reduce, re-assign, transfer, or accept identified risks. An acceptable level of risk is usually determined by the asset manager (facility manager) or owner.

### Risk avoidance

Severe risks with the potential for a high degree of loss and which may occur frequently should be avoided. These risks need to be identified prior to an

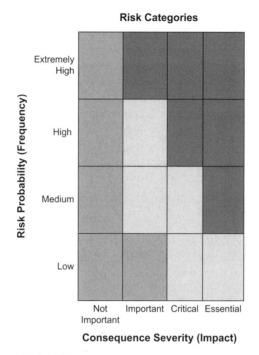

**Risk Categories**

Risk Management Guideline

These risks are very high and measures should be taken to eliminate them or transfer liability to a third party.

These risks are moderate and management may determine to address them to reduce the level of risk.

These risks are low and management may decide to retain and reduce the level of risk.

**Figure 12.3** Risk logic matrix.
*Source:* The Risk Logic Matrix was adapted from: Long, L.E., & Renfrow, N.A. (1999). A new automation tool for risk assessment. 15th Annual NDIA Security Technology Symposium. Session: Risk and Threat Assessment Techniques.

incident and avoided completely. Risks that are categorized in the red zone in Figure 12.3 should be avoided, or significant safety and security upgrades implemented to reduce risk to the greatest degree possible. For example, if a sport activity or event has a history of potentially fatal accidents or crowd management problems, the facility manager may wish to eliminate the activity or cancel the event.

## Risk reduction

Facility managers can reduce risk by developing and exercising plans and policies and ensuring staff are adequately trained in their respective roles. Risks that are categorized in the yellow zone in Figure 12.2 may be reduced. For example, if a facility manager has experienced acts of hooliganism at the facility it would be prudent for the manager to identify the culprits and ban them from future events to prevent future incidents. Alternatively, the manager may wish to implement buffer zones between rival fans to prevent confrontational issues. Sport facility managers can also reduce likelihood of threats by improving physical protection systems such as implementing access controls, closed-circuit television (CCTV) security cameras, venue lighting, personnel background checks, credentialing measures, interoperable communication networks, and developing emergency response and evacuation plans. Further safety and security measures to reduce threats and risks are presented in Chapter 13.

## Risk transfer

Average frequency and moderate severity risks can be transferred to someone who's willing to assume the risk. Risks categorized in the yellow zone in Figure 12.3 may be transferred to a third party. Commonly used transfer methods are insurance, independent contractors, liability waivers, and indemnification clauses. The two main types of insurance available to the facility manager are personal injury liability insurance and property insurance.

Personal liability coverage is needed in the event a facility patron is injured due to the action(s) or inaction(s) of the facility manager or owner. For example, a spectator is injured by a stray baseball that traveled through an undiscovered hole in the protective barrier around the field. This incident may result in a lawsuit in order for the victim to recover damages for direct injuries, and pain and suffering. Property insurance is important when considering protecting the facility and its contents from damage or destruction. There are two types of property insurance – (1) named perils and (2) all-risk insurance policy. Named perils insurance will cover only what is stated in the policy. Most commonly named perils are natural occurrences such as fire, hail, explosion, lightning, malicious mischief, tornadoes, vandalism, and smoke.

Other methods of risk transfer include waivers, independent contractors, indemnification clauses, and leasing or rental agreements. A waiver transfers risk from the facility management team or owner to the person signing the document. There are several principles to be followed for a waiver to be valid. The waiver must be voluntarily signed by an adult. The waiver must be explicit and in clear language, stating that the waiver is for the negligence of the provider and acknowledgement of inherent risks of an activity. The participant must be aware that they are signing a waiver; however, the waiver cannot release the facility management team from intentional, or willful and wanton acts, or gross negligence.

Some sport programs may wish to use independent contractors to conduct an activity or provide a service. Independent contractors can be individuals or organizations. Employees such as event staff and security officials can be utilized to transfer risk. These individuals are responsible for the liability of their services

Table 12.2 Risk control and response matrix

| Threat/risk identification | Risk probability | Consequence severity | Risk control | Financing option |
|---|---|---|---|---|
| 1 Vandalism | Medium | Not important (minor loss) | Reduce | Retention (current expensing) |
| 2 Terrorist attack | Low | Essential (catastrophic loss) | Avoid/ transfer | Transfer (insurance) |
| 3 Theft/ embezzlement | Medium | Critical/important (serious/ moderate loss) | Reduce | Retention (current expensing) |
| 4 Spectator or participant injury | Medium | Either (dependent upon extent) | Reduce/ transfer | Transfer (insurance, waiver) |

and for their own insurance coverage. The sport program may contract with private organizations to provide a program or service. For example, an organization may wish to contract with firms for concessions, facility maintenance, or security. It is important to note that when selecting an independent contractor facility management must take reasonable care to select a competent person or organization that possesses the necessary credentials. Sometimes facility management will lease or rent the facility for other events such as concerts. In this case, facility management should include an indemnification clause (sometimes referred to as hold harmless agreements) to allow the facility to be compensated by entities leasing or renting the facility, if damage occurs during the event.

## Risk retention

Facility managers may decide to retain the risk and assume responsibility. Risks categorized in the green zone in Figure 12.2 may be retained. Facilities choosing to retain the risks become financially responsible for any injuries or financial risks associated with an incident. Risk financing strategies for retention may include current expensing, unfunded reserves, funded reserves, borrowing, self-insurance, and joint pooling. In a current expensing (or 'pay-as-you-go') system the organization pays for losses as they arise out of their budget. The unfunded reserve method deducts potential losses from a bookkeeping account. This reminds management of potential future expenses for financial losses. A funded reserve is money set aside in the organizations budget to pay for future losses. Borrowing is an option for the organization when it does not have sufficient resources to pay for losses. The organization can borrow from internal or external sources, although it is often difficult to borrow from external sources to pay for a loss. Table 12.2 illustrates examples of facility risks, probability of occurrence, consequence severity, risk control response, and possible financing options.

## Chapter review

Risk is the possibility of loss from a threat. Risk increases as the consequences and probability of occurrence increase. Risk management is important to facility managers in order to meet legal obligations, prevent financial loss, and ensure business continuity. An all-hazards approach must be employed when assessing potential threats and risks (including man-made and natural events, i.e. terrorism, crowd management, natural disasters, theft, and fraud). Risk assessment involves the following key steps: identify SESAT, characterize assets, assess threats, assess vulnerabilities, evaluate consequences, analyze risk levels, and provide countermeasure improvements. Countermeasures are used to reduce the probability and consequence severity of a threat/risk. The facility manager can control risk through several strategies. They can avoid, transfer, reduce, or retain identified risks.

# 13 Security planning for facility management

## Chapter outline

## Chapter objectives

This chapter will address global security issues involved in protecting sport facilities from threats and risks identified in Chapter 12. Security best practices, systems, and planning options are provided to equip the twenty-first century sport manager with an all-hazards approach to facility security planning. Security management and planning involves the development of plans, policies, and protective measures. Protective security measures addressed in this chapter include venue design and safety, physical protection systems, perimeter control, access control and credentialing, communications, security personnel, training and exercise, crowd management, emergency management, and business continuity.

## Security management

Security management systems are employed to reduce risk and exposure to facility vulnerabilities. A facility manager is expected to act in a reasonably prudent manner regarding the safety and security of their facility, this includes (1) keeping the facility in safe repair, (2) inspecting the facility to discover hazards, (3) removing hazards or warning of their presence, (4) protecting patrons from foreseeable dangers, and (5) conducting facility operations with reasonable care for the safety of all. Sport facility managers reduce liability exposure by successfully managing risks and foreseeable actions that lead to injuries.

Security management requires the coordination and collaboration of many individuals, government agencies, and private contractors. Figure 13.1 illustrates the multiple stakeholders involved in providing a safe and secure sporting environment. Sport organizations should designate a Security

**Figure 13.1** Sport event security stakeholders.

Director to oversee security operations and coordinate security efforts with stakeholders. The security director forms a leadership (planning) team with representatives from the stakeholder groups, known as a Sport Event Security Action Team (SESAT). The facility manager, owner, or operator is normally responsible for the safety and security management of events. However, they may rely upon other agencies, locally and regionally, in the case of a major incident. Regardless of the type and criticality of an incident, the sport organization should have established a working relationship with external agencies. Multi-agency collaboration ensures effective planning, response, and recovery efforts.

Planning is a critical component to the overall security management system. In order to effectively plan, the sport manager must first identify facility risks, threats, and vulnerabilities. Addressing specific threats ensures that appropriate planning measures, such as relevant policies, procedures, and security measures, are implemented. To reduce risk, the sport facility should develop a list of essential venue safety and security policies, i.e. alcohol policy, fan conduct policy, search policy, etc. A facility emergency response plan should be developed with annexes for game day operations, evacuation procedures, incident response, and business continuity and recovery. A game day operations plan provides the general administrative, operational, and security strategies for game day. A game day operations plan may include the following items:

- Ticketing policies
- Ticket samples
- Seating policies
- Radio communications
- TV broadcast information
- Stadium staff directory
- Gate designations
- Parking information
- Parking maps
- Parking pass samples
- Traffic flow information
- Credential samples
- Tailgating policies
- Severe weather plans
- General information policies, i.e. admission, prohibited behavior/items, alcohol, cameras, first aid, disability accommodations, guest services, lost and found.

To successfully implement security plans, facility managers, event staff, security personnel, and emergency response personnel require adequate training in their respective roles and responsibilities. Crowd control methods, spectator safety, and terrorism awareness training are essential for security staff to detect suspicious behavior or criminal activity. Training should be conducted on a continuous basis and refresher courses utilized to emphasize individual tasks. Beyond basic training, security stakeholders should conduct some type of exercise to test security plans for effectiveness and to identify resource gaps.

Post 9/11, U.S. professional sport organizations enhanced security efforts. The National Football League (NFL), National Basketball Association (NBA), and National Hockey League (NHL) developed a best practices guide of recommended protective security measures to assist league members. Security management was also upgraded at the collegiate level. The National Collegiate Athletic Association (NCAA) issued a Security-Planning Options guide for American college athletic programs. The NCAA is a voluntary organization that governs American college and university athletic programs. The NCAA National Office staff consulted with Stadium Managers and law-enforcement representatives from across the United States to compile the list of options to assist NCAA members with security planning. Planning options included items related to deliveries, facility personnel, coordination with public safety agencies, lockdown, metal detectors, parking and perimeter, prohibited items, and publicity. A 38-item Game Day Security Operations Checklist of pre-event, game time, and post-event considerations is presented in Table 13.1.

**Table 13.1** Game Day Security Operations Checklist

Pre-event considerations
   write a formal risk management plan
   implement a pre-event training program for all event staff
   be aware of nearby dangerous/explosive sites
   be aware of the quantities of antidotes within the region
   coordinate your plans with the local and state police
   conduct background checks on all employees including students and seasonal
   employees
   verify that first responders have a small stockpile of drugs and medications for rapid
   response use should a biological weapon be released
   utilize 24-hour live security teams in concert with a sophisticated surveillance system
   lock down the venue prior to the event
   prohibit all concession deliveries 90 minutes prior to the event
   utilize bomb-sniffing dogs
   test air quality prior to the event
   issue holographic personal identification cards for all media
   purchase and install clear refuse bags and receptacles
   escort all cleaning crews

Game time considerations
   secure no-fly zones over the venue
   patrol air space above the venue, parking lots, and adjacent access roads
   secure the services of a mobile emergency room to be on site
   utilize portable biological detection equipment
   use undercover surveillance teams/individuals
   utilize one crowd observer for every 250 spectators
   utilize radio-equipped security personnel in parking lots and key access points
   have key personnel wear inexpensive hazmat smart strips that detect the presence of
   nerve agents, cyanide, and other chemicals
   invoke periodic broadcasts detailing security practices and restricted areas within the
   facility
   implement electronic scanning of all tickets and match these records with detailed
   records of all your season ticket holders
   frisk/wand every spectator
   ban all carry-ins and backpacks
   prohibit re-entry by spectators

Post-event and general considerations
   implement a formal post-event debriefing of all personnel
   vary your security practices so as not to create a pattern in your system

*Adapted from Pantera, M.J., et al. (2003). Best practices for game day security at athletic & sport venues. The Sport Journal, 6 (4). [On-Line]. Available from: http://www.thesportjournal.org/2003Journal/Vol6-No4/security.asp.*

## Lessons learned from the United Kingdom

---

### The Hillsborough disaster

Britain is a pioneer in the implementation of security standards through government regulation. Hooliganism in British football (soccer) has been well documented for many years and legislative and administrative changes introduced by the English Football Association (FA) and British government have helped control the problem.

The Hillsborough disaster was the worst stadium disaster in English football history, resulting in the deaths of 96 people. On April 15, 1989, the FA Cup semi-final match between Liverpool FC and Nottingham Forest at the Hillsborough football stadium was abandoned six minutes into the game due to a human stampede in the Leppings Lane end of the stadium holding Liverpool fans.

Go to the online supplements for the text to review the history of this disaster from pre-match through kick-off to the aftermath of the human crush; and an analysis of the key issues that led to this disaster.

---

Since the 1989 Hillsborough disaster and the 1990 Taylor Report on football stadium safety, new legislation has been introduced and new safety and security measures imposed on football teams. The Football Disorder Act (1989), Football Spectators Act (1989), Football Offenses Act (1991), Football Act (1999), Football Disorder Act (2000), and Football Disorder Bill (2001) were enacted by government. These pieces of legislation prohibited hooliganism; categorized the different offenses that a person would be charged with; covered both domestic and international terrorist threats to sport stadiums; and assured that individuals who were banned would be prevented from attending matches inside and outside Britain. Additionally, the Football Intelligence Unit was created to collect and disseminate information and intelligence about domestic and international issues that occur at or near sport stadiums. Football Intelligence Officers are assigned to each football team to gather intelligence and identify potential troublemakers or banned offenders from entering the stadium.

Most significant, under new safety legislation each football club is required to hold a stadium 'Safety Certificate'. The government produced and published a set of safety requirements in the 'Guide to Safety at Sports Grounds' (2008) for every club playing in the top four divisions in England. The local government authority (municipality) is responsible for issuing the Safety Certificate and ensuring that the stadium complies with the requirements issued in the safety guide. In addition, each football club is designated a Safety Officer to assist facility management with safety strategies on match day. Safety Officers are responsible for the recruitment and training of all stewards. The Safety Officers formed the Football Safety Officers Association to share best practices (www.fsoa.org.uk). Specific safety and security measures utilized in the English Football system are the following:

- Football clubs ban any person who is arrested or ejected from a stadium.
- Football clubs operate travel clubs for away matches and only issues tickets to supporters who are members.
- Each club in the top two divisions (English Premier League and Division I) is required to restrict admission of spectators to seated accommodation only.
- National legislation introduced by government outlaws: (1) the possession of alcohol on trains and/or coaches when traveling to a match, (2) entering a stadium drunk or in possession of alcohol, (3) throwing objects towards pitch or spectators, (4) entering the pitch, (5) indecent or racist chanting, and (6) ticket touting.
- Any person convicted of a football-related offense receives a banning order preventing the offender from attending matches at home or abroad for three years. Failure to obey this ban is a criminal offense.

## Protective measures

Facility managers must have adequate security measures in place to protect spectators, athletes, officials, and staff. Protective security measures reduce facility vulnerabilities and enhance preparedness among supporting agencies to respond to and resolve potential incidents. According to the U.S. Department of Homeland Security, protective measures are designed to meet one or more of the following objectives:

- Devalue: lower the value of a facility to terrorists, criminal activity, or crowd management issues, thereby making the facility less attractive as a target for illegal or unruly behavior.
- Detect: Spot the presence of suspicious people, unruly fan behavior, and/or dangerous materials, and provide responders with information needed to execute an effective response.
- Deter: Make the facility difficult to attack or less vulnerable to fan/player violence and criminal activity.
- Defend: Respond to an attack, protect the facility, and mitigate any effects of an incident.

Some protective measures are designed to be implemented on a permanent basis to serve as routine protection for a facility and are sometimes referred to as 'baseline' security measures. Other measures may be enforced as security threats arise. To establish a facility's baseline security measures, the facility manager must assess facility threats and vulnerabilities (as discussed in Chapter 12). Specific facility threats, vulnerabilities, and organizational policies provide a foundation for development of baseline protective security measures. Sport organizations should consider protective security measures in the following key areas:

- Venue design and safety
- Physical protection systems

- Perimeter control
- Access control and credentialing
- Communications
- Security personnel
- Training and exercise
- Crowd management
- Emergency management
- Business continuity.

## Venue safety and design

Venue design and safety features are pre-determined to an extent by occupational safety and health administration regulations, environmental regulations, fire codes, seismic safety codes, life safety codes, transportation regulations, and zoning regulations. However, security trends in the twenty-first century are guiding the work of sport architects and engineers in developing the next generation of facilities. Designers are now working in collaboration with security professionals and first responders during the design process.

Designers can control stadium accessibility by restricting the size of grounds surrounding the stadium to provide limited space for loitering, less space for event staff to patrol, and limit vehicle access to the stadium. Securing the facility perimeter can be established by installing vertical posts (sometimes called bollards) around the stadium to create a physical separation. Parking garages should not be attached to a facility and separated by as much distance as possible so that terrorists cannot park a vehicle loaded with explosives. The planning committee for Liverpool Football Club's new proposed stadium at Stanley Park insisted planners design the stadium to minimize openness to terrorist attacks, specifically suicide bombers. Design standards set forth by the Association of Chief Police Officers (ACPO) set parameters for construction and design of grounds to reduce crowd management issues and the likelihood of attacks. The planning scheme includes a high-level CCTV system, fully equipped control room, and its own on-site mini-prison (or custody suite).

Most stadiums built today include a modern command center (also known as a Command Post) with communication capabilities for security forces to monitor events inside and outside of the stadium. The command center controls the security functions of the sport event. The center is normally staffed with the security director, facility management (operations and security), fire, police, emergency medical services, private security, and media representatives. Copies of security plans, phone directories, and backup technology systems are normally located at this facility in case of an incident. The center has reliable communications and the capability to access the facility's public announcement system, fire alarm system, voice activation system, turnstile system, and door access control system.

# Scottish Football Association

## Stadium architecture and design safety features

- All seated grounds in respect of Safety Certificate requirements under the Safety at Sports Grounds Act 1975.
- Adequate provision of turnstiles and exit gates.
- Professional stewarding.
- Spacious internal and external concourses.
- Provision of dedicated parking areas for both 'home' and 'away' fans.
- Provision of parking areas for Emergency Service vehicles.
- Internal and external CCTV systems linked to modern police control room.
- High quality public address systems and fire alarm systems.
- Modern public address, steward's control and medical control rooms in close proximity to each other.
- Good internal and external lighting.
- No smoking policies in vulnerable areas.
- Electronic turnstile counting mechanisms.
- Provision of retractable tunnel to protect players and officials from injury by thrown objects.
- Wide, hard surface tracks around the perimeter of playing surfaces onto which fans can be evacuated in emergency situations.
- Easily opened emergency gates giving access from stands and terraces towards the playing areas.
- An absence of fencing between stands/terraces and the playing areas.
- Provision of sand buckets to quickly douse any flares or fireworks that are thrown.
- Provision of electronic scoreboards and jumbotron screens which are capable of displaying written text messages.
- Tried and tested police and stewarding operations.
- Passageway patrols by stewards.
- Substantial season ticket holdings, which means fans sit beside each other at every match and therefore settle into patterns of behavior which are acceptable to each other and the authorities.
- Policies that ensure matches are all-ticket, minimizing queues and crushing.
- The employment of Safety Officers who are empowered to take action against fans whose behavior is unacceptable.
- The employment of Ticket Center Managers and Stadium Managers who ensure that ticketing and maintenance matters are properly supervised.
- The employment of Health and Safety Managers to ensure that all procedures adopted by clubs are safety based.
- Policies of full cooperation with the police, fire, and building control authorities who regularly undertake 'spot' checks within grounds.
- Pre-match inspections 24 hours before matches.
- Pre-match meetings 48 hours before matches.
- Provision of external bins to encourage the disposal of bottles, cans, etc.
- Provision of doctors, paramedics, and first aid personnel at matches.
- Provision of first aid stations within grounds.

*Continued*

---

## Scottish Football Association—cont'd

- Provision of televisions on internal concourses, which broadcast games 'live' and therefore encourage an even distribution of fans to fast food outlets throughout matches.
- Application of plastic seals to exit gates which, without impeding emergency opening, deter unauthorized openings.
- Adoption of Ground Regulations, Safety Policies and Emergency Action Plans.
- The attendance at matches on standby of Scottish Power personnel and Lift Engineers in the event of system failures.

*Sources:* Football Safety Officers Association Scotland. Football Safety Design. Available at: http://www.footballsafety.com/design.htm.

---

### Physical protection systems

Physical security is imperative in preventing a multitude of threats and vulnerabilities. An annual structural inspection of the facility will determine current structural damage or future problems. Alarms and card-access entry points can restrict parts of the building to unauthorized persons. Stadiums design restricted areas to protect food sources, communication centers, and public media outlets. Facility managers can protect restricted areas by requiring a magnetic-striped key for entrance to ensure access to the appropriate key holder. The stadium and press box should be equipped with an Integrated Security Management System (ISMS) consisting of CCTV. Cameras may be utilized to monitor the sport facility including perimeter, concourses, playing field, and concession areas. Facility managers should monitor: (1) stadium entrances and exits, (2) spectators and employees for suspicious behavior, and (3) individuals standing in prohibited areas, taking pictures of the stadium without consent, drawing maps, or appearing in large groups outside the stadium during the event.

Sufficient lighting at gate areas is needed for adequate searching of bags and persons. Ventilation systems should be secured and capable of blocking hazardous agents such as anthrax. Air quality monitors can detect changes in air quality and identify biohazards and radioactive materials. Additionally, a mobile command center may be utilized. In England, a mobile command center known as the 'Hoolivan' is located at high-profile football matches. The Hoolivan is a vehicle equipped with CCTV for surveillance operations and maintains radio contact with officers inside and outside the stadium.

### Perimeter control

Establishing perimeter control measures helps prevent illegal entry into premises, or into the sport facility. A secure outer perimeter of at least 100 feet should be established around the facility. This normally encompasses the facility property boundary, including parking areas. Roads and streets adjacent to the facility should be blocked off when feasible. Security forces may utilize barricades, such as jersey barriers, concrete planters, or bollards. Clear ingress and egress routes are established for emergency medical services, fire, and police in case of emergencies. An inner perimeter should be established around the stadium with limited and controlled pedestrian access points 12 hours prior to an event. The stadium should be locked down 24 hours prior to an event and allow only controlled access during this period. During events, security personnel are assigned to guard vulnerable systems. All buildings located within 100 feet of the stadium should be inspected prior to the event and secured by lock or security guard. Vehicles should be requested to park more than 100 feet away from the stadium. If a vehicle needs to be parked close to the stadium, permission must be granted ahead of time by stadium officials.

### Access control and credentialing

Access control and credentialing measures are enforced to prevent unwanted persons or vehicles from entering the facility premises or restricted areas of the facility building. Access control considerations include prohibiting coolers, bags, large backpacks, containers, weapons, and outside food or beverages, except as required for medical or family needs. Some stadiums implement a no re-entry policy, except for medical emergencies. Event staff can divide spectators into two groups for stadium entry: one with bags and other items, and the other with no items. This allows for better traffic flow into the stadium. The use of portable metal detectors and standard pat-down procedures at stadium entry gates has been employed at many major sport stadiums.

Technology-based security solutions include electronic scanning of tickets or contact cards capable of capturing season ticket holder information. Several U.K. football teams (i.e. Manchester City, Wigan Athletic, Fulham, and Rangers F.C.) use a 'SmartCard' system for fans. Instead of paper-based tickets, fans are issued a plastic card containing a microchip stored with ticket and gate access information. Fans scan their card at turnstile locations at their designated gate entrances. This method of entry provides reliable information to the facility manager as spectator data is collected and analyzed in real-time. For security purposes, it minimizes queues and reveals exactly who is sitting where. The SmartCard technology is also used for marketing and customer-relationship management purposes. These cards provide consumer profiles and insight into consumer buying habits; this enables the football club to target specific audiences for matches. The SmartCard can be charged with electronic credit, allowing fans to buy match tickets, refreshments, and merchandise.

Additional technology-based security tools, such as FaceTrac and Biometric systems, are used to identify fans, run database searches, and send images to security personnel on the ground. Facial recognition technology was used by the NFL in 2001 for Super Bowl XXXV in Tampa, Florida, and at each subsequent Super Bowl. This technology locates faces, constructs facial print templates, and matches facial images with those previously stored in a database, allowing law enforcement to identify suspicious facial photos. Biometric systems are suitable for use in protecting facilities with a high-risk rating (i.e. government) or high-risk areas within a sport facility, such as a command center. During the 2006 FIFA World Cup in Germany, organizers recorded the biometric facial data of known hooligans and suspected troublemakers.

Credentialing considerations include conducting background checks on all vendors, employees, contractors, and volunteers. Credential systems can be simplified by indicating zone access and color code by game function. Management should issue photo credentials to all regular game-day employees, staff, media, vendors, and subcontractors and require those designated to pick up their credentials to do so in person, using government-issued photo ID. Management should schedule limited daily or weekly delivery times for vendors, and ensure food dispensing and handling procedures are secure to prevent contamination. Credentials need to be worn at all times and clearly displayed. Credentials will include name, photograph, personal identity number, and areas of authorized access. Additionally, a record of persons issued credentials should be maintained for control purposes.

---

## FIFA Confederations Cup South Africa 2009

## Stadium entry policy

### 3. Entry to the stadium

3.1 Entry into a stadium, which includes areas under the control of the FIFA Confederations Cup Authorities on a match day ('Stadium'), will be authorized on a match day only upon the presentation of a valid ticket by each person seeking to gain entrance, regardless of his age.

3.2 Each ticket evidences permission to enter the stadium on a match day which can, at any time, be revoked for good reason by FIFA, the 2010 FIFA World Cup™ Organising Committee South Africa ('LOC'), the 2010 FIFA World Cup™ Ticketing Centre ('FWCTC'), the FIFA Ticketing Office ('FTO'), the stadium management and/or the South African governmental entity(ies) responsible for safety and security in connection with the matches, and their respective employees, volunteers, agents, representatives, officers, and directors (together the 'FIFA Confederations Cup Authorities').

*Continued*

## FIFA Confederations Cup South Africa 2009—cont'd

3.3 All Ticket Holders must comply with the applicable safety and security rules adopted by the FIFA Confederations Cup Authorities for the stadiums on match days. These rules are summarized in the stadium code of conduct, which is published and available from the sources identified in Clause 11.2 below ('Stadium Code of Conduct'). Examples of items that may be prohibited by the FIFA Confederations Cup Authorities at any time in accordance with the Stadium Code of Conduct include, without limitation, weapons of any kind or anything that could be used as a weapon, fireworks, flares, or other pyrotechnics, commercial materials or similar items which could infringe any rights of FIFA for the Event, and other objects which could compromise public safety and/or harm the reputation of the FIFA Confederations Cup South Africa as reflected in the Stadium Code of Conduct. The Stadium Code of Conduct should be read carefully before attendance at a match.

3.4 The FIFA Confederations Cup Authorities will be entitled to carry out checks on any Ticket Holder. Tickets may be rendered null and void, and entrance into a stadium can be refused for any person who, or a Ticket Holder can be refused admission or ejected from the stadium if such Ticket Holder:

(a)   is noticeably under the influence of alcohol, narcotics or any behavior-modifying substance;

(b)   is behaving, or is likely to behave, violently, harmfully or in a manner liable to disrupt public order or cause a nuisance to other Ticket Holders; or

(c)   has failed to comply with the terms of these GTCs, the Stadium Code of Conduct or all sales regulations applicable to the Ticket Applicant outlined in the Ticket Application Form (the 'Sales Regulations'), which are all available through the sources identified in Clause 11.2 below or any relevant laws or by laws.

3.5 Individuals who have been banned from attending football matches by competent authorities or sport governing bodies in any country, or who are considered as a security risk, are prohibited from receiving tickets and from entering or remaining in the stadium.

3.6 Ticket Holders leaving the stadium will not be re-admitted unless otherwise approved by FIFA.

3.7 Each ticket is numbered to identify a specific seat. Each Ticket Holder must sit in the seat allocated to the respective ticket. The FIFA Confederations Cup Authorities reserve the right to substitute the seat identified on the ticket with another seat, if appropriate for security reasons, without compensation to the Ticket Holder.

*Continued*

---

## FIFA Confederations Cup South Africa 2009—cont'd

3.8 The FIFA Confederations Cup Authorities cannot guarantee:

(a)   that a specific player will participate in a match;
(b)   the length of time that any match will be played; or
(c)   that the Ticket Holder will have uninterrupted and/or uninhibited view of the match from the seat provided. The FIFA Confederations Cup Authorities will use reasonable efforts to identify obstructed view seats prior to purchase.

*Source*: Ticket General Terms and Conditions. FIFA Confederations Cup South Africa 2009. Available at: http://www.fifa.com/confederationscup/organisation/ticketing/termsandconditions.html.

---

### Communications

The sport organization should have an interoperable communication system in place with access to the stadium's command center. An efficient interoperable communication system may require hand-held portable multi-channeled radios, cell phones, pagers, or a combination thereof. All responding agencies must be able to communicate with each other on the same network to coordinate security management, response, and recovery efforts. Security personnel on the ground must have the capability to report problems to authorities at the center and receive relevant intelligence on disruptive behavior or suspicious activity. The NFL implemented a new text-messaging system that allows fans to report drunk or disorderly fans without confronting them. Fans send a quick text message to the stadium's command center for security to respond. Teams are able to compile databases of complaints and how they were resolved, as well as track areas in a stadium where complaints are frequent. By 2009, all NFL stadiums will have a text message line or telephone hotline installed.

In addition to possessing adequate communication equipment and systems, the sport organization should have a risk communication system in place that is operational and ready to be activated. Successful risk communication reduces the length, strength, and frequencies of controversies resulting from an incident. Sport organizations should plan for a press conference post incident with key representatives including emergency services. Risk communication needs to take into consideration the target audience, including cultural background, shared interests, concerns and fears, and social attitudes.

### Security personnel

The sport organization should appoint an experienced employee as the Security Director to deal with daily security matters and emergency incidents.

A successful security staff plan has properly screened, trained, and educated staff. An employee background screening program for all facility personnel and contracted staff should be established. All personnel and contracted staff working at events should be trained in appropriate standard operating procedures (SOPs) for emergency response, security awareness (i.e. suspicious persons and packages), and notification protocols. Recommended training for security personnel includes training in first aid, CPR, crowd management, drug awareness, emergency response, and defensive techniques. The sport organization may utilize outsourced personnel in the form of contractors, vendors, or security forces.

There should be adequate supervision and oversight of facility employees. The number of security personnel needed to staff an event or facility may vary according to the type of event, stadium capacity, or relevant intelligence. The National Fire Protection Association (NFPA) industry standards for fire prevention and safety apply to crowd-management principles. There should be one trained crowd-management professional for every 250 spectators in any facility with a capacity of over 250 people. It is important that security personnel are visible during the event. Visible security forces may deter illegal activity or unruly fan behavior; additionally, personnel are easily accessible to spectators in case of an emergency. Major sport events, such as the Olympics and FIFA World Cup, require a very large workforce. The FIFA 2006 World Cup in Germany employed 52,000 staff to oversee the security program, including 30,000 federal police officers, 15,000 private sector security professionals, and 7000 armed forces personnel.

## Training and exercise

Staff training is a key component in protecting critical infrastructures such as sport stadiums and arenas. The three main levels of staff training are (1) multi-agency team training, (2) supervisory training, and (3) event staff training. Multi-agency team training is conducted with the SESAT (leadership/planning team). Supervisory training is conducted with main supervisors in charge of event staff and security personnel. Event staff training is conducted for all other venue staff (full-time, part-time, or volunteer). These may include parking attendants, contracted security personnel, gate security, ticket takers, ushers, concessionaires, vendors, and maintenance workers. Training should be conducted at routine times, for example, pre-season, during season, and post-season. Written responsibilities and duties for each position should be provided.

Sport organizations should conduct exercises to test plans and promote awareness of staff roles and responsibilities during an incident scenario. There are seven types of exercises defined by the U.S. Department of Homeland Security Exercise and Evaluation Program (HSEEP), and these are considered either discussion-based or operations-based. Discussion-based exercises familiarize participants with current plans and policies, or may be used to develop new plans and policies. Types of discussion-based exercises include seminars, workshops, table-top exercises, or game simulations. Operations-based exercises validate plans and policies, clarify roles, and identify resource gaps in security operations. Types of operations-based exercises include drills, functional exercises, and full-scale exercises.

## Crowd management

Crowds need to be managed for several reasons. Large gatherings of people increase the odds of something happening and make changes in action slower and more complex. Furthermore, communications tend to be slower and more complicated than normal. Most importantly, in the event of an incident at a mass gathering, the possible number of injuries increases. People have been injured or killed at sport venues around the world from crowd crushes, fires, bombs, heat exhaustion, structural collapses, overcrowding, and rioting. The Australian Open has been fast gaining a reputation for fan violence. In 2007, more than 150 Serbian and Croatian fans attacked each other with flagpoles and bottles. In 2008, the tournament was overshadowed when police had to use pepper spray on unruly Greek fans. Again, in 2009, fans from the Serbian and Croatian communities clashed, hurling chairs and missiles at each other during Serbian Novak Djokovic's win over Bosnian-born Amer Delic who now represents the United States

Critical components of a crowd-management plan include the following:

1. Trained staff in crowd-control methods: staff training has been emphasized in several areas of this chapter. It is evident that human capital is critical to the effective coordination and response efforts of all security- and safety-related programs. Employees should have an understanding of the facility, including the location of emergency medical services to assist fans.
2. Established policies and procedures for possible incidents: specific policies and procedures are needed to address incidents such as disruptive and unruly fans, or public drunkenness and disorder. Parking and traffic control is critical in the management of crowds entering or exiting the facility. Poor traffic and parking control can result in stalled crowd ingress, delaying the event's start, or fuel aggressive behavior by fans because of frustration.
3. Effective communication systems: an effective communication network integrated with the stadium command center allows for efficient reporting of incidents and response and recovery efforts.
4. Appropriate signage: adequate signage is the final component of the crowd management plan. There should be prominent signage providing guidance on responding to and reporting suspicious behavior.

A crowd-management plan should include an alcohol policy. Protective measures concerning alcohol include staff training in alcohol management, identification checks to prevent underage drinking, limiting the number of alcoholic drinks sold to one individual, and ending alcohol sales at a certain point during the event. The NFL requires stadiums to stop selling beer at the end of the third quarter and is considering more drastic measures to prevent unruly fan behavior. In fall 2008, the NFL and all 32 NFL clubs issued a fan code of conduct to promote a positive fan environment and address behavior that detracts from the fan experience.

---

## NFL fan code of conduct

'The National Football League and its teams are committed to creating a safe, comfortable, and enjoyable experience for all fans, both in the stadium and in the parking lot. We want all fans attending our games to enjoy the experience in a responsible fashion. When attending a game, you are required to refrain from the following behaviors':

- Behavior that is unruly, disruptive, or illegal in nature.
- Intoxication or other signs of alcohol impairment that results in irresponsible behavior.
- Foul or abusive language or obscene gestures.
- Interference with the progress of the game (including throwing objects onto the field).
- Failing to follow instructions of stadium personnel.
- Verbal or physical harassment of opposing team fans.

'Event patrons are responsible for their conduct as well as the conduct of their guests and/or persons occupying their seats. Stadium staff will promptly intervene to support an environment where event patrons, their guests, and other fans can enjoy the event free from the above behavior. Event patrons and guests who violate these provisions will be subject to ejection without refund and loss of ticket privileges for future games.'

*Source* : McCarthy, M. (2008, August 8). NFL unveils new code of conduct for its fans. USATODAY.com

---

### Emergency management

The four primary components to all-hazards emergency management are mitigation, preparedness, response, and recovery. Mitigation activities try to prevent emergencies or lessen the damage of unavoidable disasters. Preparedness activities such as training and exercise drills enhance the ability of agencies to respond quickly in the aftermath of an incident. Response activities focus on damage assessment or assisting the affected population. Recovery actions, such as providing economic aid, ensure the successful recovery of the affected location. Figure 13.2 depicts the interrelated components and offers potential considerations under each area.

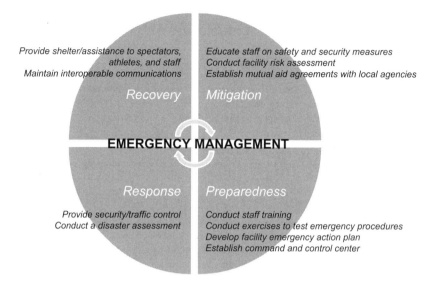

**Figure 13.2** Principles and components of sport event emergency management. Adapted from Hall, S., Marciani, L., & Cooper, W.E. (2008). Emergency management and planning at major sports events. *Journal of Emergency Management*. January/February, Vol. 6, No.1, p. 43–47.

## Business continuity

Business continuity involves developing measures and safeguards allowing an organization to continue to operate under adverse conditions. The development of a business continuity program includes the formation of a sound contingency plan. A contingency plan includes the steps taken before, during, and after an incident. Contingency plans include the facility's emergency management policy, personnel responsibilities, potential emergency scenarios, and location of response operations. The plan highlights how core elements of the emergency management system will be organized, such as communications, community outreach, recovery and restoration of systems, operations, administration and logistics. Supporting documentation to the plan may include building and site maps, floor plans, escape routes, emergency equipment inventories, emergency procedures, and personnel call lists. The London 2012 Olympic Games Organizing Committee has a contingency budget of 2.7 billion pounds sterling. Additionally, contracts should be in place for immediate restoration and secondary locations identified to hold event bookings in case of an incident. For example, in 2006, the English FA provisionally booked Cardiff's Millennium Stadium in case Wembley Stadium in London was not completed in time to host the 2007 FA Cup Final. The ultimate goal is to return the facility and its stakeholder's quality of life to the same level it was before the incident.

## FIFA World Cup 2002 Japan/Korea

## Security measures

1. South Korean Armed Forces positioned mobile surface-to-air missiles at stadium to prevent terrorist attacks.
2. South Korean Air Force jets patrolled the skies over world cup stadiums and no-fly zones over venues were established for other aircrafts.
3. Japan's airliner, All Nippon Airlines (ANA), stationed sky marshals on flights into Japan to guard against possible terrorist/hooligan attacks.
4. Japanese riot police conducted disaster drills – 200 police in riot gear and biohazard suits removed a car bomb and hazardous materials from a soccer stadium in central Japan.
5. 800–1000 security personnel were assigned at every event.
6. Security checks at gates included 17 banned items including alcohol, umbrellas, helmets, and frozen substances.
7. Fans used different entrances/exits.
8. Fans were separated into different sections.
9. FIFA banned the showing of replays on giant TV screens in stadiums during matches to prevent the replaying of controversial incidents or goals.
10. 'Spotters' utilized – European security personnel working under cover, seated among fans.
11. A hooligan register (database) was sent to Japanese police prior to the event.
12. Korea's anti-hooligan task force were equipped with water cannons, police trained in martial arts like tae kwon do and judo, and they used trained police dogs.
13. Match tickets featured holograms to enhance security. Security production and distribution of tickets were paramount: 3.2 million tickets for 64 matches spread over 20 venues in two different countries, with 32 nations taking part. To tighten security and minimize black market activity: (1) tickets were personalized to an individual or sponsor, (2) no more than four members of a household could purchase tickets, (3) tickets were non-transferable to prevent block booking, and (4) all tickets for second round matches and beyond were issued smart cards which could be read at special kiosks at each venue.

*Source* : Korean Security Measures (2002); Holograms Provide Security for FIFA World Cup 2002, (2002, August).

## Chapter review

Security management systems are employed to reduce risk and exposure to facility vulnerabilities. Facility managers are responsible for keeping the facility in safe repair, discovering potential hazards, and protecting patrons from foreseeable dangers. Security management requires the coordination and collaboration of many stakeholders including individuals, government agencies, and private contractors. The facility manager should develop a facility emergency response plan with annexes for game-day operations, evacuation procedures, and incident response to various emergency scenarios.

Industry best practices, planning options, and guidelines are available to the facility manager for assistance in security planning. Britain has successfully implemented national legislation and standard stadium requirements and protocols to combat hooliganism. Protective security measures are designed to devalue, detect, deter, and defend the facility from attack or illegal activity. Baseline protective security measures should be implemented on a permanent basis as routine inspection for a facility. Protective security measures should be considered in the following key areas: venue site design, safety and sustainability, physical protection systems, perimeter control, access control, communications, security personnel, training and exercise, crowd management, emergency management, and business continuity and recovery.

# Section Four

## Effectiveness of Management and Operations

# 14 Performance management and benchmarking

## Chapter outline

## Chapter objectives

Performance management and benchmarking are important techniques for facility managers, for three key reasons. First, they help facility managers to achieve better results by enabling them to understand the drivers of performance and how to influence them. This is achieved by both data benchmarking, comparing statistical performance with others; and process benchmarking, comparing the key decisions made to achieve good performance. Second, benchmarks provide much more authoritative reporting of performance than an organization's performance reported in isolation. Third, when benchmarking/performance management techniques become established as part of organizational culture, they provide the basis for a clear focus on the business essentials as well as the direction for continuous improvement. This capstone chapter will ensure that the book concludes on a high note by bringing together various concepts that out of necessity have been treated separately earlier in the book such as strategic management; financial management; the four es of economy, efficiency, effectiveness and equity; customer satisfaction; and service quality. It will draw on the principal benchmarking systems internationally, including the Sport England National Benchmarking Service, and the CERM Performance Indicators (PIs) PIs system from Australia.

This chapter will draw together various strands of performance management referred to throughout the book, for example, staff turnover ratios (human resources), extraction ratios, e.g. dollars per head of secondary spend; return on investment in marketing (e.g. coupons returned as a function of promotion cost) and so on. The basic point is that which gets measured gets managed, so therefore managers need to be clear about what their priorities are and what measures they need to monitor in order to demonstrate personal, team, facility, and corporate effectiveness.

## Introduction to performance management and benchmarking

It might be tempting to suggest that good managers are intuitive, with natural skills for dealing with people and making decisions, using inspiration and flair. This romantic vision of management probably fits a few inspirational entrepreneurs. However, it is totally inappropriate for the large majority of good managers. All the principles of good management suggest that as well as personal skills, it is important to have, among other things, evidence to guide decisions. At the heart of this chapter, therefore, is the concept of good performance evidence. It is this evidence that will:

- Demonstrate whether or not strategies and objectives are being realized;
- Identify key financial changes and guide financial decision-making;
- Demonstrate how customers are feeling about products or services and guide marketing decisions; and
- Identify the quality of service provision and guide human resource decisions.

Furthermore, it is not advisable to just examine evidence for one's own organization in isolation. Comparisons are also important in order to judge how the organization is doing in relation to other providers of similar products or services, whether or not they are competitors, and also in relation to previous periods. Comparison is the essence of benchmarking, which is another key element to this chapter.

Utilizing appropriate evidence about organizational performance in order to improve decision-making and comparing this evidence with similar providers and past achievements are the essentials of performance management and benchmarking. This chapter first provides examples of performance management frameworks, the organizational processes which stimulate the right evidence and the right use of it. Second, concepts of performance are examined, demonstrating that it is a multi-faceted phenomenon. Third, appropriate performance indicators are discussed (i.e. the pieces of data which are selected to represent organizational performance). Finally, benchmarking is considered, with the help of a case study of a benchmarking service used for sport facilities in the UK.

The term 'performance management' is often used interchangeably with 'quality management' because they cover very similar principles.

- Performance management is defined by IDeA, the improvement and development agency for local government in the UK, as 'taking action in response to actual performances to make outcomes for users and the public better than they would otherwise be' (IDeA, 2009). It is a process of improving organizational performance by informing management decisions with appropriate planning, objectives, targets, performance measurement, and review.
- Quality management is defined by The Chartered Institute of Quality as 'an organization-wide approach to understanding precisely what customers need and consistently delivering accurate solutions within budget, on time and with the minimum loss to society' (Chartered Institute of Quality, 2009). Typically broader in

concept, this incorporates measuring and analyzing performance in a process designed to achieve continual improvement in products, services and the processes that deliver them to the customer.

# Performance management frameworks

A number of frameworks have been devised to facilitate performance management. They are used interchangeably as performance management frameworks or quality management frameworks. We examine two – one a general model for any organization (EFQM) and the other a framework specifically designed for public sector cultural services in the UK (TAES).

## The European Foundation for Quality Management (EFQM) Excellence Model

EFQM was established on the premise that to be successful, an organization needs to establish an appropriate management system. The EFQM Excellence Model is a practical tool to help organizations do this. It does so by measuring where they are on the path to excellence, helping managers to understand the weaknesses in performance, and then stimulating solutions through actions.

Introduced in 1992, the EFQM Excellence Model, also known as the Business Excellence Model, is a management framework that can be used to provide continuous improvement to any organization, in any area of activity. It works by self-assessment by an organization's managers, rather than external assessment. An organization is assessed by its managers against the relevant criteria which go to make up quality performance and a score is allocated.

By matching the organization against the model's criteria, strengths and weaknesses are identified. Within this non-prescriptive approach, there are some fundamental concepts which underpin the model:

- Results orientation: satisfying the needs of all stakeholders.
- Customer focus: the essence of service quality is to identify the needs of customers and satisfy these needs.
- Leadership and constancy of purpose: without effective leadership in seeking continuous improvement, it is unlikely to be achieved.
- Management by processes and facts: i.e. systematic management based on reliable evidence.
- People development and involvement: realizing the potential of staff through a culture of trust and empowerment.
- Continuous learning, innovation, and improvement: requiring sharing and an organizational culture which embraces change and development.
- Partnership development: mutually beneficial relationships based on trust.
- Corporate social responsibility: an ethical approach to service delivery which demonstrates responsibility to the wider community.

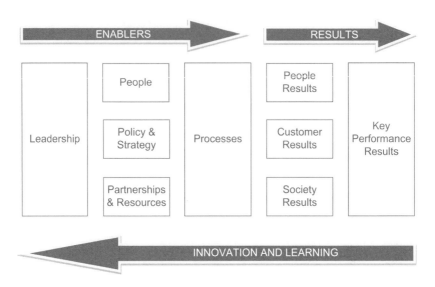

**Figure 14.1** Business excellence model: EFQM.
*Source*: EFQM at http://ww1.efqm.org/en/Home/tabid/36/Default.aspx.


The model is based on nine criteria, and is reproduced in Figure 14.1. Five of these criteria are 'Enablers', covering what an organization does. Four are 'Results', covering what an organization achieves. Feedback from Results helps to improve the Enablers.

The EFQM is the most widely used organizational framework in Europe and has become the basis for many national and regional Quality Awards, including a quality accreditation system in the UK designed specifically for sport and leisure services – Quest (see: http://www.questnbs.info/).

### Towards an excellent service (TAES)

TAES was introduced in 2006 by IDeA, the improvement and development agency for local government in the UK. It is a national framework for performance management in cultural services. It was developed in consultation with a number of other agencies, including the relevant government department (Department of Culture, Media and Sport), the government watchdog for public services (Audit Commission), and major professional institutes in sport and leisure (The Institute for Sport, Parks and Leisure, The Institute of Sport and Recreation Management, and the National Association for Sports Development).

TAES is a self-assessment and improvement planning toolkit, which is designed to complement and embrace other quality frameworks and awards such as EFMQ. It is described by IDeA as a 'journey' rather than a scheme, because it is a continuous process of improvement. Continuous improvement is necessary because of continuous changes in both community needs and customer expectations. Continuous improvement requires an organization to:

- Clearly establish what it is trying to achieve, i.e. objectives;
- Establish what causes success;
- Identify current performance;
- Take actions to improve on a continuous basis; and
- Go back to step one and carry on (IDeA, 2006).

TAES identifies eight key 'themes' that influence the quality of cultural services, with 'equality' and 'service access' integrated into every theme:

1. Leadership
2. Policy and strategy
3. Community engagement
4. Partnership working
5. Use of resources
6. People management
7. Standards of service
8. Performance measurement and learning (IDeA, 2006).

The similarity of these criteria with those of the EFQM Excellence Model is deliberate – it is designed to complement EFQM. Within each of the themes, there are criteria which define key aspects of high-quality service. A number of 'descriptors' for the criteria allow performance in them to be measured. The system is evidence-based – evidence schedules identify the sorts of evidence required to demonstrate whether a particular criterion has been met or not – 'the evidence schedules are vital to the integrity of the framework' (IDeA, 2006, p. 12). From the evidence emerging from self-assessment, an organization can identify its position in relation to four levels of performance: poor, fair, good, and excellent. It is not surprising that a lack of evidence automatically leads to a rating of 'poor' under the TAES self-assessment.

IDeA focuses on the improvement plan as the most important part of the TAES process – 'it is the very reason for carrying out the self assessment in the first place' (IDeA, 2006, p. 12). Key attributes of an improvement plan are:

- Improvements are prioritized, focusing first on those which will make the biggest impact.
- The plan must be such that specific tasks are identified which are realistic, resourced, with clear accountability and deadlines set for delivery.
- The improvements are themselves measurable and you can monitor if the actions planned are having the desired effect (IDeA, 2006, p. 12).

## Performance management principles

A well-designed performance management system must be based on a systematic analysis of the relationships between the objectives of the organization, the performance indicators employed in representing these objectives, the management targets set for the performance of the organization and the actions taken to realize these targets. To some sport managers, as indicated by the Audit Commission (1989) in Britain, the differences between these concepts have been vague. However, since that seminal report, a range of performance management systems has been devised to help managers achieve continuous improvement.

The Audit Commission (2000a) has made clear why performance measurement is at the heart of good performance management – see Figure 14.2. It is evident that without the right evidence, it is not easy to see where you are, let alone what is right or wrong with an organization.

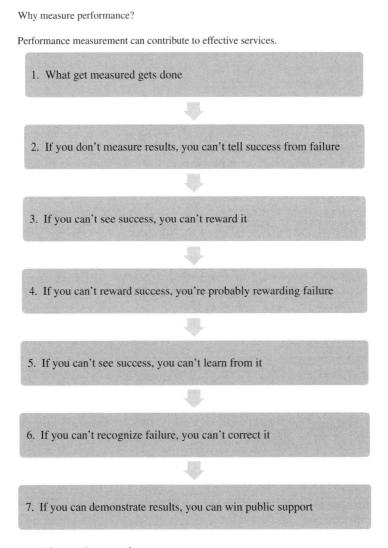

Why measure performance?

Performance measurement can contribute to effective services.

1. What get measured gets done

2. If you don't measure results, you can't tell success from failure

3. If you can't see success, you can't reward it

4. If you can't reward success, you're probably rewarding failure

5. If you can't see success, you can't learn from it

6. If you can't recognize failure, you can't correct it

7. If you can demonstrate results, you can win public support

**Figure 14.2** Why measure performance?
*Source*: Audit Commission, 2000a

## *Objectives*

An essential first stage in performance management is setting appropriate organizational objectives. An objective is a desired future position. Taylor (1996) identifies a number of desirable attributes for organizational objectives:

- Objectives should be specified so that, at the end of an appropriate period, it is clear whether or not they have been achieved. This means that objectives need to be quantifiable. Each objective requires appropriate performance indicators, by which measurement of performance is possible.
- Objectives are concerned with ends, not means. For example, it is not an objective to 'set low prices for disadvantaged groups in the community'; the objective here is 'to increase visits to the service by people from such disadvantaged groups' and this objective can be served by a number of means, of which pricing is just one.
- The prioritization of objectives is important. Sometimes objectives may conflict, for example 'increase revenue' might conflict with 'increase usage of a sport facility by the lowest socio-economic groups in the community'. Where trade-offs between conflicting objectives are apparent, priorities need to be identified. Failure to specify such priorities means that targets and management actions become compromised.

The attributes of appropriate objectives can be summarized in the mnemonic MASTER:

M = measurable
A = actionable
S = specific
T = time-specified
E = ends not means
R = ranked

It has often been the case, particularly in the public sector, that organizational objectives are expressed vaguely or generally, so that it is difficult if not impossible to identify whether or not they have been achieved. Such inaccurately specified objectives include 'achieving sport for all', 'serving the community's needs', and 'providing a high quality sporting experience'. These are 'aims' rather than objectives – they are broadly based and non-measurable. They require more specific, measurable objectives to be monitored through performance indicators, which in turn are used for management decision-making.

Objectives for public sector sport organizations are likely to be more complicated than those of private, commercial firms – the reason being that social, non-profit objectives such as usage by disadvantaged groups are of importance to public sector organizations as well as financial and customer satisfaction objectives. Social objectives extend to the impacts of public services, such as improved health and citizenship, and reduced crime and vandalism. Impacts are typically less easily expressed in a measurable form than operational objectives.

## Performance

Performance for a sport organization can mean any number of things, depending on what objectives are specified. It is possible, however, to generalize about the nature of performance, and do so in the context of any type of organization. Before discussing specific performance indicators, it is important to identify the different aspects of performance that sport managers will be interested in.

The most common type of performance found in the private sector is financial performance (see Chapter 7). This is often simplified to mean profits, but in fact financial performance means much more than this. It can include revenue, costs, debts, liquidity, and security. But for both operational and strategic appraisal purposes it is necessary to examine the different strands of performance, as accountancy does.

Related to financial performance is the concept of economy. This is solely concerned with the input side of the production process and with costs. It is not concerned with outputs. Economy is achieved if inputs are acquired at minimum cost. Overemphasis on economy is not wise unless it is seen as the main reason for weak performance. In the public sector it has often been the case that performance has been 'measured' by expenditure on inputs, i.e. increased spending is taken to automatically mean an increase in service output. But of course this is no measure of performance at all. It says nothing of the actual outputs of the service, which could be highly ineffective, inefficient, and wasteful of resources despite the rising expenditure.

Efficiency is concerned with achieving objectives and targets at minimum cost and considers the best possible relationships between inputs and outputs. Efficiency is sometimes given the terms 'cost effectiveness' or 'cost efficiency', and is also what is meant by the terms 'productivity' and 'value for money'.

Effectiveness is concerned solely with the achievement of output targets. It does not, therefore, consider the costs of achieving the output targets. A basic measure of effectiveness is throughput volume, such as the number of visits in a given time period, an example being the number of bathers at a swimming pool. However, this is a rather basic indicator because it contains no indication of the types of visitors who have been attracted, nor the extent to which the service has met the needs of the visitors.

Effectiveness is an important performance aspect in public sector leisure services, since they are concerned with social objectives that are largely non-financial in nature. These objectives include education, notably with services such as swimming and other activity classes. They also include increasing visits by specified disadvantaged target groups.

In the public sector, organizations are also interested in the effectiveness of services in terms of achieving impacts in society. Therefore, whilst throughput is concerned with the volume of visitors, and outputs are concerned with direct effects such as the type of visitors, or the revenue they provide, impacts are concerned with broader effects on society, such as improvements in health, citizenship, or quality of life.

In addition to economy, efficiency, and effectiveness, sometimes another 'e' is added to the list of important performance dimensions, particularly in public sector organizations. This is equity, which implies fairness in the treatment of all customers. This has a variety of interpretations, such as equality of opportunity to visit, prioritizing visits by the poorest members of society, or alternatively service benefits distributed according to how much tax people have paid to support the service.

Another performance dimension which is increasingly common is customer satisfaction, which can be measured directly by such methods as questionnaire surveys, comments slips, or complaints. A variant of this which is not unusual in the public sector is satisfaction with services by local citizens, regardless of whether or not they have actually used the service. This may seem contradictory – if a person has not actually used a service, how can he or she possibly comment? However, it is often the case that the community has a collective interest in the performance of a service. An example is sport for young people at risk. A wide range of people will have a view on whether or not such a service is satisfactory, from parents and neighbors to anyone with a fear of nuisance or worse from bored young people.

## Performance indicators

Ideally, indicators of performance should have certain qualities to make them suitable for management purposes. A set of performance indicators should:

- Reflect all the objectives of the leisure service accurately;
- Cover different dimensions of performance, such as effectiveness and efficiency;
- Be capable of being measured for separate parts of the service, since it is likely that different objectives and different targets are applicable to different parts of the service, even within the same facility;
- Be administratively manageable and easily understood; and
- Be consistent over time and between service elements and different organizations – this is particularly important for benchmarking.

In the UK public sector the Audit Commission (2000b and 2007) has provided two forms of advice in relation to performance measurement. Although designed for the public sector, much of this general advice is transferable to other sectors. First, it is necessary to consider the general characteristics of indicators that can help to ensure that proposed indicators will be useful and effective (Audit Commission, 2000b). Second, it is important that the data collected is reliable (Audit Commission, 2007). Good quality data is the essential ingredient for reliable performance information.

The Audit Commission (2000b) identified 13 criteria for assessing the robustness of a performance indicator – see Table 14.1. Devising a performance indicator that fulfills all of the criteria in this table is challenging. Inevitably a performance indicator will score less well against one or two criteria. For

**Table 14.1** Criteria for good performance indicators

| Criteria | Explanation |
| --- | --- |
| Relevant | Indicators should be relevant to the organization's strategic goals and objectives. They should also be relevant to the people providing the data. |
| Clear definition | The performance indicators should have a clear and intelligible definition in order to ensure consistent collection and fair comparison. |
| Easy to understand and use | Performance indicators should be described in terms that the user of the information will understand. |
| Comparable | Indicators should be comparable on a consistent basis between organizations and this relies on there being agreement about definitions. They should also be comparable on a consistent basis over time. Comparability of performance indicators should include consideration of the context within which the comparison is taking place because external or internal circumstances can differ to such a degree that comparison is invalid. For example, inter-authority comparisons could be misleading if there is considerable variation in the characteristics of the areas being compared. |
| Verifiable | The indicator also needs to be collected and calculated in a way that enables the information and data to be verified. It should therefore be based on robust data collection systems, and it should be possible for managers to verify the accuracy of the information and the consistency of the methods used. |
| Cost-effective | There is a need to balance the cost of collecting information with its usefulness. Where possible, an indicator should be based on information already available and linked to existing data collection activities. |
| Unambiguous | A change in an indicator should be capable of unambiguous interpretation so that it is clear whether an increase in an indicator value represents an improvement or deterioration in service. |
| Attributable | Service managers should be able to influence the performance measured by the indicator. |
| Responsive | A performance indicator should be responsive to change. An indicator where changes in performance are likely to be too small to register will be of limited use. |

Table 14.1 Criteria for good performance indicators—Cont'd

| Criteria | Explanation |
| --- | --- |
| Avoid perverse incentives | A performance indicator should not be easily manipulated because this might encourage counter-productive activity. |
| Allow innovation | Indicators that focus on outcome and user satisfaction are more likely to encourage such innovation to take place than indicators that are tied into existing processes. |
| Statistically valid | Indicators should be statistically valid and this will in large part depend on the sample size. |
| Timely | Data for the performance indicator should be available within a reasonable time-scale. |

*Source: derived from Audit Commission (2000b).*

national indicators, the Audit Commission advises that a performance indicator should be clearly defined, comparable, verifiable, unambiguous, and statistically valid. Indicators that are published for the benefit of the local community should first and foremost be relevant and easy to understand.

The Audit Commission (2007) defined six key characteristics that can be used to assess the quality of data used to construct performance indicator scores – see Table 14.2. Most of these criteria directly echo those stipulated for performance indicators in Table 14.1 – i.e. not only relevance, validity, and timeliness, but also reliable (=comparable) and accurate (=verifiable). The one additional consideration in Table 14.2 is completeness – an important reminder that validity and reliability are as much dependent on what is missing as on what is collected.

Having stated these requirements, however, it is necessary to stress that any set of indicators is unlikely to fulfill all of these properties. This is simply because these qualities are difficult to achieve – all indicators have their good points and their bad points.

## Private, commercial sector

For a private, commercial organization, performance is, in the main, specified in financial terms, although there are other important considerations. Business accounting ratios are designed principally for planning purposes (strategic appraisal) and control purposes (operational appraisal). The ratios are concerned not just with profit, but also with liquidity, asset utilization, capital structure, and investment potential. A sample of such ratios is given in Table 14.3.

These financial ratios, and many more, are detailed for individual companies and industry sectors by commercial sources such as ICC British Company Financial Datasets, a part of Dialog's company and industry intelligence service which covers nearly half a million companies worldwide, as well as market share

**Table 14.2** Criteria for suitable performance indicators' data

| Dimension | Description |
| --- | --- |
| Accuracy | Data should be sufficiently accurate for its intended purposes, representing clearly and in sufficient detail the interaction provided at the point of activity. Data should be captured once only, although it may have multiple uses. Accuracy is most likely to be secured if data is captured as close to the point of activity as possible. Reported information that is based on accurate data provides a fair picture of performance and should enable informed decision-making at all levels. The need for accuracy must be balanced with the importance of the uses for the data, and the costs and effort of collection. For example, it may be appropriate to accept some degree of inaccuracy where timeliness is important. Where compromises have to be made on accuracy, the resulting limitations of the data should be clear to its users. |
| Validity | Data should be recorded and used in compliance with relevant requirements, including the correct application of any rules or definitions. This will ensure consistency between periods and with similar organizations. Where proxy data is used to compensate for an absence of actual data, organizations must consider how well this data is able to satisfy the intended purpose. |
| Reliability | Data should reflect stable and consistent data collection processes across collection points and over time, whether using manual or computer-based systems, or a combination. Managers and stakeholders should be confident that progress towards performance targets reflects real changes rather than variations in data collection approaches or methods. |
| Timeliness | Data should be captured as quickly as possible after the event or activity and must be available for the intended use within a reasonable time period. Data must be available quickly and frequently enough to support information needs and to influence the appropriate level of service or management decisions. |
| Relevance | Data captured should be relevant to the purposes for which it is used. This entails periodic review of requirements to reflect changing needs. It may be necessary to capture data at the point of activity which is relevant only for other purposes, rather than for the current intervention. Quality assurance and feedback processes are needed to ensure the quality of such data. |
| Completeness | Data requirements should be clearly specified, based on the information needs of the organization and data collection processes matched to these requirements. Monitoring missing, incomplete, or invalid records can provide an indication of data quality and can also point to problems in the recording of certain data items. |

*Source: Audit Commission (2007).*

**Table 14.3** Performance ratios for commercial organizations

*Profitability*

$$\frac{\text{Either gross or net profit}}{\text{Sales}}$$
No rules of thumb. It varies widely between industries and firms.

$$\frac{\text{Net profit after tax}}{\text{Total assets}}$$
'Return on Capital Employed'. No standard definitions, so care is needed in making comparisons between firms and industries.

*Liquidity*

$$\frac{\text{Current Assets}}{\text{Current liabilities}}$$
'Current Ratio'. Rule of thumb = 2:1

$$\frac{\text{Current assets} - \text{inventories}}{\text{Current liabilities}}$$
'Acid Test', 'Quick' or 'Liquidity' Ratio. A more discriminating test of ability to pay debts.

$$\frac{\text{Balance sheet trade debtors} \times 365}{\text{Total credit sales}}$$
Average collection period of trade debts, i.e. average number of days before an account is paid.

*Asset utilization*

$$\frac{\text{Sales}}{\text{Fixed assets}}$$
Indicates the effectiveness in using fixed plant to generate sales.

$$\frac{\text{Cost of goods sold}}{\text{Inventories}}$$
'Stock Turnover'. Varies a lot between industries.

$$\frac{\text{Sales}}{\text{Number of employees}}$$
Indicates revenue productivity of labor.

*Capital structure*

$$\frac{\text{Net Worth}}{\text{Total assets}}$$
Indicates shareholders' interest in the business. (Net Worth is ordinary shares + preference shares + reserves.)

$$\frac{\text{Borrowing}}{\text{Net worth}}$$
'Gearing'. An indication of the riskiness of the capital structure.

*Investment*

$$\frac{\text{Dividend per share}}{\text{Market price per share}}$$
'Dividend Yield'. Indicates rate of return on investment in shares.

$$\frac{\text{Net profit} - \text{Preference Share Dividend}}{\text{Number of ordinary shares}}$$
Earnings per ordinary share.

$$\frac{\text{Market Price per Share}}{\text{Earnings per share}}$$
'Price/Earnings Ratio'. Indicates the market's evaluation of a share.

Source: *Gratton and Taylor (1988).*

and sales, business directories, and financials on 14 million US and international companies.

A major advantage of ratios is that they put performance into a consistent perspective. For instance, a business may declare a profit of $100,000, but this figure takes on more meaning if it is put in the context of turnover, or capital, as 'rate of return' figures do. Ratios commonly involve two monetary sums, such as the ratio of a firm's debt to its equity; so, they enable financial comparisons to be made over time, without having to worry about adjusting for inflation. The use of ratios hides potentially sensitive or confidential information which may be more preferable than disclosing absolute values – e.g. labor costs expressed as a percentage of total operating costs.

Ratios have to be interpreted very carefully. Many are more appropriate for comparing a single firm's performance over time than for comparing different firms, particularly if the firms are from a different industry or sector. Some ratios involve estimates which can be done in various ways; so, comparing like with like can be problematic – for example, valuing inventories and intangible assets. Some ratio values are annual averages; so, getting the information from balance sheets is unreliable, merely averaging the beginning and end of the year situations, when more observations during the year are really required – e.g. liquidity ratios.

Private firms are also interested in other aspects of performance apart from financial ratios. Market share is an important objective that is normally measurable, even at the local or regional level. Market share is one indicator for a major concern for organizational performance – the demand for the product. It is vital for any organization, from whatever sector, to be informed about changes in demand for the service it is providing. Market research is a typical means of generating this evidence.

Most large private leisure organizations have marketing departments, with market research functions. As well as continual monitoring of demand for their goods and services by this means, they regularly employ outside market research agencies or consultancies to conduct specialist market research. In addition, some consultancies produce regular reports with market research information alongside financial data for different industries. Recent reports from Mintel, for example, include Sport and the Media (February 2009), Motor Sports (January 2009) and Golf in the UK (March 2009). Key Note has recent market reports on the Sports Market (April 2008), Sports Clothing and Footwear (May 2009), and Sports Equipment (April 2009).

## Public sector

Public sector sport providers have had to become accustomed to performance measurement in the UK, with the advent of first, Comprehensive Performance Assessment (CPA), and more recently Comprehensive Area Analysis (CAA). These government requirements have obliged local authorities to publish performance information for a set of national performance indicators. Table 14.4, however, shows that the indicators relevant to public sector cultural

**Table 14.4** Public sector national indicators for culture in the UK

**(a) CPA 2007/08**

Visits to/usage of museums and galleries (including research enquiries and Website hits) per 1000 population
Visits to museums and galleries in person per 1000 population
Visits to museums & galleries by pupils in organized groups
Compliance with Public Library Service Standards

**(b) CAA, 2009+**

| National Indicator name | Local area agreements including NI/152 | |
|---|---|---|
| | Number | Rank/152 |
| Participation in regular volunteering | 42 | 43 |
| Adult participation in sport and active recreation | 82 | 16 |
| Use of public libraries | 10 | 95 |
| Visits to museums and galleries | 2 | 142 |
| Engagement in the arts | 24 | 65= |
| Children and young people's participation in high-quality PE and sport | 24 | 65= |
| Young people's participation in positive activities | 75 | 75 |
| Children and young people's satisfaction with parks and play areas | 0 – definition still to be agreed | N.A. |

*Source: Audit Commission, http://www.audit-commission.gov.uk/localgov/audit/bvpis/pages/guidance.aspx.*
*Source: IDeA, http://www.idea.gov.uk/idk/core/page.do?pageId=8399555.*

services have been very restricted under CPA. Under CAA the list covers more activities, although now local authorities can choose which indicators to report, and the final column shows that this take-up is variable for cultural indicators.

At the local level and in specific consultancy services, however, a much more comprehensive list of performance indicators can be found. For example, Sport England's National Benchmarking Service (NBS) for sport and leisure centers compiles data for 47 performance indicators across four dimensions of performance. These are listed in Table 14.5.

This NBS list illustrates the compromise that is often necessary between what indicators are desirable and what indicators can be measured reliably and at reasonable cost. The NBS does not attempt to measure wider impacts of sport provision, such as improvements in health, improved quality of life, reduced crime and vandalism, or education benefits – these are considered too difficult to measure regularly in the specific context of sport provision. However, the NBS does provide indicators relevant to another impact objective – social inclusion – the access indicators do this. The NBS also does not measure non-users' attitudes and barriers – this would require research in local communities, which is

**Table 14.5** Performance indicators for Sport England's National
Benchmarking Service

## (a) Access
*Key*

  % Visits 11–19 years ÷ % catchment population 11–19 years
  % Visits from NS-SEC classes 6 and 7 ÷ % catchment population in NS-SEC classes 6
  and 7*
  % Visits 60+ years ÷ % catchment population 60+ years
  % Visits from black, Asian, and other ethnic groups ÷ % catchment population in
  same groups
  % Visits disabled, <60 years ÷ % catchment population disabled, <60 years

*Other*

  % Visits 20–59 years ÷ % catchment population in same group
  % Of visits which were first visits
  % Visits with discount cards
  % Visits with discount cards for 'disadvantage'**
  % Visits female
  % Visits disabled, 60 years+ ÷ % catchment population disabled, 60+ years
  % Visits unemployed

* NS-SEC classes 6 and 7 are the two lowest socioeconomic classes in the official classification used in the UK.

** Disadvantage eligibility for discount cards includes over 50s, students, unemployed, disabled, single parents, government support, government funded trainees, widows, exercise referrals, and elite performers.

## (b) Utilization
*Key*

  Annual visits per sq. m. (of usable space, i.e. excluding offices and corridor space).

*Other*

  Annual visits per sq. m. (of total indoor space, including offices and corridor space).
  % Of visits casual, instead of organized
  Weekly number of people visiting the center as % of catchment population

## (c) Financial
*Key*

  Subsidy per visit

*Other*

  % Cost recovery
  Subsidy per resident
  Subsidy per sq. m.
  Total operating cost per visit
  Total operating cost per sq. m.
  Maintenance and repair costs per sq. m.
  Energy costs per sq. m.
  Total income per visit
  Total income per sq. m.
  Direct income per visit
  Secondary income per visit

**Table 14.5** Performance indicators for Sport England's National
Benchmarking Service—Cont'd

**(D) Service attributes for customer satisfaction and importance scoring**
*Accessibility*
    Activity available at convenient times
    Ease of booking
    The activity charge/fee
    The range of activities available

*Quality of facilities/services*
    Quality of flooring in the sport hall
    Quality of lighting in the sport hall
    Quality of equipment
    Water quality in the swimming pool
    Water temperature of swimming pool
    Number of people in the pool
    Quality of car parking on site
    Quality of food and drink

*Cleanliness*
    Cleanliness of changing areas
    Cleanliness of activity spaces

*Staff*
    Helpfulness of reception staff
    Helpfulness of other staff
    Standard of coaching/instruction

*Value for money*
    Value for money of activities
    Value for money of food/drink

*Overall – satisfaction only*
    Overall satisfaction with visit

expensive; nor the views, behavior, etc. of young people under 11 years, who are not considered suitable for the questionnaire survey employed.

It is really up to each organization to choose a manageable array of indicators to reflect its objectives and performance priorities. For a public sector provider, this may include throughput indicators for particular groups of clients, such as women, the elderly, lower socioeconomic groups, and the disabled, since this would monitor the effectiveness of the organization in dealing with target groups. It may also include very conventional indicators of financial performance such as those relevant to the private supplier in Table 14.3, particularly for parts of the service which have no particular 'social service' function, such as the bar, cafe, vending machines, and other merchandise sales.

How often should performance indicators' evidence be produced? It is very common for performance indicators to be calculated on an annual average basis. However, there are good reasons for wanting operational performance indicators to be available on a far more regular basis. Decisions about promotion, programming, and staffing arrangements may be modified at any time; so, a regular flow of up-to-date information assists such decisions.

## Targets

Targets are precise statements of what is to be achieved by when. They are an obvious implication of measuring performance indicators which reflect management objectives. A target provides a concrete and unambiguous reference point against which to ask 'is this objective being achieved?' A target typically takes the form of a numerical target. So, for example, given the objective of increasing usage by the disabled, and using as an indicator the ratio of % of visits by the disabled to % of local population who are disabled, a target figure of 1 would mean trying to increase usage by the disabled to a level which is representative of their numbers in the local population. This is a good example of the way in which a target can provide specificity to an objective.

Evidence of previous performance or evidence of the performance of similar organizations elsewhere provides a quantitative basis for setting targets. Such evidence enables the target setter to reach the difficult balance between ambition and realism. Targets need to be challenging but they also need to be achievable. If they are too easily reached, or if they are impossible to reach, they quickly fall into disrepute. Targets can and do change in the course of time. They need to remain under continuing scrutiny for their relevance to the operating circumstances of the organization.

## Balanced scorecard

One of the best known models for performance measurement is the Balanced Scorecard, a system devised by Kaplan and Norton (1992). A motivation for the Balanced Scorecard was to add strategic non-financial performance measures to the traditional financial measures, to give a more 'balanced' view. The structure of the Balanced Scorecard is presented in Figure 14.3.

The figure demonstrates not just the development of performance measurement beyond the financial, but also a consistent process of specifying objectives, devising measures for these, setting targets, and devising initiatives to achieve the targets. It is the last of these processes that turns the Balanced Scorecard into a performance management system, not just a performance measurement tool.

# Benchmarking

So far we have been discussing evidence that is appropriate for an organization to collect in order for its managers to know how the organization is performing

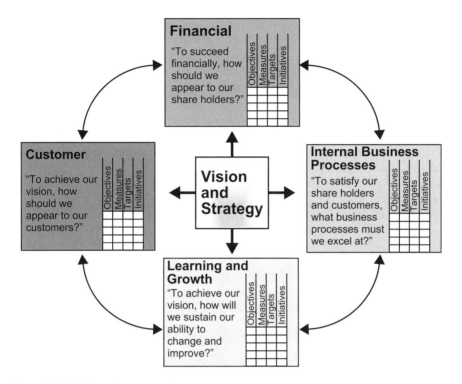

**Figure 14.3** Balanced scorecard structure.
*Source*: http://www.balancedscorecard.org/.

and whether changes are occurring as a result of their decisions (or in spite of them!). However, it is also likely that the organization will want comparisons to be made with other similar organizations. Benchmarking is a process which facilitates this.

- Data benchmarking involves comparison with numerical standards (e.g. averages) calculated for performance indicators in a particular service. They are typically organized into relevant categories or 'families' of similar organizations.
- Process benchmarking involves comparison of different procedures adopted in different organizations. Used in conjunction with performance data, process benchmarking facilitates an understanding of the procedures which improve performance.

External benchmarks for performance are important because they enable a judgment to be made on the relative performance of an organization, which in turn gives a competitive impetus to the organization. They also enable other bodies to assess the relative performance of each organization. This is particularly important in the public sector where the central government, through such bodies as the Audit Commission in the UK, is very interested in monitoring the relative performance of individual local government services, if only because it directly funds around half the costs of these local services in the UK.

Comparative performance information is available in both the private sector and the public sector. In the private sector, for example, ICC British Company Financial Datasheets provides detailed evidence for individual companies, including industry comparisons for a number of key business ratios. Similarly, Key Note provides Business Ratio Reports for each UK industry sector.

In the public sector in the UK, benchmarks are provided for sport in two publications by the Chartered Institute of Public Finance and Accountancy (CIPFA). These are 'Culture, Sport and Recreation Statistics' and 'Charges for Leisure Services'. The former in the main contains financial statistics, and they are estimates rather than outturns. Furthermore, CIPFA does not group the data for comparative purposes; so, care needs to be taken in selecting authorities to compare with.

Three other explicit benchmarking services can be identified for sport. First, in Australia and New Zealand, the CERM Performance Indicators Project is operated by the University of South Australia. Designed for public aquatic centers and leisure centers, it now extends to a range of sport and leisure services, including golf courses, caravan and tourist parks, campgrounds, skate parks, and outdoor centers. CERM PIs provides benchmarks for 26 performance indicators, including services (e.g. program opportunities per week), marketing (e.g. promotion cost as a proportion of total cost), organization (e.g. cleaning and maintenance cost per visit), and finance (e.g. surplus/subsidy per visit).

In the UK there are two benchmarking services relevant to sport – APSE Performance Networks and Sport England's National Benchmarking Service for sport and leisure centers (NBS). APSE's service, operating since 1998, covers all local authority services, with separate reporting for each – sport and leisure facility management being one. It provides data on management and finance with customer satisfaction as an optional extra. APSE compares an individual local authority's performance with other local authorities of a similar type in terms of local policy, demography, and size and type of operation. Sport England's NBS is featured in the case study below.

## Sport England's National Benchmarking Service (NBS)

The NBS measures performance standards for indoor sport and leisure centers with one or both of the following core facilities: a sport hall of four badminton courts or more; and/or a swimming pool of at least 20 metres length. This helps to ensure that the service is focussed on similar types of facilities. The performance indicators measured in this service are identified in Table 14.5. They are designed to cover as many dimensions of performance as are practical for a reasonable cost. However, as noted earlier, they do not cover many of the broader impacts of sport in the community, such as improvements in health and education.

# Sport England's National Benchmarking Service (NBS)—cont'd

To generate the data the NBS requires clients to conduct a survey of customers and submit a form with management and finance information. In addition, population data for the local catchment area is derived from the National Census by the University of Edinburgh. Data from clients is checked carefully – there can be considerable discrepancies and inaccuracies in quite basic pieces of management information, such as throughput counts and cost estimates. Similarly, the administration of the user survey has to ensure valid and reliable results. An NBS guidance document is designed to give advice to try to ensure as much consistency in data as possible between clients.

The NBS results for access, finance, and utilization performance are compared with benchmarks for four families which have been empirically tested and proven to have structural effects on performance:

- Type of center – wet, dry (with/without outdoor facilities), and mixed (with/without outdoor facilities).
- The socioeconomics of a center's location – high deprivation, medium deprivation, and low deprivation – measured by the percentage of the catchment population in the bottom two socioeconomic classes.
- Size of the center – large, medium, and small.
- Management type at the center – in-house local authority, trust, and commercial contractor.

Three benchmarks are employed. The 25%, 50%, and 75% benchmarks are the quarter, half, and three-quarter points in the distribution of scores for a PI, if all the centers' scores were organized from the lowest score at the bottom end of the distribution to the highest score at the top end.

For the importance and satisfaction attributes (see Table 14.5), the NBS reports on the satisfaction scores in comparison with industry averages for wet, dry, or mixed centers; the gaps between importance and satisfaction mean scores from customers; and the percentage of customers dissatisfied with each attribute. These methods of reporting satisfaction are preferred by customers to the comparison with benchmarks employed for the other performance indicators.

Another important feature of the NBS output is the information on facility users from the user survey. Frequency distributions of responses to all the user survey questions include visit characteristics (e.g. activities done, frequency of visit); and the profile of visitors (e.g. travel distance and time, travel mode, home postcodes).

*Continued*

## Sport England's National Benchmarking Service (NBS)—cont'd

NBS clients have emphasized a number of benefits from the service. These include:

- Awareness of the state of the service, often confirming preconceived ideas but objectively.
- Challenges to preconceived ideas held by managers and politicians, causing a reassessment of priorities and delivery methods.
- Real data to help set targets for objectives.
- Experience of research data develops an awareness of further information needs, helping to develop an evidence-based management culture.
- Benchmarking data enables selection of process benchmarking partners with whom to discuss how to generate better performance for specific performance indicators.

In addition, NBS clients have demonstrated a number of commendable responses to the processes of performance management:

- generating the right information;
- interpreting the results meaningfully;
- utilizing the results in performance planning – i.e. immediate action plans, and longer-term contract specification and strategy development.

### Suggested discussion topics

1. Take one of the NBS indicators from each of the categories of access, utilization, and financial identified in Table 14.5, and consider its merits against the Audit Commission criteria in Table 14.1.
2. As a sport facility manager, why would you want to compare the performance of your facility with NBS benchmarks for other facilities?

## Conclusions about performance management and benchmarking

Performance management and benchmarking are essential tools in the quest for continuous improvement. At the heart of these systems is appropriate evidence of performance. However, acquiring appropriate evidence is not an easy matter. Performance indicators have to be selected which fully represent an organization's objectives. One of the problems encountered with the NBS is that feasible performance measurement falls short of desired performance measurement in public sector sport facilities. Much of the modern emphasis in justifying taxpayers' subsidies to such facilities rests on social impacts, particularly in improving users' health. However, measuring improvements in health and relating them specifically to visiting sport facilities is a difficult task, and one beyond the cost of a reasonable performance measurement system.

Another threat to the promise of performance management is the difficulty in assembling accurate and consistent measurement data. Financial data may be subject to accounting regulations but even so there is considerable variation in the way in which some standard ratios are calculated and 'creative accounting' can be used to disguise problems if the wrong organizational culture has set in. Another increasingly essential component of management evidence is market research of customers, but there are enough precedents at the national and local levels to warn that market research can all too easily be conducted in an inappropriate manner, which can bias samples, or that lead respondents into answering questions in certain ways.

Nevertheless, if these constraints can be overcome, the promised land of performance management beckons, where the right evidence enables weaknesses to be identified, plans to be made, actions to be taken and outcomes to be improved. The last two decades in particular have seen an accelerated take-up of performance management and measurement systems. Benchmarking is increasingly the norm. This can only help to secure continuously improving performance in sport facilities.

## Chapter review

This chapter started by showing the similarity between two concepts – performance management and quality management. Two examples of performance management frameworks are described – EFQM and TAES. EFQM is one of the oldest generic systems and it is possible to see similarities between this and many other systems which have been subsequently developed. TAES is a system devised specifically for cultural services in the UK public sector.

Objectives are a cornerstone of good performance management and they need to be expressed much more specifically than organizational aims. Criteria for good objectives are given.

The meaning of 'performance' is discussed and whilst it is driven in an organization by its objectives, there are many different facets to performance. The major elements relevant to sport facility management are detailed.

Performance indicators have to be devised to represent the performance that is relevant to objectives. Indicators are the way in which performance is measured and this chapter discusses the criteria for good performance indicators, and the requirements for good data from which to calculate performance indicator values. Differences between performance indicators in the commercial and public sectors are demonstrated.

As well as measuring performance indicators, it is important for organizational improvement to set targets for them. These targets will be determined by the objectives of the facility.

The Balanced Scorecard is an example of a performance measurement system, designed for the commercial sector, to reflect more than simply financial performance. The Balanced Scorecard reinforces the essential principles of performance management – objectives, targets, measurement, action, and review.

Finally, the concept of benchmarking is explained – i.e. comparing performance with either other facilities, or with previous performance. Examples of benchmarking systems for sport facilities are identified and one in particular, the NBS, is featured in a case study.

# Glossary

**Acceptance** agreeing to the terms of a contract tendered via an offer.

**Access indicator** a measure of the type of customers who are accessing a service; and normally used in the context of disadvantaged groups such as disabled people or people from minority ethnic groups.

**Accommodative style** an appeasement style of conflict resolution that is more concerned with taking care of another's concerns before one's own concerns.

**Achievement** the need for personal accomplishment through being self-fulfilled or having high self-esteem and/or prestige.

**Achievement-oriented leadership** a type of leader behavior that involves setting challenging goals, expecting high performance levels, and expecting workers to assume responsibility.

**Action plan** what an organization wants to accomplish – articulated through goals, objectives, and strategies; and within the parameters of policies and procedures.

**Administrative law** rules and regulations created, implemented, and enforced by a specifically authorized agency.

**Administrative level** also known as middle managers; professional staff who are accountable for the day-to-day operations of specific departments or operations within a sport facility, and connect both the upper and lower levels of management within the sport facility.

**Adverse** description of an unfavorable variance between actual and budgeted financial performance, for example expenditure on wages has been higher than expected.

**Advertising** the process of attracting public attention to a sport product or sport business through paid announcements in the print, broadcast, or electronic media.

**Affections** the actual emotions emitted as a result of the perception.

**Affiliation** the most basic concept of social interaction; the need for interaction with other human beings and to be in an atmosphere of connectedness and belonging.

**All-hazard emergency management** includes the four primary components such as mitigation, preparedness, response, and recovery.

**Ambush marketing** the attempt by a third party to create a direct or an indirect association with a sport facility, the event it is hosting, or its participants without their approval, hence denying official sponsors', suppliers', and partners' parts of the commercial value derived from the 'official' designation.

**APICS** Association for Operations Management; the largest and most widely recognized association in operations management.

**Appraisal systems** a tool utilized in performance review for making decisions about employee advancement, retention, and termination; salary increases; and employee improvement.

**Architect** the individual responsible for designing a functional facility by drawing drafts, building scale models, and be a resource to the planning committee for pre-construction processes including site studies, surveying, and securing permits.

**Assault** when one individual tries to physically harm another in a way that makes the second person under attack feel immediately threatened; there does not need to be actual physical contact – threats, gestures, and other actions that would raise the suspicions of a reasonable person can constitute an assault.

**Asset**   items that are of value to a business such as buildings (fixed assets) and cash (current assets).

**Asset-backed securitizations**   similar to private-placement bonds, however only the most financially viable revenue streams are bundled into the bond offering.

**Atmospherics**   the utilization of the design of visual communications in an environment to entice the sport consumer's perceptual and emotional responses to purchase the sport product or service.

**Attitude**   a mental state of readiness that is learned and organized through experience.

**Autocratic leadership**   a style of leadership where the leader tells the human resources what to do, and limits discussion about alternative courses of action.

**Avoidant style**   a neglecting style of conflict resolution where the person is indifferent to the concerns of either party and may withdraw from the conflict.

**Balance sheet**   a listing of the assets and creditors (or liabilities) of a business at a point in time which enables readers to identify the net worth (or capital of a business). The balance sheet equation is ASSETS minus CREDITORS (or LIABILITIES) equals CAPITAL.

**Battery**   the unlawful and unwanted physical contact by one person to a second person with the intention to harm.

**Benchmarking**   the process of measurement based on a specific set of standards of comparison.

**Benchmarks**   individual management tools used by an organization to plan for evaluation, measurement, and improvement.

**BIFM**   British Institute of Facilities Management.

**Bonds**   interest-bearing certificates that are issued by either a jurisdiction or a business that is a binding promise to repay the initial investment of money, and an agreed upon level of interest at a specified date in the future.

**Budget**   the goals of a business expressed in financial terms, for example 'to achieve a profit of $2 m in the next financial year'; an organization's budget will typically be produced on a spreadsheet and will model how the agreed business goals are intended to pan out in practice.

**Burnout**   a pattern of emotional, physical, and mental exhaustion in response to job-related stressors.

**Business continuity**   involves developing measures and safeguards allowing an organization to continue to operate under adverse conditions.

**Bylaws**   the rules adopted to define and direct the internal structure, policies, and procedures of an entity.

**Capital**   the net worth of a business; capital is what is left over once all creditors have been paid off – it comes in two forms: first, the investment of the owners in a business; and, second, profits that are retained within the business as a result of successful trading (in commercial businesses capital is also known as shareholders' funds).

**Capital costs**   the expenses incurred on land, buildings, construction, and equipment related to the management and operation of a facility.

**C-Corporation**   see corporation.

**Certificates of obligation**   bonds that are secured by unlimited claims on tax revenues, have a low interest rate, and are easily obtained through governmental sources because the issuance does not require approval by vote of the population.

**Certificates of participation**   a non-guaranteed bond that involves a jurisdiction purchasing a facility and leasing parts of the facility back to the general public or associated agencies; the revenue from those lease payments is then utilized to pay off the capital expenses for the sport facility.

**Climate**   forecasting the factors that will have a direct effect on the internal and external functioning of the sport facility.

**Close corporation**   similar to a C-Corporation, however it is designed for businesses that have a corporate structure with as few as one owner (a sole proprietor who chooses to use a corporation structure) to a maximum of usually no more than 50 owners/ shareholders.

**Collaborative style**   an integration style of conflict resolution concerned with a win-win situation for both parties; therefore, both parties are fully satisfied with the outcome.

**Command center (also known as a Command post)**   The place that controls the security functions of the sport facility, and has communication capabilities for security forces to monitor events inside and outside of the facility.

**Command groups**   A formal group that is specified in organizational charts, including employees reporting to a supervisor or manager.

**Common law**   laws that are created based on past legal decisions (precedence).

**Common size analysis**   see vertical analysis.

**Competing values model**   a model of organizational effectiveness where effectiveness is measured based on the interaction between four sets of competing values: (1) internal focus and integration; (2) external focus and differentiation; (3) flexibility and discretion; and (4) control and stability.

**Competitive style**   a dominating style of conflict resolution in which the person wants to win at the expense of another's concerns.

**Consequence evaluation**   measuring the 'criticality' impact of loss; classified as essential (catastrophic loss), critical (serious loss), important (moderate loss), or not important (minor loss).

**Consideration**   the exchange of value between two parties, hence there is a benefit to both parties.

**Consumer**   an individual or organization that purchases or obtains goods and services for direct use or ownership.

**Constitution**   a document that outlines the purpose, structure, and limits of an organization.

**Constitutional law**   laws embedded in the constitution or charter of a country or region.

**Constraints (of a project)**   specific restrictions that may have an adverse effect on the scope of a project and its related actions.

**Consumer behavior**   the conduct that consumers display in seeking out, ordering, buying, using, and assessing products and services that the consumers' expects will satisfy their needs and wants.

**Contingency plan**   the steps taken before, during, and after an incident.

**Contingency theory of leadership**   explains that the most effective style of leadership is dependent on factors relating to employees and the work environment itself.

**Contractor**   the main builder for a sport facility.

**Controlling**   see coordinating.

**Coordinating**   monitoring resources and processes to achieve goals and objectives in an efficient manner.

**Corporation**   a business ownership structure created under the laws and regulations of governmental authority made up of a group of individuals who obtain a charter authorizing them as a legal body where the powers, rights, authority, and liabilities of the entity are distinct from the individuals making up the group.

**Countermeasures**   methods and tools used to reduce the probability and consequence severity of a threat/risk.

**Copyright**   intellectual property that gives the owner of an artistic creation the exclusive right to copy, reproduce, distribute, publish, perform, or display the work.

**Creditor**   a trading partner, business, or agency to whom money is owed. Creditors might include staff, suppliers, and tax authorities. Creditors are also known as 'liabilities'.

**Criminal law**   laws enacted to protect the general health, safety, and welfare of the public.

**Current assets**   items of value that are used for day-to-day trading activities and there is an expectation that current assets are either cash or will be turned into cash (for example debtors paying up) in the next year.

**Current ratio**   a model for measuring a business' liquidity; defines the company's ability to meet short-term debt obligations.

**Customer satisfaction**   the extent to which service attributes meet the needs of facility users.

**Data benchmarking**   involves comparison with numerical standards (e.g. averages) calculated for performance indicators in a particular service.

**Debentures**   see permanent seat licenses.

**Debt financing**   money or capital from those who are prepared to loan money for the development of a business in return for a fixed rate of interest and the knowledge that in the event of business failure they will get their money back.

**Debtor**   a trading partner, a business, or an agency which owes money to a business – most commonly for sales made on credit.

**Debt ratio**   a measure of how much an organization's assets are funded by its creditors.

**Decision-making**   Management role that includes initiating change, resolving disputes, and conducting negotiations with internal and external entities.

**Defamation**   written (libel) or verbal (slander) communication of non-factual information with the intent to create a negative image.

**Delegating**   one of Hersey and Blanchard's situational leadership styles; the leader provides little instruction, direction, or personal support to employees.

**Delivery**   the concept of producing or achieving what is desired or expected by the consumer.

**Democratic leadership**   a participative style of leadership when human resources are involved with the decision-making and problem-solving processes.

**Development**   the further education of an employee to further his/her skills, and value to an organization.

**Directive leadership**   a type of leader behavior involving setting standards and communicating expectations to workers.

**Discussion-based exercises**   steps taken to familiarize participants with current plans and policies, or may be used to develop new plans and policies.

**Domestic terrorism**   the unlawful use, or threatened use, of force or violence by a group or individual based and operating entirely within the home country.

**Economic impact**   the net economic change in a host community that is directly attributable to a facility or an event.

**Economic impact study**   a commissioned analysis that attempts to model the future economic impacts of a sport facility or to measure the actual economic impact of a facility or an event.

**Economy**   is solely concerned with the input side of the production process and with costs; is achieved if inputs are acquired with minimum cost.

**Effectiveness**   is concerned solely with the achievement of output targets, and does not consider the costs of achieving the output targets – particularly important in the public sector as providers in this sector have social objectives that are largely non-financial in nature.

**Efficiency**   is concerned with achieving objectives and targets at minimum cost; considers the best possible relationships between inputs and outputs and is often called 'cost effectiveness', 'cost efficiency', 'productivity', or 'value for money'.

**Embedded knowledge**   the information which is articulated within rules and regulations, and organizational policies and procedures.

**Embodied knowledge**   the practical skills, understandings, and applications of concepts exhibited by employees and management.

**Embraced knowledge**   the theoretical/conceptual/cognitive skills exhibited by employees and management.

**Emotional motive**   involves the selection of goals according to individual or subjective criterion.

**Employment**   the process of making a living through work or conducting business.

**Encultured knowledge**   the collective intelligence, values, and beliefs of an entire organization.

**Environmental management**   the process of managing the interaction between the human environment and the physical environment/habitats.

**Equity**   is a subset of effectiveness and is concerned with the fairness of how a service is being delivered, such as the need to know what type of people are accessing a service as well as how many people are accessing it.

**Equity financing**   money or capital drawn from those who wish to risk their money on taking a stake in a business by buying the right to share in future profits.

**EurOMA**   the European Operations Management Association.

**Event life cycle**   a schedule or timeline of events scripted to the minute.

**Executive level**   professional staff within an organization who has the most power and authority, is made up of senior or top managers, and they are usually responsible for the majority of the overall management and operation of the organization.

**Facility event marketing plan**   a comprehensive framework for identifying and achieving a sport facility's marketing goals and objectives through the event.

**Facility management**   an all-encompassing term referring to the maintenance and care of commercial and non-profit buildings, including but not limited to sport facilities.

**Facility operations manual**   the central document that articulates accurate and current information regarding the operational policies and procedures of the sport facility.

**Fault-driven model**   a model of organizational effectiveness where effectiveness seeks to eliminate traces of ineffectiveness in its internal functioning through the design of backup plans to be reliable even if some components fail.

**Favorable**   description of a desirable variance between actual and budgeted financial performance, for example sales have been higher than expected.

**Feasibility study**   an examination of the likelihood that an idea or concept can be transformed into a business entity.

**Financial accounting**   the classification and recording of monetary transactions of an entity in accordance with established concepts, principles, accounting standards and legal requirements, and their presentation, by means of profit and loss accounts, balance sheets, and cash-flow statements, during and at the end of an accounting period.

**Financial indicator**   an indicator that is concerned with the performance of an organization expressed in monetary terms such as profitability, growth, or return on investment, and is often used for analyzing financial statements and measuring concepts such as cost or income per square meter, or secondary spend per customer.

**Financial management**   the group of concepts including financial reporting, budgeting and break-even analysis that are vital to the fiscal health of the sport facility, and hence the ability to continue business operations.

**Financial statements**   the prescribed format in which financial accounts are presented, namely, the profit and loss account (also called the income and expenditure statement); the balance sheet; the cash-flow statement; and an integral set of notes.

**Financing**   the act of obtaining or providing money or capital for the purchase of a business enterprise.

**Fixed assets**   items of value that are not usually traded in the normal course of business and tend to have long-term value (more than one year) to a business.

**Friendship group**   An informal group made up of employees who have something in common, such as age, ethnic background, or even similar sporting interests.

**FMA Australia**   the Facility Management Association of Australia.

**General obligation bonds**   bonds that are repaid with a portion of the general property tax and are backed by the full faith and credit of the issuing body.

**General partnership**   the most basic form of partnership; is an ownership structure where two or more partners are responsible for all business operations and management responsibilities for a business.

**General staff**   are the specialists within individual units who complete the tasks as assigned by the management structure.

**Goal model**   a model of organizational effectiveness where the achievement of specific organizational goals determines effectiveness, and is designed to enhance strategic planning by linking program goals and resource allocation levels.

**Greening**   the process of transforming a space into a more environmentally friendly area.

**Hard taxes**   assessments that are applied to the entire population.

**Hazard**   an occurrence that can cause personal injury, property damage, or economic loss.

**Herzberg's two-factor theory**   proposes two different sets of job factors: (1) intrinsic motivators and (2) extrinsic hygiene factors.

**High-performing system model**   a model of organizational effectiveness where effectiveness is a measurement that compared itself with other similar organizations.

**Horizontal analysis**   a financial analysis technique used to measure changes in performance between one financial period and another; primarily used to measure business growth (for example in sales or profit). Also known as year-on-year analysis.

**Human capital management**   the process of planning, organizing, directing, and controlling the most important asset within an organization – the people.

**Human relation model**   a model of organizational effectiveness where effectiveness is measured based on the development of the organization's personnel.

**Human resource management**   the logical and strategic supervision and managing of the most important asset within an organization – the employees; without a quality group of individuals working for the facility, goals and objectives could not be met, tasks would not be completed, and customers would not be served.

**Human resource manual**   the central document that articulates accurate and current information regarding the policies and procedures of the sport facility as they relate to employees/personnel/volunteers/other associated human resources.

**HVAC**   heating, ventilation, and air conditioning.

**IAAM**   International Association of Assembly Managers.

**IFMA**   International Facility Management Association; the world's largest and most widely recognized international association for professional facility managers.

**Ideal self**   human resource management concept where a manager needs to recognize whom the human resource wants to be.

**Images**   the pictures that are formed in the mind to differentiate what is perceived.

**Impact**   how a facility will have a direct effect on the future development of an action.

**Importance**   the value that customers place on particular service attributes of a facility.

**Income**   all monies that have been received or are receivable (e.g. debtors) by an organization in a given period of time.

**Income and expenditure statement**   see profit and loss account.

**Informational roles**   Management that includes disseminating pertinent information to staff members and acting as a spokesperson to external constituencies.

**Intellectual property**   creative intangible assets that have commercial value.

**Intentional tort**   a civil wrong (criminal act) based on an intentional act.

**Interest**   an amount of money paid, in addition to principal, as a fee for borrowing principal.

**Interest group**   an informal group formed to achieve a mutual objective among the group, not related to objectives of the organization.

**Internal process model**   see process model.

**Internal reports system**   a framework part of the marketing information system that allows the organization to examine the internal operations of the sport organization to enhance their marketing efforts.

**International terrorism**   the unlawful use of force or violence against persons or property committed by a group or an individual who has some connection to a foreign power or whose activities transcend national boundaries.

**Interpersonal roles**   Management that is social in nature and includes serving as a figurehead or 'face' of the organization.

**Invasion of privacy**   interference with the right to be left alone.

**Inventory of assignments**   sequenced, priority listing of responsibilities to ensure which tasks are accomplished first, and how long it should take to complete the tasks.

**Job allotment**   the allocation of tasks to employees.

**Job analysis**   a common technique used to help a manager match the individual to a specific job; is the process of examining and evaluating the specific tasks to be completed within an organization and determining the best way to design a method for completing them in the most timely and relevant way.

**Job description**   a document that articulates the job responsibilities of a position opening and the expected competencies of candidates for the position.

**Job enrichment**   refers to adding variety, responsibility, and managerial decision-making to make the job more rewarding.

**Job evaluation**   providing direct feedback about the employees' work so that necessary changes can be made.

**Key assets**   individual targets whose destruction could create local disaster or damage to the nation's morale or confidence.

**Knowledge management**   the acquisition, sharing, and use of intelligence, understanding, and expertise within a sport organization to aid in the accomplishment of tasks, processes, and operations.

**Laissez-Faire leadership**   where the leader defers decision-making and problem-solving to the human resources because of their extensive experience, skill, and knowledge about a given process; a hands-off style of leadership.

**Laws**   a body of rules that govern individual or collective actions and conduct as defined by an authorized governing body and having binding legal force.

**Leadership**   the process of influencing followers (employees) to attain organizational goals.

**Leading**   entails providing direction for the sport organization and its staff and influencing staff to follow the desired direction.

**Leaseback agreements**   where a municipal agency uses a facility it has leased from a private owner.

**Legitimacy model**   a model of organizational effectiveness where effectiveness is measured by acting lawfully and ethically in the eyes of the internal and external environments.

**Liabilities**   see creditors.

**Libel**   written defamation (see defamation)

**Life-cycle costs**   the maintenance of physical asset cost records over the entire asset lives, so that decisions concerning the acquisition, use, or disposal of the assets can be made in a way that achieves the optimum asset usage at the lowest cost to the entity.

**Limited liability corporation (LLC)**   hybrid corporate structure with characteristics of both a partnership and a corporation, it is formed by members of the organization, not shareholders.

**Limited liability partnership (LLP)**   see limited partnership.

**Limited partnership**   an ownership structure where owners provide financial backing for a business, but do not take an active role in the day-to-day operation and management of the business.

**Liquidity**   a measure of an organization's ability to meet its obligations (payments to creditors) as they fall due; can be measured using ratios such as the current ratio or the quick ratio.

**Maintenance**   preventative work necessary to maintain facilities and equipment.

**Management**   the process of planning, organizing, directing, and controlling tasks to accomplish goals, meet the mission of the organization, and work towards a vision.

**Management accounting**   the process of identification, measurement, accumulation, analysis, preparation, interpretation, and communication of information used by management to plan, evaluate, and control within an entity and to assure appropriate use of and accountability for its resources.

**Marketing concept**   a consumer-oriented philosophy that suggests that satisfaction of consumer needs provides the focus for product development and marketing strategy to enable the firm to meet its own organizational goals.

**Marketing decision support system**   the culminating technique within a marketing information system that assists managers and other decision makers within an organization by taking advantage of information that is available from the various sources and using that information to make strategic decisions, control decisions, operational decisions, and marketing decisions.

**Marketing information system**   a procedure to collect the various data available in one place for use in making sport marketing decisions through an intricate structure involving the interacting of people, infrastructure, and techniques to gather, sort, analyze, evaluate, and distribute relevant, well-timed, accurate information for use by sport facility directors so that they can develop, implement, and manage marketing plans.

**Marketing intelligence system**   an element of the marketing information system that examines the external environment affecting organizations and their associated functions.

**Marketing research system**   the process of designing, gathering, analyzing, and reporting information that is utilized to solve a specified sport marketing issue or problem.

**Maslow's hierarchy of needs**   a model that emphasizes five levels of individual needs – basic physiological needs, safety needs, social needs, self-esteem needs, and self actualization.

**Master plan**   a strategy for taking a vision for a sport facility and plot a path for making it a reality.

**Middle managers**   see administrative level.

**Mission**   the purpose of an organization; serves as the frame of reference for goals and objectives.

**Motivation**   the influence that initiates the drive to satisfy wants and needs.

**Motives**   emotional or psychological needs that act to stimulate an action.

**Multiparty arrangements**   where multiple financial partners initiate complex agreement to finance a facility.

**Multiple constituency model**   a model of organizational effectiveness where effectiveness is not internally judged, but is based on the judgment of its constituents.

**Municipal bonds**   interest-bearing certificates issued by a governmental agency where the interest is tax-exempt.

**Negligence**   also known as an unintentional tort; is a failure to act in a manner equal to how a reasonable person would act under the same circumstances – for there to be negligence, four elements must be proved: (1) duty, (2) the act itself, (3) proximate cause, and (4) damages.

**Non-profit corporation**   a business whose purpose is not to make a profit, but rather to offer services that are beneficial to the general public; most are tax-exempt.

**Objective**   a desired future outcome, good objectives are consistent with the MASTER mnemonic.

**Offer**   the tendering of a contract.

**Organizational behavior**   the study of human behavior in the work environment.

**Organizational culture**   a system of shared values, beliefs, assumptions, and understandings that influences worker behavior.

**Open system model**   a model of organizational effectiveness where effectiveness is measured as a result of the degree that an organization acquires inputs from its environment and has outputs accepted by its environment.

**Operations-based exercises**   steps taken to validate plans and policies, clarify roles, and identify resource gaps in security operations.

**Operations management**   focuses on administrating the processes to produce and distribute the products and services offered through a facility through the maintenance, control, and improvement of organizational activities that are required to produce products and services for consumers of the sport facility.

**Organizational effectiveness**   the concept of how efficient a business is in achieving the outcomes set forth in the planning processes.

**Organizational goals**   the tasks that need to be completed to achieve the mission.

**Organizational healing**   the efforts related to repairing the social aspects of the organization, including issues related to continuity, vision, and broken self-concepts that are needed if an organization is to operate in a strong, fit, and well manner after an actual or other perceived negative situation.

**Organizational management**   the planning, organizing, leading, and coordinating functions within a business for creating an environment that supports continuous improvement of personnel, the organization, and the customers.

**Organizational mission**   focuses on the reason for the sport facility and the guiding managerial principles.

**Organizational objectives**   the specific methods to be utilized to accomplish organizational goals.

**Organizational philosophy**   focuses on what is important to the sport facility from a business values and beliefs standpoint.

**Organizational politics**   the use of informal strategies and tactics to gain power.

**Organizational vision**   focuses on the future and where the sport facility and associated organizations ultimately want to be.

**Organizing**   identifying resources and allocating those selected resources to meet specific goals and objectives established during the planning stage.

**Orientation**   the process of introducing new employees to an organization.

**Participant**   an individual who is involved or plays a part in a spectacle – such as a sport event or concert.

**Participating**   one of Hersey and Blanchard's situational leadership styles where the leader and employees share in the decision-making process to complete a quality job.

**Participative leadership**   a type of leader behavior that involves consulting with workers to solicit suggestions and including them in the decision-making process.

**Partnership**   an ownership structure where more than one individual shares the overall administration and business operations of a business.

**Patent**   an intellectual property represented by any new and/or useful invention or improvement on a process, machine, or manufacturing method.

**Path-goal theory of leadership**   a contingency theory that focuses on how leaders influence employee perceptions of work goals, self-development goals, and paths to goal attainment.

**PDCA cycle**   plan, do, check, and act; the sequential categories of total quality management.

**Perceived self**   human resource management concept where a manager needs to recognize how the human resource believes that they are viewed by others.

**Perception**   gaining an understanding of the individual values, attitudes, needs, and expectations of an individual by scanning, gathering, assessing, and interpreting those insights.

**Performance indicator**   a piece of empirical data representing performance that can be compared over time or with similar organizations.

**Performance management**   a visionary process of setting goals and evaluating progress towards accomplishing those goals by taking action in response to actual performances to make outcomes for users and the public better than they would otherwise be.

**Permanent seat licenses**  a fee paid to buy tickets for a specific seat within a specific sport facility.

**Personality**  the unique and personal psychological characteristics of an individual which reflects how they respond to their social environment.

**Personal seat licenses**  see permanent seat licenses.

**Philosophy**  the values and beliefs of an entity that serves as a framework for all that organization engages in.

**Planning**  selecting and prioritizing goals and objectives and the methods to be used to achieve desired results, such as strategic planning, business planning, project planning, and staff planning.

**Plant operations**  the necessary infrastructure used in the support of facility operations and maintenance.

**POMS**  the Production and Operations Management Society.

**Positioning**  how a company seeks to influence the perceptions of potential and current customers about the image of the company and its products and services.

**Power**  the ability to influence decisions and control resources and is obtained in a variety of ways.

**Precedence**  see common law.

**Preliminary planning**  a process involving all of the initial tasks that need to be completed in preparation for a specific course of action.

**Principal**  an initial investment of money.

**Private financing**  providing funding for capital investments by non-governmental individuals and/or businesses to provide products and services to the public under the management and operation of the private entity, and the public usually has to pay a fee to utilize the products and services.

**Private-placement bonds**  are long-term, fixed-interest, taxable certificates issued by a non-municipal organization developing a business to venture capitalists and other private lenders of funds, and are secured by the total revenues generated by the business.

**Private pump-priming**  where a private entity uses its assets to force a public entity to invest in a facility project.

**Private sector leasing**  see leaseback agreements.

**Private sector takeovers**  where a private organization takes over responsibility for operation of a facility owned by the public sector because the municipality does not have either the expertise or finance to appropriately manage/operate the facility.

**Process benchmarking**  involves comparison of different procedures adopted in different organizations; is used in conjunction with performance data; process benchmarking facilitates an understanding of the procedures which improve performance.

**Process model**  a model of organizational effectiveness that focuses on the effectiveness of the internal transformation process; places an emphasis on control and the internal focus; and stresses the role of information management, communication, stability, and control.

**Professional staff**  the employees of a sport organization who are hired to perform specific jobs/tasks in exchange for some form of remuneration.

**Profit and loss account (also known as the income and expenditure statement)**  an analysis of how an organization's capital has changed over a given period as a result of trading; profit is calculated by deducting all expenses from income in order to determine what is left over at the end of trading.

**Pro forma budget**   the anticipated general costs of conducting operations, such as the costs of hosting an event that will be incurred by a sport facility.

**Program analysis**   a study that focuses on needs for the facility in terms of the programs that are either already established or are planned to be established.

**Program statement**   summarizes the major components of a master plan.

**Project description**   a general overview of a proposed new or modified facility, including square footage, inclusions, and amenities.

**Promotions**   a communications process that aids in providing information about the sport facility to consumers through the promotional mix (in sport facilities – advertising, sponsorship, public relations, and atmospherics).

**Protective measures**   procedures designed to be implemented on a permanent basis to serve as routine protection for a facility and are sometimes referred to as 'baseline' security measures.

**Psychic income**   the emotional and psychological benefit that the residents of a municipality perceive that they receive, even though they do not physically attend events at a facility, and are not involved in organizing them.

**Public financing**   involves the collection of taxes from those who receive benefits from the provision of public goods by the government, and then uses those tax revenues to produce and distribute the public goods to the beneficiaries.

**Public grants**   type of non-guaranteed municipal bond where awards of financial assistance from a municipality are provided to carry out a project of support or stimulation for the good of the public – the financing does not have to be repaid since it is technically not categorized as governmental assistance or individual loans.

**Publicly traded corporations**   refers to a business entity that has registered securities such as stocks and/or bonds that can be sold to the general population through stock offerings.

**Public–private partnerships**   agreements between government and the private sector regarding the provision of public services or infrastructure – the public municipality transfers the burden of capital expenditures and risks of cost overruns to the private entity, but maintains a partnership in the offering of products and services to the public.

**Public relations**   the collection of activities, communications, and media coverage that conveys what the sport organization is and what they have to offer, all in the effort to enhance their image and prestige.

**Public sector leasing**   private entities pay a lease fee in order to use the publically funded and managed facility.

**Public sector takeovers**   the seizing of a struggling or failing private sport facility should in the effort to keep an existing sport asset within the municipality because without it the sport/entertainment opportunity would cease to exist in the area.

**Quality management**   an organization-wide approach to understanding precisely what customers need and consistently delivering accurate solutions within budget, on time, and with the minimum loss to society.

**Quick ratio**   a model for measuring a business' liquidity; defines the company's financial strength or weakness.

**Rational goal model**   see goal model.

**Rational motive**   entails selecting goals based on objective criterion.

**Recovery planning**   developing a plan to salvage a situation after a problem has occurred.

**Reference group self**   human resource management concept where a manager needs to recognize how the human resource interacts with their reference group.

**Repair** curative restoration of damaged or worn-out facilities and equipment, or to a normal operating condition.

**Replacement** an exchange or substitution of one fixed asset for another having the capacity to perform the same function.

**Revenue bonds** interest-bearing certificates that are backed exclusively from the revenue that accrues from a business or its associated revenue sources.

**Revenue projections** the forecasting of sales and other income sources to offset expenses and predict net profit or loss.

**Reward systems** the policies and strategies utilized by an organization that focus on compensating employees in a fair, equitable, consistent, and transparent manner.

**Risk** the possibility of loss from a hazard such as personal injury, property damage, or economic loss.

**Risk analysis** the process of determining how frequently a risk may occur.

**Risk assessment** the process of evaluating security-related risks from threats to an organization, its assets, or its personnel.

**Risk communication** verbal and written interactions that reduce the length, strength, and frequencies of controversies resulting from an incident.

**Risk management** the process of avoiding, reducing, transferring, or retaining hazards to reduce legal exposure, prevent financial and human loss, protect facility assets, ensure business continuity, and minimize damage to the sport organization's reputation.

**Sales** the amount of income or turnover that an organization derives from supplying goods and services to customers; is a subset of total income because it does not include items such as bank interest and in the case of not-for-profit organizations, grants and donations.

**Scope (of a project)** the processes that are required to define and control the work necessary to complete a project.

**S-Corporation** a corporate structure formed in a similar manner to C-Corporations, however its tax structure is similar to a sole proprietorship or partnership – with the income from the S-Corporation passed on to the shareholders and they pay the taxes on the profit (or take the deduction in case of a loss) rather than the corporation.

**Segmentation** the concept of dividing a large, diverse group with multiple attributes into smaller groups with distinctive characteristics.

**Selling** one of Hersey and Blanchard's situational leadership styles where the leader provides employees with instructions and is supportive.

**Sensations** the most basic element of perception, as they are the immediate and direct responses from the sensory organs.

**Share** an investment in a business that gives the owner the right to a 'share' in the profits of that business resulting from its trading performance.

**Shareholders** individuals in charge of a corporation based on their investment in a business.

**Sharing style** a compromising style of conflict resolution that results in moderate or incomplete satisfaction for both parties involved.

**Site selection** the proposed location of a facility including attractiveness of location, acreage/hectare available, natural and environmental conditions, ease of access, and community support.

**Situational leadership theory** theory developed by Hersey and Blanchard that states as the employee's readiness level increases, the leader should focus more on relationship behavior and less on task-oriented behavior.

**Slander** spoken defamation (see defamation).

**Soft taxes**   assessments applied to specific product users or to non-residents of a municipality.

**Sole proprietorship**   the most basic form of business ownership; a business that has only one individual as owner, hence that individual is responsible for the overall administration of the business, is accountable for all business operations, including the management of all assets, and having personal responsibility for all debt and liabilities incurred by the sport facility.

**Special authority bonds**   a non-guaranteed municipal bond that provides financing through public organizations that have jurisdictional power outside the normal constraints of the government.

**Spectator**   an individual who is present and observes a spectacle such as a sport event or concert.

**Sponsorship**   involves acquiring the rights to be affiliated with a sport product or business in order to obtain benefits from that association.

**Sport facility event planning process**   the development of the event from conceptualization through activation to implementation and eventual evaluation by event managers.

**Statutory law**   laws created and affirmed by sanctioned legislative bodies.

**Straight governmental appropriations**   non-guaranteed municipal bond where public funding from a municipality's budget is set aside for a specific purpose.

**Strategic constituencies model**   a model of organizational effectiveness where effectiveness is determined by the extent to which the organization satisfies all of its strategic constituencies.

**Strategic human resource management**   an integrative approach to creating human resource strategies that seeks to accomplish goals based on the desired outcomes for an organization.

**Strategic significance**   the potential of having a positive, long-term impact based on the vision of an organization.

**Succession management**   the process of making provisions for the development, replacement, and strategic application of key people over time.

**Supervisory level**   professional staff who are responsible for the day-to-day operations within a specific unit in a department, are responsible to ensure that the specific tasks within their unit are completed based on the directives from their middle manager, and are the connection between the specialists working in each unit.

**Supportive leadership**   a type of leader behavior emphasizing concern for the well-being of the workers and developing mutually satisfying relationships by treating workers as equals.

**Sustainability**   the process of being renewable for an indefinite period without damaging the environment.

**SWOT**   Acronym meaning (internal) strengths, (internal) weaknesses, (external) opportunities, and (external) threats.

**Systems resources model**   a model of organizational effectiveness where effectiveness is determined in terms of the ability to attract and secure valuable resources, such as operating capital, physical resources, and quality human resources.

**Target**   a precise statement of what is to be achieved by when; can be tangible (such as a stadium or arena) or intangible (mission and vision).

**Targeting**   the process of seeking to find the best way to get a product's image into the minds of consumers, and hence entice the consumer to purchase the product accomplished by focusing on the 5 Ps of sport marketing (product, price, place, promotion, and publicity).

**Task group**  A formal group that is formed to complete a particular job or project.

**Taxable bonds**  interest-bearing certificates usually issued by corporations that do not offer the same tax-exempt benefits of a municipal bond.

**Tax-increment financing**  a non-guaranteed municipal bond utilized when there is an area identified as needing some type of renewal or redevelopment – the jurisdiction freezes the tax base in that area until the development or renewal takes place, and then taxes are raised to pay off the bond.

**Team**  A formal group consisted of individuals who work closely together and share a common vision or goal.

**Telling**  one of Hersey and Blanchard's situational leadership styles where the leader defines roles and tells employees what, where, how, and when to perform specific tasks.

**Threat**  a product of intention and capability of an adversary to take action which would be detrimental to an asset.

**Timelines**  The listing of specific benchmarks, deadlines, and schedules related to effective and efficient management and operation.

**Total quality management (TQM)**  a comprehensive, structured approach to operations management that seeks to improve the quality of facility services through constant refinements in response to feedback from users and staff.

**Trademark**  intellectual property represented by a word, phrase, symbol, or design; or a combination of words, phrases, symbols, or designs, which identifies and distinguishes the source of the goods of one party from those of others.

**Training**  the education of an employee in their job task.

**Trusts**  a catch-all description for organizations that is specifically set up to run local authority leisure services independently, and for public good rather than individual gain.

**Turnover**  total income (see above) for an organization.

**Unintentional tort**  see negligence.

**Utilization indicator**  a measure of the throughput or usage of a facility, such as the number of visits per square meter for sport facilities or the capacity of seats sold for spectator events.

**Variance**  the difference between actual financial performance and budgeted financial performance. Actual minus Budget equals Variance.

**Vertical analysis**  a financial analysis technique used to express all items on a financial statement as a percentage of a key variable; the most common use of vertical analysis is to express the items on the profit and loss account as a proportion of turnover which is given the value of 100%. Also known as common size analysis.

**Vision**  where an organization wants to be in the future.

**Volunteer**  a non-employee who willingly becomes involved with an organization or event for no compensation to assist with a need that could not otherwise be offered.

**Vulnerability**  an exploitable security weakness or deficiency at a facility.

**Work breakdown structures**  itemized responsibilities by task, personnel, and operational area.

**Year-on-year analysis**  see horizontal analysis.

# Further reading

Ackerman, A.M., 1994. Privatization of public-assembly-facility management. Cornell Hotel and Restaurant Administration Quarterly 35 (2), 72. Retrieved April 9, 2009, from ABI/INFORM Global database (Document ID: 274774).

Adler, P.S., Kranowitz, J.L., 2005. A Primer on Perceptions of Risk, Risk Communication and Building Trust. The KeyStone Center. Available from: http://www.netl.doe. gov/technologies/carbon_seq/refshelf/reg-issues/TKC%20Risk%20Paper.fin.pdf

Ammon, R., Southall, R., Blair, D., 2004. Sport Facility Management: Organizing Events and Mitigating Risks. Fitness Information Technology, Inc., Morgantown, WV.

Anand, A., Milne, F., Purda, L., 2006. Voluntary adoption of corporate governance mechanisms. <http://law.bepress.com/expresso/eps/1277> (accessed 16.03.09.).

Analoui, F., 2007. Strategic Human Resource Management. Thomson Learning, London.

Appenzeller, H., 2000. Risk assessment and reduction (chapter 24). In: Appenzeller, H., Lewis, G. (Eds.), Successful Sport Management: A Guide to Legal Issues. Carolina Academic Press. ISBN-13: 9780890896617.

Argyle, M., 1990. Bodily Communication, second ed. Madison, CT: International Universities Press, Madison, CT.

Armstrong, M., 2007. A Handbook of Human Resource Management Practice, 10th ed. Kogan Page, London.

Avolio, B.J., Waldman, D.A., McDaniel, M.A., 1990. Age and work performance in nonmanagerial jobs: the effects of experience and occupational type. Academy of Management Journal 33 (2), 407–422.

ASIS.org., 2008. ASIS International. <http://www.asisonline.org/about/history/index. xml> (accessed 15.12.08.).

Audit Commission, 2007. Improving Information to Support Decision Making: Standards for Better Quality Data. Audit Commission, London.

Audit Commission, 2000a. Aiming to Improve: the Principles of Performance Measurement. Audit Commission, London.

Audit Commission, 2000b. On Target: The Practice of Performance Indicators. Audit Commission, London.

Audit Commission, 1989. Sport for Whom? Clarifying the Local Authority Role in Sport and Recreation. HMSO, London.

Baade, R.A, 2003. Evaluating subsidies for professional sports in the United States and Europe: a public-sector primer. Oxford Review of Economic Policy 19 (4), 585–597. Retrieved March 19, 2009, from ABI/INFORM Global database.

Baade, R.A., Matheson, V.A., 2006. Have public finance principles been shut out in financing new stadiums for the NFL? Public Finance and Management 6 (3), 284–305, 307–320.

Balanced Scorecard Institute, 2009. What is the balanced scorecard? <http://www. balancedscorecard.org/BSCResources/AbouttheBalancedScorecard/tabid/55/Default. aspx> (accessed 05.08.09.).

Bakamitsos, G.A., Siomkos, G.J., 2004. Context effects in marketing practice: the case of mood. Journal of Consumer Behaviour 3 (4), 304–314.

Baker, K., Branch, K., 2002. Concepts Underlying Organizational Effectiveness: Trends in the Organization and Management Science Literature. <http://www.au.af.mil/au/awc/awcgate/doe/benchmark/ch01.pdf> (accessed 28.02.09.).

Barr-Smith, A., Calow, D., 2003, February 4. New boundaries for brands under South African law. The Times Retrieved from EBSCOHost.

Beech, J., Chadwick, S. (Eds.), 2004. The Business of Sport Management. Prentice Hall Financial Times, Essex, UK.

Bennis, W., 1997. Organizing Genius: The Secrets of Creative Collaboration. Boston: Addison-Wesley, Boston.

Bennett, G., Sagas, M., Dees, W., 2006. Media preferences of action sports consumers: differences between Generation X and Y. Sport Marketing Quarterly 15 (1), 40–49.

Bhattacharjee, S., Rao, G., 2006. Tackling ambush marketing: the need for regulation and analysing the present legislative and contractual efforts. Sport in Society 9 (1), 128–149.

Big D Disaster, 2009, May. Sports Illustrated 110 (19), 30. Retrieved June 21, 2009 from Research Library Core database.

Bovaird, T., 2007. Beyond engagement and participation: user and community coproduction of public services. Public Administration Review 67 (5), 846–860.

Brauer, R.L., 1992. Facilities Planning. Amacom Books, New York.

Bridges, F.J., Roquemore, L.L., 2004. Management for Athletic/Sport Administration, fourth ed. ESM Books, Decatur, GA.

Brook, S., 2005. What do sports teams produce? Journal of Economic Issues 39 (3), 792–797.

Buratto, A., Grosett, L., 2006. A communication mix for an event planning: a linear quadratic approach. Journal of Operations Research 14 (3), 247–259.

Bushardt, S.C., Debnath, S.C., Fowler, A.F., 1990. A contingency approach to organizational effectiveness through structural adaptation. American Business Review 8 (1), 16–24.

Careless, S.A., Wearing, A.J., Mann, L., 2000. A short measure of transformational leadership. Journal of Business and Psychology 14 (3), 389–405.

Castellano, J., Perea, A., Alday, L., Hernández-Mendo, A., 2008. The measuring and observation tool in sports. Behavior Research Methods 40 (3), 898–905.

Chadwick, S., 2005. Sport marketing: a discipline for the mainstream. International Journal of Sports Marketing and Sponsorship 7 (1), 7.

Chadwick, S., Thwaites, D., 2004. Advances in the management of sports sponsorship: fact or fiction? Evidence from English professional soccer. Journal of General Management 30 (1), 39–59.

Chartered Institute of Management Accountants, 1996. Management Accounting: Official Terminology. CIMA, London.

Chelladurai, P., 2006. Human Resource Management in Sport and Recreation, second ed. Human Kinetics, Champaign, IL.

Clement, A., 2004. Law in Sport and Physical Activity, third ed. Sport and Law Press, Miami Shores, FL.

Coderre, F., St-Laurent, N., Mathieu, A., 2004. Comparison of the quality of qualitative data obtained through telephone, postal and email surveys. International Journal of Market Research 46 (3), 347–357.

Cotts, D.G., 1999. The Facility Management Handbook, second ed. AMACOM, New York.

Coates, D., Humphreys, B.R., 2003. Professional sport facilities, franchises and urban economic development. Public Finance and Management 3 (3), 335–357.

Coots, D.G., 1992. The Facility Management Handbook, second ed. Amacom Books, New York.

Conger, J.A., Kanungo, R.N., 1998. Charismatic Leadership in Organizations. Sage, Thousand Oaks, CA.

Connolly, E., 2009. Balkan fans riot at Australian Open tennis. The Guardian. <http://www.guardian.co.uk/world/2009/jan/24/australian-open-riot> (accessed 12.02.09.).

Cotten, D.J., Wolohan, J.T., 2003. Law for Recreation and Sport Managers, third ed. Kendall/Hunt Publishing Company, Dubuque, IA.

Covell, D., Walker, S., Hess, P.W., Siciliano, J., 2007. Managing Sport Organizations: Responsibility for Performance, second ed. Butterworth-Heinemann//Elsevier, Oxford, UK.

Covello, V.T., Allen, F.A., 1988. Seven Cardinal Rules of Risk Communication. U.S. Environmental Protection Agency, Washington, DC.

Crafton, Tull, Sparks, n.d. Developing a master plan: step two in building a facility for a winning sports program. <http://www.craftontullsparks.com/assets/0000/0507/MasterPlan.pdf> (accessed 05.02.09.).

Crompton, J.L., 2004. Conceptualization and alternate operationalizations of the measurement of sponsorship effectiveness in sport. Leisure Studies 23 (3), 267–281.

Cunningham, J.B., Eberie, T., 1990. A guide to job enrichment and redesign. Personnel 67 (2), 56–61.

Davis, T., 2001. What is sports law? Marquette Sports Law Review 11, 211–244.

Department of Homeland Security, 2004, July 23. Department of Homeland Security Hosts Security Forum for Sports Executives. Office of the Press Secretary. <http://dhs.gov/dhspublic/display?content=3863> (accessed 15.09.08.).

Department of Homeland Security, 2008. Protective Measures Guide for US Sports Leagues.

Decker, R.J., 2001. Key Elements of a Risk Management Approach. United States General Accounting Office (on-line). Available from: <http://www.gao.gov/new.items/d02150t.pdf>.

DHS.gov., 2005. DHS Organization. http://www.dhs.gov/dhspublic/disply?theme=9&content=4624> (accessed 13.09.05).

Doukas, S.G., 2006. Spring. Crowd management: past and contemporary issues. The Sport Journal (9), 2.

Downes, S., 2009, June 3. Facility notes. <http://www.sportsbusinessdaily.com/index.cfm?fuseaction=sbd.preview&articleID=130672> (accessed 11.06.09.).

DuBrin, A.J., 2002. The Winning Edge: How to Motivate, Influence, and Manage Your Company's Human Resources. South-Western College Publishing, Cincinnati, OH.

Durling, R.L., Price, D.E., Spero, K.K., 2005. Vulnerability and risk assessment using the homeland-defense operational planning system (HOPS). <http://www.llnl.gov/tid/lof/documents/pdf/315115.pdf> (accessed 04.10.05.).

EFQM, 2009. The EFQM excellence model. <http://ww1.efqm.org/en/Home/aboutEFQM/Ourmodels/TheEFQMExcellenceModel/tabid/170/Default.aspx> (accessed 05.08.09.).

Emery, P.R., 2002. Bidding to host a major sports event: the local organising committee perspective. The International Journal of Public Sector Management 15 (4/5), 316–335.

Erdener, E., 2003. Linking programming and design with facilities management. Journal of Performance of Constructed Facilities 17 (11), 4–8.

Evans, R., 1996. Bogus tickets blamed for overflow crowd. Amusement Business 108 (44), 15.

Evans, D.M., Smith, A.C.T., 2004. Internet sports marketing and competitive advantage for professional sports clubs: bridging the gap between theory and practice. International Journal of Sports Marketing and Sponsorship 6 (2), 86–98.

Fahy, J., Farrelly, F., Quester, P., 2004. Competitive advantage through sponsorship: a conceptual model and research propositions. European Journal of Marketing 38 (8), 1013–1030.

Farmer, P.J., Mulrooney, A.L., Ammon, R., 1996. Sport Facility Planning and Management. Fitness Information Technology, Inc., Morgantown, WV.

Filley, A.C., House, R.J., Kerr, S., 1976. Managerial Process and Organizational Behavior, second ed. Scott Foresman, Glenview, IL.

Filo, K., Funk, D.C., 2005. Congruence between attractive product features and virtual content delivery for Internet marketing communication. Sport Marketing Quarterly 14 (2), 112–122.

Fletcher, G.P., Sheppard, S., 2005. American Law in a Global Context: The Basics. Oxford University Press, Cary, NC.

Flynn, R.B., 1995. Panning Facilities for Athletics, Physical Education, and Recreation. American Alliance for Health, Physical Education, Recreation, and Dance, Reston, VA.

Friday, S., Cotts, D.G., 1994. Quality Facility Management: A Marketing and Customer Service Approach. Wiley, New York.

Fried, G., 2005. Managing Sports Facilities. Human Kinetics, Champaign, IL.

Fried, G., Shapiro, S.J., DeSchriver, T.D., 2008. Sport Finance, second ed. Human Kinetics, Champaign, IL.

Funk, D.C., James, J.D., 2004. Exploring origins of involvement: understanding the relationship between consumer motives and involvement with professional sport teams. Leisure Sciences 26 (1), 35–61.

Funk, D.C., James, J.D., 2004. The fan attitude network (FAN) model: exploring attitude formation and change among sport consumers. Sport Management Review 7 (1), 1–26.

Gardner, W.L., Avolio, B.J., 1998. The charismatic relationship. Academy of Management Review 2 (1), 32–58.

Garner, B.A. (Ed.), 2004. Black's Law Dictionary, eighth ed. Thompson West, Eagan, MN.

Goldman, A.J., 2006. Optimal facility-location. Journal of Research of the National Institute of Standards and Technology 111 (2), 97–101. Retrieved January 29, 2009, from ProQuest Science Journals database.

Goss, B., Jubenville, C., MacBeth, J.L., 2003. Primary principles of post-9/11 stadium security in the United States: transatlantic implications from British practices. Available from: <www.iaam.org/CVMS/Post%20911%20Stadium%20Security.doc>.

Graham, P.J., Ward, R., 2006. Public Assembly Facility Management: Principles and Practices. International Association of Assembly Managers, Coppell, TX.

Grapentine, T., 2005. Segmenting the sales force. Marketing Management 14 (1), 29–34.

Greenberg, M.J., 2004. The stadium game. In: Rosner, S.R., Shropshire, K.L. (Eds.), The Business of Sports. Jones and Bartlett Publishers, Sudbury, MA, pp. 113–126.

Greenwich Leisure Limited, 2009. London's Most Successful Social Enterprise. <http://www.gll.org> (accessed 11.05.09.).

Griffin, R.W., 1991. Effects of work redesign on employee perceptions, attitudes, and behaviors: a long term investigation. Academy of Management Journal 34 (2), 425–435.

Griffin, R.W., Moorhead, G., 1986. Organizational Behavior. Houghton Mifflin, Boston.

Hall, S., 2006. Fall. Effective security management of university sport venues. The Sport Journal 9, 4.

Hall, S., 2006. Effective security management of university sport venues. The Sport Journal 9 (4), 1–10.

Hall, S., Marciani, L., Cooper, W.E., 2008. Emergency management and planning at major sports events. Journal of Emergency Management January/February 6 (1), 43–47.

Hall, S., Marciani, L., Cooper, W.E., 2008. Sport venue security: planning and preparedness for terrorist-related incidents. Sport Management and Related Topics Journal 4 (2), 6–15.

Hall, S., Marciani, L., Cooper, W.E., Rolen, R., 2007, August. Securing sport stadiums in the 21st century: think security, enhance safety. Anser Homeland Security Institute: Journal of Homeland Security, 1–7.

Hall, S., Marciani, L., Cooper, W.E., Rolen, R., 2007. Introducing a risk assessment model for sport venues. The Sport Journal 10 (2), 1–6.

Harbottle, Lewis, December 2003/January 2004. Ambush marketing. <http://www.legal500.com/devs/uk/en/uken_065.htm> (accessed 03.03.06.).

Harzing, A., Van Ruysseveldt, J., 1995. International Human Resource Management. Sage Publications, London.

Hater, J.J., Bass, B.M., 1988. Superiors' evaluations and subordinates' perceptions of transformational and transactional leadership. Journal of Applied Psychology 73 (4), 695–702.

Henderson, N.R., 2005. Twelve steps to better research. Marketing Research 17 (2), 36–37.

Henricks, M., 2007. A blueprint for building success. IAAM Facility Manager. http://www.iaam.org/Facility_manager/Pages/2007_Oct_Nov/Feature_3.htm> (accessed 12.02.09.).

Henry, P.C., 2005. Social class, market situation and consumers' metaphors of (dis)-empowerment. Journal of Consumer Research 31 (4), 766–778.

Hersey, P., Blanchard, K.H., 1988. Management of Organizational Behavior: Utilizing Human Resources, 5th ed. Prentice Hall, Englewood Cliffs, NJ.

Hequet, M., 1994. Giving good feedback. Training 31 (9), 72–76.

Hess, R.L., Rubin, R.S., West Jr., L.A., 2004. Geographic information systems as a marketing information system technology. Decision Support Systems 38 (2), 197–212.

Herzberg, F., 1974. The wise old Turk. Harvard Business Review 52 (5), 70–81.

Hofstede, G., 1980. Culture's Consequences: International Differences in Work-Related Values. Sage, Beverly Hills, CA.

Hoksport.com., 2009. HOK Sport Sustainability Case Studies. <http://www.hoksport.com/sustainable/casestudies.html> (accessed 12.02.09.).

Holograms Provide Security for FIFA World Cup 2002, 2002, August. Holography News (16), 6. <http://ihma.org/upload/file/HN%202002%20FIFA.pdf> (accessed 30.01.09.).

Homeland Security Exercise and Evaluation Program (HSEEP), 2007. Volume I: HSEEP Overview and Exercise Program Management. Available from: https://hseep.dhs.gov/support/VolumeI.pdf

Hopwood, M.K., 2005. Applying the public relations function to the business of sport. International Journal of Sports Marketing and Sponsorship 6 (3), 174–188.

Hou, X., 2007. Fundamental research on development management of sports facility in Beijing universities. Journal of Shenyang Institute of Physical Education 26 (4), 36–38.

House, R.J., 1971. A path-goal theory of leadership effectiveness. Administrative Science Quarterly 16 (3), 321–329.

House, R.J., Mitchell, T.R., 1974. Path-goal theory of leadership. Journal of Contemporary Business 3, 81–97.

Howard, D.R., Crompton, J.L., 2004. Financing Sport, second ed. Fitness Information Technology, Morgantown, WV.

Hums, M.A., MacLean, J.C., 2009. Governance and policy in sport organizations. Holcomb Hathaway Publishers, Scottsdale, AZ.

Hums, M.A., Barr, C.A., Guillion, L., 1999. The ethical issues confronting managers in the sport industry. Journal of Business Ethics 20 (1), 51–66.

Hurst, R., Zoubek, P., Pratsinakis, C., 2007. American sports as a target of terrorism: the duty of care after September 11th (on-line). Available from: www.mmwr.com/_uploads/UploadDocs/publications/American%20Sports%20As%20A%20Target%20Of%20Terrorism.pdf.

Hypes, M.G., 2006. Planning and designing facilities. Journal of Physical Education, Recreation, and Dance 77 (4), 18–22.

IAAM, 2002. Safety and Security Task Force Best Practices Planning Guide. Center for Venue Management Studies. <http://www.iaam.org/CVMS/cvms.htm> (accessed 20.09.08.).

IDeA, 2006. Towards an Excellent Service: A Performance Management Framework for Cultural Services. IDeA, London.

International Organization for Standardization, 2009. ISO 14000 essentials. <http://www.iso.org/iso/iso_14000_essentials> (accessed 06.06.09.).

Ironside, S., 2008. Major events management act 2007. Managing Intellectual Property (184), 122. <http://www.managingip.com/Article/2041356/ Major-Events-Management-Act-2007.html> (accessed 06.05.09.).

Ivancevich, Matteson, 1999. Organizational Behavior and Management, fifth ed. McGraw-Hill, New York.

Jackson, T.W., 2005. CRM: from 'art to science'. Journal of Database Marketing and Customer Strategy 13 (1), 76–92.

James, J.D., Ross, S.D., 2004. Comparing sport consumer motivations across multiple sports. Sport Marketing Quarterly 13 (1), 17–25.

Jamrog, J.J., Vickers, M., Overholt, M.H., Morrison, C.L., 2008. High-performance organizations: finding the elements of excellence. Human Resource Planning 31 (1), 29–38.

Kaiser, R., Robinson, K., 2005. Risk management. In: Management of Park and Recreation Services. National Recreation and Park Association, Washington D.C.

Kaplan, R.S., Norton, D.P., 2005. The balanced scorecard – measures that drive performance. Harvard Business Review 83 (7), 172–180.

Kass, S., 1999. Employees perceive women as better managers than men, finds five year study. APA Monitor 30 (8), 6.

Kinney, J.A., 2003. Securing stadiums: keeping them safe for successful special events. Stadium Visions (2), 1, 10. Available from: <http://www.iapsc.org/uploaded_documents/stadiumPDF.pdf>.

Kirmeyer, S.L., Dougherty, T.W., 1988. Work load, tension, and coping: moderating effects of supervisor support. Personnel Psychology 41 (1), 125–139.

Koger, D., 2001. Expanding sports facilities. American School & University 73(11), 48.

Korean Security Measures, 2002. World Cup Soccer News. <http://soccerphile.com/archives/wc2002/ne/mfb.html> (accessed 01.02.09.).

Kotter, J.P., 1990. What leaders really do. Harvard Business Review 68 (3), 103–111.

Kwok, S., Uncles, M., 2005. Sales promotion effectiveness: the impact of consumer differences at an ethnic-group level. Journal of Product and Brand Management 14 (3), 170–186.

Kwon, H.H., Armstrong, K.L., 2004. An exploration of the construct of psychological attachment to a sport team among students: a multidimensional approach. Sport Marketing Quarterly 13 (2), 94–103.

Laabs, J., 1998. Satisfy them with more than money. Workforce 77 (11), 40–43.

Larue, R.J., Sawyer, T.H., Vivian, J., 2005. Electrical, mechanical, and energy management. In: Sawyer, T.H. (Ed.), Facility Design and Management, for Health, Fitness, Physical Activity, Recreation, and Sports Facility Development, 11th ed. Sagamore Publishing, Champaign, IL 2002.

Lawler III, E.E., 1977. Reward systems. In: Hackman, J.R., Suttle, J.L. (Eds.), Improving Life at Work. Goodyear Publishing, Santa Monica, CA, pp. 163–226.

Leonidou, L.C., Theodosiou, M., 2004. The export marketing information system: an integration of the extent knowledge. Journal of World Business 39 (1), 12–36.

Lewin, K., 1935. A Dynamic Theory of Personality. McGraw-Hill, New York.

Lilien, G.L., Rangaswamy, A., Van Bruggen, G.H., Starke, K., 2004. DSS effectiveness in marketing resource allocation decisions: reality vs. perception. Information Systems Research 15 (3), 216–235.

Locander, W.B., Luechauer, D.L., 2005. Are we there yet? Marketing Management 14 (6), 50–52.

Long, L.E., Renfrow, N.A., 1999. A new automation tool for risk assessment. In: 15th Annual NDIA Security Technology Symposium. Session: Risk and Threat Assessment Techniques. Available from: <http://www.dtic.mil/ndia/technology/smith.pdf>.

Maloy, B.P., 1993. Legal obligations related to facilities. The Journal of Physical Education, Recreation & Dance 64 (2), 28–30.

Marber, A., Wellen, P., Posluszny, S., 2005. The merging of marketing and sports: a case study. Marketing Management Journal 15 (1), 162–171.

Marsden, A.W., 1998. Training railway operating staff to understand and manage passenger and crowd behaviour. Disaster Prevention and Management 5 (7), 401–405. Retrieved February 13, 2009 from EBSCO database.

Maskus, K., 2000. The global policy framework: intellectual property rights and wrongs. <http://www.iie.com/publications/chapters_preview/99/6iie2822.pdf> (accessed 27.01.09).

Maslach, C., Leiter, M.P., 1997. The Truth About Burnout: How Organizations Cause Personal Stress and What to Do About It. Jossey-Bass, San Francisco.

Masterman, G., 2004. Strategic Sports Event Management: an International Approach. Butterworth-Heinemann/Elsevier, Oxford, UK.

Martinez-Tur, V., Piero, J.M., Ramos, J., 2001. Linking service structural complexity to customer satisfaction: the moderating role of type of ownership. International Journal of Service Industry Management 12 (3/4), 295–306.

deMause, N., Cagan, J., 2008. Field of Schemes: How the Great Stadium Swindle Turns Public Money into Private Profit (rev. ed.). Nebraska Press, Lincoln, NE.

McAdam, R., 2000. Three leafed clover?: TQM, organisational excellence and business improvement. The TQM Magazine 12 (5), 314.

McCarthy, M., 2008, December 22. A security tool or the 'rat line'? NFL targeting the unruly fan. USATODAY.com. http://www.usatoday.com/sports/football/nfl/2008-12-18-fan-conduct-cover_N.htm> (accessed 01.02.09.).

McCarthy, M., 2008, August 8. NFL unveils new code of conduct for its fans. USATODAY.com. <http://www.usatoday.com/sports/football/nfl/2008-08-05-fan-code-of-conduct_N.htm> (accessed 15.12.08.).

McNamee, M.J., Fleming, S., 2007. Ethics audits and corporate governance: the case of public sector sports organizations. Journal of Business Ethics 73 (4), 425–437.

Miller, W.S., 1998. Sport facility issues, part one. The boom in stadium construction and financing new facilities. For The Record (Marquette University Law School) 9 (4), 7.

Miner, J.B., 1988. Organizational Behavior: Performance and Productivity. Random House, New York.

Mintzberg, H., 1975. The manager's job: folklore and fact. Harvard Business Review 53 (4), 49–61.

Moore, J.E., 2000. Why is this happening? A casual attribution approach to work exhaustion consequences. Academy of Management Review 25 (2), 335–349.

Muret, D., March 6–12, 2006. Staying on guard. Street & Smith's Sports Business Journal 43 (8).

Muret, D., February 11–17, 2008. NFL, stadiums rethinking alcohol policies. Street & Smith's Sports Business Journal 41 (10).

Miller, N., 2007. Ambush marketing and the 2010 Vancouver-Whistler Olympic Games: a prospective view. <http://www.imakenews.com/iln/e_article000867643.cfm?x=b11,0, w> (accessed 11.05.09.).

Miller, D., Desmarais, S., 2007. Developing your talent to the next level: five best practices for leadership. Organization Development Journal 25 (3), P37–P43.

Nalbantian, H.R., Guzzo, R.A., Kieffer, D., Dohery, J., 2003. Play to Your Strengths. Managing Your Internal Labor Markets for Lasting Competitive Advantage. McGraw-Hill Trade, New York.

Naoum, S., 2001. People and Organizational Management in Construction. Thomas Telford, London.

National Intramural-Recreational Sport Association, 2009. Campus Recreational Sports Facilities: Planning, Design, and Construction Guidelines. Human Kinetics, Champaign, IL.

National Counterterrorism Security Office, 2006. Counter Terrorism Protective Security Advice for Stadia and Arenas. Association of Chief Police Officers in Scotland. Available from: <http://www.nactso.gov.uk/documents/Stadia%20Doc. pdf>.

National Ski Areas Association, 2009. The environment. <http://www.nsaa.org/nsaa/environment/sustainable_slopes/> (accessed 04.06.09.).

Naylor, D.J., 2001. Managing Your Leisure Service Budget. Ravenswood Publications Limited, London.

NCAA. org., 2008. About the NCAA. Available from: <http://www.ncaa.org/wps/ncaa?ContentID=2> (accessed 10.12.08.).

Neild, L., October 31, 2007. Police fear new Liverpool stadium could be terrorist target. Liverpool Daily Post. <www.liverpooldailypost.co.uk>; (accessed 10.02.09.).

Newell, K., 2004. If you rebuilt it, they will come: renovating your athletic facility is a win-win situation. Coach & Athletic Director 73 (6), 64–70.

Pantera, M.J., 2003. Architectural design and game day considerations for new or retrofitted sport facilities. The Sport Supplement 11 (4). <www.thesportjournal.org>; (accessed 26.09.05.).

Pantera, M.J., et al., 2003. Best practices for game day security at athletic & sport venues. The Sport Journal 6 (4) (on-line). Available from: <http://www.thesportjournal.org/2003Journal/Vol6-No4/security.asp>.

Papadimitriou, D., Apostolopoulou, A., Loukas, I., 2004. The role of perceived fit in fans' evaluation of sports brand extensions. International Journal of Sports Marketing and Sponsorship 6 (1), 31–48.

Papadimitriou, D., 2007. Conceptualizing effectiveness in a non-profit organizational environment: an exploratory study. The International Journal of Public Sector Management 20 (7), 571–587.

Parks, J.B., Quarterman, J., Thibault, L., 2007. Contemporary Sport Management, third ed. Human Kinetics, Champaign, IL.

Parkhouse, B.L., 2004. The Management of Sport: Its Foundation and Application. McGraw-Hill Higher Education, New York.

Pate, D.W., Moffitt, E., Fugett, D., 1993. Current trends in use, design, construction, and funding of sport facilities. Sport Marketing Quarterly 2 (4), 9–14.

Pearson, G., 2006. Fig Fact-Sheet Four: Hooliganism. <http://www.liv.ac.uk/footballindustry/hooligan.html> (accessed 11.10.07.).

Penquite, C., 2002. Urban ballpark design: a holistic strategy toward vitalization. (Masters Thesis, University of Cincinnati, 2002). <http://www.ohiolink.edu/etd/send-pdf.cgi/PENQUITE%20CRAIG.pdf?acc_num=ucin1084940472> (accessed 19.03.09.).

Petersen, J.C., Piletic, C.K., 2006. Facility accessibility: opening the doors to all. Journal of Physical Education. Recreation & Dance 77 (5), 38–44.

Plochg Business Psychology Consulting, 2009. Dysfunctional patterns in leadership. Retrieved April 22, 2009, from http://businesspsychologistconsulting.com.

Powell, G.N., 1990. One more time: do female and male managers differ? Academy of Management Executive 4 (3), 68–75.

Potoski, M., Prakash, A., 2005. Green clubs and voluntary governance: ISO 14001 and firms' regulatory compliance. American Journal of Political Science 49 (2), 235–248.

Quester, P., 1997. Sponsorship returns: the value of naming rights. Corporate Communications 2 (3), 101–108.

Rebeggiani, L., 2006. Public vs. private spending for sports facilities – the case of Germany 2006. Public Finance and Management 6 (3), 395–424, 429–435.

Rhodes, C., 2000, December 13. Rangers launch smart card. BBC News. Available from: <http://news.bbc.uk/2/hi/uk_news/1066797.stm>.

Robinson, L., 2004. Managing Public Sport and Leisure Services. Routledge, London.

Rosandich, T.J., 2005. Facility maintenance. In: Sawyer, T.H. (Ed.), Facility Design and Management, for Health, Fitness, Physical Activity, Recreation, and Sports Facility Development, 11th ed. Sagamore Publishing, Champaign, IL.

Rosentraub, M.S., 2009. Sport facilities, a new arena in Edmonton, and the opportunities for development and a city's image: Lessons from successful experiences. <http://www.ottawa.ca/calendar/ottawa/citycouncil/pec/ 2009/ 02–24/8-CSS0013-Document%201%20Appendix%20F%20-%20Lessons%20from %20Successful% 20Experiences%20-%20Edmonton.pdf> (accessed 03.04.09.).

Rosentraub, M.S., Swindell, D., 2009. Of devils and details: bargaining for successful public/private partnerships between cities and sports teams. Public Administration Quarterly 33 (1), 118–148.

Rosentraub, M., Swindell, D., 2009. Of devils and details: bargaining for successful public/private partnerships between cities and sports teams. Public Administration Quarterly 33 (1), 118–148.

Rouzies, D., Anderson, E., Kohli, A.K., Michaels, R.E., Weitz, B.A., Zoltners, A.A., 2005. Sales and marketing integration: a proposed framework. Journal of Personal Selling and Sales Management 25 (2), 113–122.

Russell, D., Patel, A., Wilkinson-Riddle, G.J., 2002. Cost Accounting: An Essential Guide. Pearson Educational Limited, London.

Sauter, M.A., Carafano, J.J., 2005. Homeland Security: A Complete Guide to Understanding, Preventing, and Surviving Terrorism. McGraw Hill, New York.

Sawyer, T.H., 2002. Financing facility development. In: Sawyer, T.H. (Ed.), Facilities Planning for Health, Fitness, Physical Activity, Recreation and Sports: Concepts and Applications, 10th ed. Sagamore Publishing, Champaign, IL, pp. 45–66.

Sawyer, T.H., 2006. Financing facilities 101. Journal of Health, Physical Education, Recreation, and Dance 77 (4), 23–28.

Schein, E.H., 1985. Organizational Culture and Leadership. Jossey-Bass, San Francisco.

Schuler, M., 2004. Management of the organizational image: a method for organizational image configuration. Corporate Reputation Review 7 (1), 37–53.

Schwarz, E.C., Hunter, J.D., 2008. Advanced Theory and Practice in Sport Marketing. Elsevier Inc., Oxford, UK.

Schwarz, E.C., 2009. The evolution of global anti-ambush marketing laws. In: Paper Presented at the Seventh Annual Conference of the Sport Marketing Association, Cleveland, Ohio.

Schwepker, C., Good, D.J., 2004. Marketing control and sales force customer orientation. Journal of Personal Selling and Sales Management 24 (3), 167–179.

Schwepker, C., Good, D.J., 2004. Sales management practices: the impact of ethics on customer orientation, employment and performance. Marketing Management Journal 14 (2), 134–147.

Security and Policing, 2005. In U.K. Sport, Staging Major Sports Events: The Guide. Available from: <http://www.uksport.gov.uk/pages/major_sports_event_the_guide/>.

Seidler, T., 2000. Safe facilities: the facility risk review (Chapter 29). In: Appenzeller, H., Lewis, G. (Eds.), Successful Sport Management: a Guide to Legal Issues. Carolina Academic Press, Durham, NC.

Seippel, O., 2002. Volunteers and professional in Norwegian sport organizations. Voluntas: International Journal of Voluntary and Nonprofit Organizations 13 (3), 253–270.

Shibli, S., 1994. Leisure Manager's Guide to Budgeting and Budgetary Control. ILAM/ Longman, London.

Simon, H.A., 1960. The New Science of Management Decision. Harper & Row, New York.

Slack, T., Parent, M.M., 2006. Understanding Sport Organizations: The Application of Organization Theory, second ed. Human Kinetics, Champaign, IL.

Smolianov, P., Shilbury, D., 2005. Examining integrated advertising and sponsorship in corporate marketing through televised sport. Sport Marketing Quarterly 14 (4), 239–250.

Spangler, J., 2001, September 30. Meeting the threat. Deseretnews.com. <http:// deseretnews.com/dn/sview/1,3329,320006966,00.html> (accessed 16.09.05.).

Speegle, M., 2006. Process Technology Plant Operations. Delmar Cengage Learning, Florence, KY.

Spoor, D.L., Cox, S., 1998. Athletic facilities: Planning, designing, and operating today's physical-education centers. American School & University 70 (10), 3.

Sport England, 2004. Funding sport pack. In: Building a sport facility (Chapter 2.10). <http://www.sportengland.org/funding_guidance_building_facilities.pdf> (accessed 29.01.09.).

Stadia Safety and Security, 2005. The Prevention of Football Related Violence. FA Student Research Source. Available from: <http://www.thefa.com/NR/rdonlyres/ CEEB70F9-695A-4F70-8898-8BBE6BBC16BB/95078/1982Sec9.pdf>.

Steinbach, P., 2006. September. Storm: a year removed from the dark days of hurricane Katrina, college athletic departments are now being viewed in a new light – as disaster response specialists. Athletic Business, 38–46.

Steinberg, G.M., Singer, R.N., Murphey, M., 2000. The benefits to sport achievement when a multiple goal orientation is emphasized. Journal of Sport Behavior 23 (4), 407–422.

Stevens, A., 2007. Sports Security and Safety: Evolving Strategies for a Changing World. Sport Business Group.

Stice, S., Stice, W., 2007. A good design is no accident. Athletic Administration 33 (3), 18–19.

Stimac, J., 2000. Put "awe appeal" into your community center: crucial elements in planning for and designing a facility that will "wow" your community. Parks & Recreation 35 (8), 96–102.

Supovitz, F., Goldblatt, J., 2004. The Sports Event Management and Marketing Playbook. Wiley, Hoboken, NJ.

Tackling Football Violence, n.d. Football Violence in Europe: Tackling the Problem. Social Issues Research Center. <http://www.sirc.org/publik/fvtackle.html> (accessed 10.02.09.).

Tang, N.K.H., Benton, H., Love, D., Albores, P., Ball, P., MacBryde, J., Boughton, N., Drake, P., 2004. Developing an enterprise simulator to support electronic supply-chain management for B2B electronic business. Production Planning and Control 15 (6), 572–583.

Taylor, I., 1987. Putting the boot into a working-class sport: British soccer after Bradford and Brussels. Sociology of Sport Journal 4 (2), 171–191.

Taylor, P.D., 1996. The role of management information systems in the provision of recreation. In: Ashworth, G., Dietvorst, A. (Eds.), Tourism and Special Transformation. CAB International, Wallingford, UK.

Taylor, J., 2006. A Survival Guide for Project Managers. AMACOM Division, American Management Association. ISBN: 081440877X.

Thomas, K.W., 1979. Organizational conflict. In: Steven, Kerr (Ed.), Organizational Behavior. Grid Publishing, Columbus, OH, pp. 151–185.

Thomaselli, R., 2005. Ambushing the super bowl: ordinance to pare back sneak ad attacks in host city Detroit scaled down. Advertising Age 76 (26), 3.57.

Thompson, J., 1967. Organizations in Action. McGraw-Hill, New York.

Thompkins, J.A., White, J.A., Bozer, Y.A., Tanchoco, J.M.A., 2003. Facilities Planning, third ed. John Wiley and Sons, Hoboken, NJ.

Tichy, N.M., Devanna, M.A., 1990. The Transformational Leader. Wiley, New York.

Tilley, C., Whitehouse, J., 1992. Finance and Leisure. ILAM/Longman, London.

Torkildsen, G., 2005. Leisure and Recreation Management, fifth ed. Routledge, London.

Tracey, W.R., 1994. The Human Resource Management and Development Handbook, second ed. American Management Association, New York.

Trail, G.T., Anderson, D.F., Fink, J.S., 2005. Consumer satisfaction and identity theory: a model of sport spectator conative loyalty. Sport Marketing Quarterly 14 (2), 98–111.

Trenberth, L., 2003. Managing the Business of Sport. Dunmore Press Limited, New Zealand.

Trevino, L.K., Nelson, K.A., 1995. Managing Business Ethics: Straight Talk About How to Do It Right. Wiley, New York.

UK Sport, 2005. Running events. In: UK Sport Major Sport Events – the Guide. UK Sport, London, pp. 1–8. <http://www.uksport.gov.uk/assets/File/Generic_Template_Documents/Publications/Major_sports_events_The_guide/RUNNING_EVENTS.pdf> (accessed 17.06.09.).

UK Sport, 2005. Writing your major event strategy. In: UK Sport Major Sport Events – The Guide. UK Sport, London, pp. 1–8. <http://www.uksport.gov.uk/assets/File/Generic_Template_Documents/Publications/Major_sports_events_The_guide/EVENT_STRATEGY.pdf> (accessed 17.06.09.).

Unison, 2006. Leisure Trusts Briefing 148 December 2006: Charitable trusts delivering public leisure and cultural services. <http://www.unison-scotland.org.uk/briefings/leisuretrusts.html> (accessed 11.05.09.).

United States Green Building Council, 2009. LEED. <http://www.usgbc.org> (accessed 04.06.09.).

U.S. Public Health Service, 1995, February/March. Risk communication: working with individuals and communities to weigh the odds. Prevention report. <http://odphp.osophs.dhhs.gov/pubs/prevrpt/Archives/95fml.htm> (accessed 12.02.09.).

Vakratsas, D., Feinberg, F.M., Bass, F.M., Kalyanaram, G., 2004. The shape of advertising response functions revisited: a model of dynamic probabilistic thresholds. Marketing Science 23 (1), 109–119.

Vassallo, E., Blemaster, K., Werner, P., 2005. An international look at ambush marketing. The Trademark Reporter 95 (6), 1338–1356.

Veal, A., 2002. Leisure and Tourism Policy and Planning. CABI Publishing, Wallingford, Oxon, UK.

Walker, M.L., Stotlar, D.K., 1997. Sport Facility Management. Jones and Bartlett, Sudbury, MA.

Wang, G., Huang, S.H., Dismukes, J.P., 2005. Manufacturing supply chain design and evaluation. International Journal of Advanced Manufacturing Technology 25 (1–2), 93–100.

Waters, K., 2006, Dec./2007, Jan. A practical step-by-step guide to organising successful events. The British Journal of Administrative Management. Retrieved January 30, 2009 from ABI/INFORM Global.

Watt, D.C., 2003. Sports Management and Administration, second ed. Routledge, London.

Webster, M., 2007, January 16. Ethnic Rivalry Mars First Day of Aussie Open (Echosport Edition). Northern Echo, pp. 19. Retrieved June 22, 2009 from ABI/INFORM Trade & Industry database.

Westerbeek, H., Smith, A., Turner, P., Emery, P., Green, C., van Leeuwen, L., 2006. Managing Sport Facilities and Major Events. Routledge, London.

White, H., Karabestos, J., 1999. Planning and designing facilities. In: Sawyer, T.H. (Ed.), Facilities Planning for Physical Activity and Sport: Guidelines for Development, ninth ed. Kendall-Hunt, Dubuque, IA, pp. 11–28.

Wilson, J.Q., 1993. The Moral Sense. The Free Press, New York.

Wilson, R., Joyce, J., 2008. Finance for Sport and Leisure Managers. Routledge, London.

Woodall, T., 2004. Why marketers don't market: rethinking offensive and defensive archetypes. Journal of Marketing Management 20 (5–6), 559–576.

Wolff, A., Cazeneuve, B., Yaeger, D., 2002, August. When the terror began. Sports Illustrated 97 (8), 58–72. Retrieved June 21, 2009 from Research Library Core database.

World Wrestling Entertainment, Inc., 2009, June. WWE vs. NBA. Entertainment Business Newsweekly 45. Retrieved June 21, 2009 from ABI/INFORM Trade & Industry database.

Yones, M., 2009. Dysfunctional leadership & dysfunctional organizations. International Institute of Management Executive Journal. <http://www.iim-edu.org/dysfunctionalleadershipdysfunctionalorganziations/index.htm> (accessed 22.04.09.).

Yoon, S.-J., Choi, Y.-G., 2005. Determinant of successful sports advertisements: the effects of advertisement type, product type and sports model. Journal of Brand Management 12 (3), 191–205.

Yukl, G.A., 2002. Leadership in Organizations, fifth ed. Prentice Hall, Upper Saddle River, NJ.

1993, May. Savage assault. Sports Illustrated 78(18), 18–21. Retrieved June 21, 2009 from Research Library Core database.

2001. Recycling at the University of Pittsburgh. Facilities management recycling at the University of Pittsburgh. <http://www.facmgmt.pitt.edu> (accessed 16.03.08.).

2002. TQM: a snapshot of the experts. Measuring Business Excellence 6(3), 54–57. Retrieved June 7, 2009, from ABI/INFORM Global database.

2003. From the archives: June 1985, World Soccer 43 (9), 82.

2003. General Security Risk Assessment Guideline (on-line). ASIS International. Available from: <http://www.asisonline.org/guidelines/guidelinesgsra.pdf>.

2003. Vulnerability assessment report. Office of Domestic Preparedness, U.S. Department of Homeland Security. <http://www.ojp.usdoj.gov/odp/docs/vamreport.pdf> (accessed 31.05.05.).

2004, October 1. CRS Report for Congress. Critical Infrastructure and Key Assets: Definition and Identification. (on-line). Available from: <http://www.fas.org/sgp/crs/RL32631.pdf>.

2005, January. Threat and Risk Assessment (Local Jurisdiction), third ed. Texas Engineering Extension Service (TEEX), College Station, TX.

2008. Guide to Safety at Sports Grounds. The Stationary Office, London.

2008. Merriam-Webster.com. Vandalism. Retrieved: November 10, 2008.

2008, March 6th. Recycling with Razorbacks keeps tons of material out of landfill. States News Service. Retrieved March 16th, 2008 from Lexis-Nexis Academic database.

2009. What is the international facility management association? http://www.ifma.org/about_ifma/index.cfm (accessed 19.06.09.).

2009. <http://www.apics.org/About> (accessed 19.06.09.).

# Index